misLeading Indicators

misLeading Indicators

How to Reliably Measure
Your Business

Philip Green and George Gabor

 PRAEGER

AN IMPRINT OF ABC-CLIO, LLC
Santa Barbara, California • Denver, Colorado • Oxford, England

Library of Congress Cataloging-in-Publication Data

Green, Philip, 1959–
  MisLeading Indicators : how to reliably measure your business / Philip Green and George Gabor.
    p. cm.
  Includes bibliographical references and index.
  ISBN 978-0-313-39595-6 (hbk. : alk. paper) — ISBN 978-0-313-39596-3 (ebook)
1. Management—Statistical methods. 2. Economic indicators. 3. Work measurement. 4. Performance—Statistical methods. I. Gabor, George. II. Title.
  HD30.215.G74   2012
  658.0072'7—dc23   2011039499

ISBN: 978-0-313-39595-6
EISBN: 978-0-313-39596-3

16 15 14 13 12   1 2 3 4 5

This book is also available on the World Wide Web as an eBook.
Visit www.abc-clio.com for details.

Praeger
An Imprint of ABC-CLIO, LLC

ABC-CLIO, LLC
130 Cremona Drive, P.O. Box 1911
Santa Barbara, California 93116-1911

This book is printed on acid-free paper (∞)

Manufactured in the United States of America

658.
6

To Louise and Julie

Contents

Preface

Misleading indicators, and the misleading use of indicators, abound: indicators of business performance, process performance, performance dashboards, statistical process control, the measurement of global mean surface temperature in climate research, the rating of securities, the measurement of inflation, and the measurement of all sorts of social and political trends, or supposed trends, such as discrimination, poverty, and opinion polls, to name a few.

We decided there would be value in a book that provided laymen with a practical framework, based on sound theory, to judge which measurements they could trust, and why. Green's concern was damage such measurements cause in business and society; Gabor's was with their defiance of fundamental laws of physics and logic.

Another motivation for the book was that the misleading use of orthodox statistical methods has gained the upper hand in training programs taken by business managers. These programs are run in industry by a throng of consultants promulgating methods such as "Six-Sigma" and in academia by professors of both business and statistics.

Chapter one is an overview of misleading indicators, the use of measurement to make inferences, and the four principles of reliable measurement. Each chapter illustrates the principles: sufficient background information, accuracy and precision, reasonable inferences, and reality checks—in different situations. Chapters two and four describe the three fundamental ways of measuring—with instruments, counting, and rating—and how to apply the principles and identify misleading indicators in the actual act of measurement. Chapters five through ten show how indicators and measurements are used and misused, and the four principles violated, by people in business, government, finance, economics, and science, and in high-profile issues such as climate change. Finally, chapter eleven tries to dispel the dangerous notion that you can measure risk.

The use of the first person in the book always refers to Green, although both Green and Gabor contributed. Both authors are statisticians, albeit from opposite ends of the spectrum. Green has worked for more than twenty-five years as a business consultant almost exclusively in industry, where his focus is decidedly practical. Gabor is an academic theoretician, working on the fundamentals of statistics.

We maintain a blog and website at **www.misleadingindicators.com** in which we comment on misleading indicators in the news and the principles explained in this book.

DISCLAIMER

We have used several fictitious characters (Rachel Benaly, Melvyn Cunahan, Bart Crawford, Andy, Balpreet Singh, and Jessica Vilati) and places (Royal Valley Hospital) in the book in some short stories whose purpose is to illustrate certain principles. Any resemblance to any persons or places, real or imagined, is pure coincidence.

Acknowledgments

A number of people contributed to this book in a variety of ways. Louise Royer, PhD, Green's wife and a physicist, willingly accepted the impact of time spent writing a book rather than generating consulting revenue, and was supportive at all times. She also helped with some of the physics. Les and Marion Green provided ongoing support during the whole project, particularly at the critical junctures where success seemed most unlikely. Henry Regier, retired professor emeritus from the University of Toronto, gave helpful input on measurement in complex systems. Professor Clarence Virtue, Department of Physics, Laurentian University, and Sudbury Neutrino Observatory in Sudbury, Ontario, read parts of the manuscript and provided useful comments on measurement, probability, and particle physics. Alok Dobriyal, PhD, a statistician and consulting colleague of Green's, has been a font of ideas and lively discussion on measurement for twenty years. Chantal Medri, MSc, helped look up a large number of research articles. Dr. Douglas Hamilton, MD, Dr. Stephen Freedman, MD, and Genevieve Courant, NP, provided helpful information and feedback on matters related to measurement of health. A number of researchers willingly shared data and engaged in useful email exchanges on a wide variety of topics. These included Dr. Phil Jones, director of the Climatic Research Unit (CRU), School of Environmental Sciences, University of East Anglia, Norwich; Dr. John Kennedy, climate monitoring and research scientist, Met Office Hadley Centre, Exeter; Dr. Willie Soon, Harvard-Smithsonian Center for Astrophysics, Cambridge, Massachusetts; Dr. Vincent Courtillot, Institut de Physique du Globe de

Paris, Université de Paris, Institut Universitaire de France; and Dr. Richard McPeters, principal investigator, Earth Probe TOMS, NASA Goddard Space Flight Center. Others who made contributed information or ideas were Paul Langston, Coretec Inc., Roberto LoVerde, European Space Agency; Alan Medri, BA, Urban Haven Landscapes; John Sabiston, P.Eng; and Serge Théberge, PhD.

ONE

What Indicators Indicate

A man with one watch knows the time. A man with two watches is never quite sure.

—Attributed to Lee Segall

The aim of this book is to reveal the hidden and potentially misleading nature of measurements that can make or break a business. It shows how to measure accurately and precisely so that the measured information that businesses depend on is reliable. It shows how to determine which measurements and indicators can be trusted, and which mislead.

The stakes are enormous. Measurement problems lurk behind the daily headlines.

Many of the decisions that led to the 2007–2009 Credit Crunch were based on faulty measures of risk in the banking industry—measures with the allure of scientific precision. The banks invented a measure called "value at risk," and then used it as an indicator of their risk exposure. They were misled. They lost billions. Governments bailed out the financial sector to the tune of hundreds of billions of dollars as the economy headed into a tailspin.

Nations around the world began retooling their economies to prevent global warming when scientists measured the global mean temperature and drew charts for the United Nations Panel on Climate Change that showed it shooting up. Mainstream scientists, media, politicians and others attacked the credibility of scientists who proposed alternative ways of measuring the global mean temperature than those used in official reports and that contradicted official findings. Then the computers at the Climatic Research Unit were hacked and emails were leaked with phrases like "trick" and "hide the decline." This in turn cast doubts on the temperature measurements the CRU produced and the UNPCC used in its reports to policy makers.

Governments regularly change the way they measure inflation; some independent estimates of inflation peg it as much as 6 percent higher than recent government measures. Ever since Joseph Lowe published his proposal for measuring inflation in 1822,[1] critics have charged that governments use inflation measurements to hide the depreciation of money from the public.

Today managers are more reliant on measurements than ever before. Commerce is increasingly conducted through electronic transactions rather than personal relationships; and businesses are relentlessly replacing employees with information technology to pursue productivity gains. In response to these trends, enterprise software that collects measurements and produces indicators is proliferating. Meanwhile, business professors, consultants, accountants, and authors are continually devising new methods of measuring business performance. As we shall see, many of them grossly mislead.

IF YOUR MEASUREMENTS MISLEAD YOU'LL MISMANAGE

There is a common saying that "if you can't measure it you can't manage it." Many people mistakenly think the reverse is true: that if they can measure it, or something they call "it," they can manage it. What they ignore is an old lesson from some of the greatest scientists: just because you can obtain numbers from measuring does not mean the thing you think you are measuring actually exists. What then are you managing? Businesses measure and create all sorts of indicators without asking whether they indicate what they think they indicate. Often they do not.

What is a misleading indicator? It is a measurement from which an unreasonable, unwarranted, or plain wrong, inference is made, explicitly or implicitly.

The easiest way to avoid such an inference is to distinguish between what should and can, and what should not or cannot, be measured.

People manage most aspects of their lives without recourse to measurement, whether it is their child's struggles at school, their relationship with their spouses or their boss, or their choice of wines. My piano tuner, like many piano tuners, tunes our baby grand piano beautifully and very precisely without measuring anything, relying only on his acute sense of hearing and his musical skills. Entrepreneurs launch great new business ventures on hunches and their own vision without measurement; great leaders have inspired their followers to untold feats without measurement.

Peter Drucker[2] wrote that a central problem of managers is to strike the right balance between the measurable and the unmeasurable. It is a mistake to rely too heavily on quantification and overlook vital, but unmeasurable, information. Few business people do this deliberately. They carefully spell out what they want to measure and do not ask themselves to what unmeasurable information they should be paying attention.

Drucker wrote that some of the things that have the biggest effect on businesses, such as the sudden launch of better competing products, are not measurable until it is too late to act. V.E. (Andy) Anderson, once a senior executive with Tennessee Eastman, a division of Kodak at the time, told me that when he was the manager of their large chemical plant, he would clandestinely watch employees coming to and from work through the plant's gate at shift change. If they came in with feet dragging and left with a bouncy gait, he knew that they dreaded work and that they were happy to leave it, indicating there was trouble coming. Drucker describes how senior executives know that a company is bound for extinction when it cannot attract or hold able people.

Lord Kelvin's lecture to the Institute of Civil Engineers in 1883 has become an indictment of sorts of those who attempt to discriminate between the measurable and the unmeasurable, and has encouraged people to measure everything they manage. He said, "I often say that when you can measure what you are speaking about, and express it in numbers, you know something about it; but when you cannot measure it, when you cannot express it in numbers, your knowledge is of a meager and unsatisfactory kind." People wrongly interpret that comment to mean, "If you cannot measure it, you are ignorant."

ARE YOU MEASURING WHAT YOU THINK YOU ARE MEASURING?

But it is not what Lord Kelvin meant. False interpretation of his remark has caused a lot of damage. Lord Kelvin (or William Thomson, his given name) was more concerned with the existence of intelligible physical properties than with their measurability.[3] He knew that you have to be very careful about what inferences or conclusions you can draw from measurements. He knew that you cannot infer the thing you think you are measuring actually exists just because you obtain numbers from measuring what you presume to be that thing. A measurement is not proof of some underlying property of the thing you are measuring. If such a property exists, however, Kelvin thought you must measure it to gain a satisfactory knowledge of it. Likewise, you cannot make an inference about something based on a measurement, if that thing does not actually exist, or does not exist in the form you imagine it to exist.

Kelvin was concerned with the measurement of properties such as the velocity of light and electrical currents. In his time, there was uncertainty about what light and electric currents actually were and about what properties were being measured or could be measured. Today we measure things that would have probably have seemed absurd to Kelvin, rarely questioning whether our conclusions about some presumed underlying property are warranted, and whether the property even exists in a sufficiently definite form to lend itself to measurement.

The *Wall Street Journal*, in an article titled "Happiness Inc.,"[4] described how researchers are developing new techniques to measure "happiness or fulfillment." The article described how companies are adapting the research to find the best way to market their products, and lawyers are contemplating using it to measure a "loss of happiness" and thus calculate damages in divorce proceedings. Nikolas Sarkozy, the president of France, announced in 2009 with a group of leading economists that countries needed to find a way to measure happiness as well as raw economic numbers such as growth.

Is there really an underlying property called happiness that is sufficiently uniform in its behavior that it can be measured? Or are these researchers just measuring something related to happiness and labeling it "happiness"? Can we actually draw an inference from such measurements about happiness?

Many companies use a performance indicator to measure on-time delivery, clearly an important issue for their customers.

The CEO of a company I knew once came to a major client armed with an impressive chart of his company's on-time delivery, a key performance indicator. The client did not believe his measurements. Their own measurements showed his firm's deliveries were often late, causing expensive production delays. They canceled their contract. Humiliated and furious, the CEO investigated. He found that when his orders were late, his planners rescheduled them. His enterprise software then used the new date to calculate on-time delivery, making late deliveries appear on time in the performance indicator. His company was not measuring on-time performance, it was measuring something it called on-time performance. Managers then presumed that because that's what they said they were measuring, they were.

SOME MEASUREMENTS HAVE STOOD THE TEST OF TIME . . .

We measure things every day without even thinking about it and could not live without these measurements. In the morning, once your time-measuring device has woken you up, you might look at the thermometer to decide whether you need a sweater. You measure the level on your coffee maker as you pour water into it. In your car you check your gas gauge before you drive to the commuter train station, and keep an eye on the speedometer as you drive.

Each and every one of these measurements will affect a decision you make, from the trivial (stop pouring water into the coffee maker) to the critical (filling your gas tank).

Most people trust routine, mundane measurements explicitly because they know from experience that the inferences they make from them are reasonable. But you should not lower your guard. Be suspicious of any measurement or indicator that is not routine and well established, and of many that are.

Even many mundane measurements are not as simple as they seem. Most of us stand on the bathroom scale from time to time to measure our weight. Perhaps you do it only after Thanksgiving or Christmas, or perhaps you are somewhat compulsive and do it daily. The number you read when the dial stops spinning or the electronic display stops flashing is, supposedly, your weight. If you got off the scale and right back on it again, you might very well get a similar but slightly different weight. Is this also your weight? They cannot both be your weight. As the chapter's motto says, a man with one watch knows the time (or thinks he does!), a man with two watches is never quite sure.

I once did a simple experiment and moved my scale to different parts of my house. I left it at each spot for an hour or so before weighing myself again and did not eat or drink anything. The spread between my lightest and heaviest weight was about 10 pounds. The basement was cool and somewhat moist; my upstairs bathroom, which faces southeast, was warm. Presumably the temperature difference changed the stiffness of the springs inside the scale, resulting in different weights.

I am in good company with this experiment. Lord Kelvin's mirror-galvanometer, an electrical device used in the late 1800s to measure electric current, had to be used in the basement. It was almost useless in any other room because of disturbances caused by slight vibrations in the house. Users also had to remove their keys, as I do when I stand on the bathroom scale, because keys would affect the readings.[5]

Many, if not most, of the things we measure are dynamic in nature. They are always changing, even if ever so slightly. They may change over time; they may change depending on their location. The accuracy of the measurement process itself is also dynamic, as with Kelvin's mirror-galvanometer.

Consider your weight. Depending on what type of scale you use, the measurement accuracy changes when the temperature changes, and your weight itself changes according to the flow in and out of your body fluids and solids. When we speak of weight, we assume your body is actually imbued with a property that for convenience we call "weight."

It is not. Astronauts on space walks are weightless. They do not become headless or legless or heartless—just weightless. Weight is not some property of their bodies that changes when they go into space; it is the interaction between the mass of their bodies and surrounding bodies or gravity. That same interaction varies on a lesser scale on Earth. You weigh slightly more near a big heavy mountain than on sandy plains; you weigh more near sea level where you are closer to the Earth's center of gravity (and thus closer to its gravitational pull) than at 30,000 feet in an airplane, because the gravitational acceleration acting on your body varies by latitude, altitude, and location on Earth. The orbiting moon adds its pull too, just as it does with the tides, so your weight also changes with the phase of the moon.

For most of us the concept of weight is a very sharp concept—even though none of us have a specific property called weight. We use weight as a useful concept to measure ourselves, our groceries, the fish we catch, and many other things in day-to-day life, and we generally understand what we are talking about. We do, of course, have a mass, although the leading—but still unproven—theory to explain mass is that it results from interactions of subatomic particles. The Large Hadron Collider, the massive international physics project near Geneva, was built to find the proof.

Since 1889, in Paris, France, locked in a safe in the *Bureau International des Poids et Mesures* (BIPM), sits a 39mm high cylindrical block composed of an alloy of platinum and iridium, contained within three concentric glass bells to separate it from the surrounding air. It is against this chunk of expensive metal that all comparisons of mass, and thus weight, are based. They call it *Le Grand K*, for this little cylinder is the standard of mass by which the kilogram is defined around the world. Eighty close copies of this kilogram are stored in standards institutes across the globe. Together, they are the arbiters of every weighing scale in the world.

The Paris kilogram, like its copies, has a problem; it is losing mass, up to 50 micrograms in the last century.[6] Pollutants from the dirty air of the 1880s, when it was forged, could be slowly leaching out of the surface of the kilogram,[7] reducing its mass.

The metal artifact sits in "the ordinary humid air of the suburbs of Paris," which has all kinds of contaminants that could build up on its surface, despite the glass bells, according to BIPM director Terry Quinn.[8] Officials at the BIPM clean the kilogram before using it to calibrate any copies[9] but its weight still wanders.

If *Le Grand Kilo* has lost 50 micrograms (or 50 billionths of a kilo), then any object in the universe that had a mass of one kilogram one hundred years ago, and that has not lost any bits since, now has a mass of 50 micrograms more because *Le Grand Kilo* is still a kilogram. You too, dear reader, have gained weight as a result, through no doing of your own. A small amount, to be certain, a few millionths of a kilo, but it creates a fundamental problem—what is a kilogram?

In the deepest sense, then, we can never know the true weight of an object because it has no true weight, nor even a weight property. Weight, however, is a useful and very practical concept, and we know that it can be compared with and arbited by *Le Grand Kilo*, imperfect though it is.

Measurement is not a tool for revealing the absolute truth, but for providing quantitative information of practical value. Even though "true weight" is beyond our grasp, we can define weight sharply enough for most practical applications, such as determining whether you ate too much turkey and pie or figuring out how much to pay for your tomatoes at the grocers.

. . . AND MANY HAVE NOT

The questions that must be asked to determine whether measurements can be trusted, and what you can infer from them, are asked too infrequently. As a result, the business world is replete with misleading indicators.

In recent years the importance of asking these questions of financial measurements has become increasingly acute. One has only to read the daily financial papers to realize that many top business executives are still struggling with performance measurement problems. Headlines have screamed out "restatement of earnings" on an almost daily basis. The

Washington Post reported that there were 270 restatements of earnings before the Sarbanes-Oxley Act was enacted in 2001, and 1,200 in 2005.

When children are small and they amass their first collection of coins, they count their money by simply counting their coins, irrespective of the nominal value of each coin. When they can master that bit of abstract thought, they measure their cash holdings by putting the coins into piles of equal value, counting the coins in each pile and thus determining how many dollars and cents they have. They will probably recount their money several times until they think they have counted it correctly. At that level it is a simple enough measurement problem whose inaccuracies are merely the fruit of the child's difficulties with counting, abstraction, and perhaps with, well, honesty.

Some investors think companies should just count the cash and record it on their balance sheets. But abstractions are everywhere. When do you record a sale for a deal that will occur over several future periods? What constitutes cash? What is inventory worth? What discount rate and depreciation rate should be applied to the calculations?

The National Center for Children in Poverty[10] stated that "we still have one of the highest child poverty rates in the developed world. 29 million American children live in low-income families."

There is no platinum-iridium object encased in triple glass bells somewhere near Paris (or anywhere else) that gives the absolute measure of child poverty. Is child poverty an absolute quantity, wherein if a child lives in a family (what's a family?) with less than a specific amount of wealth P (*Le Grand P*) he or she is poor? Or is a *poor* child one whose family has less than the income that some supposed expert has decided the family needs to buy basic goods, goods that another expert has decided are basic to their needs? Or are poor children those who live in families that spend more than a certain proportion of their income (a proportion that more experts have decided is the right proportion) to buy all of the goods locally that yet more experts have decided they need? And if all these experts disagree with each other, then you, dear reader, are left with the feeling that you cannot really be sure about all this, but that if all the experts are arguing over child poverty it must be a pretty serious problem indeed—which is, of course, exactly what you are supposed to think, measurement or no measurement.

In business and other organizations, managers quantify their organizations and their organizations' performance by developing and watching "key performance indicators," or KPIs. This is a good but slippery idea. As we saw with the example on measuring weight, even a sharp concept presents challenges to measure (challenges on which bright minds expend considerable effort).

Performance is not a sharply defined concept. There is no standard, like the platinum-iridium kilo, against which all reliable measurements of performance are based. Performance must be defined for each organization, and for each aspect of its performance. The definition of performance is the prerogative of the company, or the person, designing the measurement.

That unfortunate CEO's on-time delivery story is common. I have seen the following definitions of on-time delivery in use for commercial deliveries in situations where there are several items in one load, such as a truckload, to customers:

1. Percentage of loads that arrived before or at the supplier's scheduled delivery time
2. Percentage of loads that arrived within one day of the supplier's scheduled delivery time
3. Percentage of loads that were shipped on the latest date on which they were originally scheduled or rescheduled to be shipped, rather than when the customers originally wanted them
4. Percentage of loads that were delivered before or at the time the customer wanted them
5. Percentage of loads that were delivered within the interval the customer specified
6. Percentage of loads that contained exactly the items the customer ordered, and that were delivered within the interval the customer specified, not before or after

All of these are key performance indicators that define on-time delivery differently. They do not allow you to make the same inferences about performance. All mean something different, all measure something different, and all measure to different standards of on-time performance. A company with a very high performance rating using the first method might achieve a very low rating with the sixth. In the first and second measures, the supplier, not the customer, sets the standards for on-time delivery time without reference to the contents of the delivery. The fourth one uses the customer's delivery time as the standard, but does not consider that some customers want deliveries within an interval, not just before the scheduled time.

In each case, somebody or something has to measure the time of shipment or arrival of the load, and compare it to the standard against which it is being measured, to determine whether the load is on time or not on time. This process is error-prone, just like counting money is error-prone. Somebody or something else has to determine whether the load was what the customer ordered. This is also subject to error. Then the data has to be assembled, the key performance indicator calculated, and the results communicated.

On-time performance, like most corporate performance indicators, is a relative measurement, not an absolute one. Phil Rosenzweig puts it this way: "A company can get better and fall further behind at the same time."[11] Your own on-time performance indicator can be getting better, but if your competitors' gets better faster than yours, to your customers you will be falling behind.

Industrial health and safety performance measures can be similarly misleading. Typically companies count the number of injuries and illnesses that take workers off the job, causing what they call "lost time." To make it possible to compare different factories, warehouses, construction sites, and so on, the numbers are scaled according to a simple formula, so that the numbers represent, approximately, the number of injuries and illnesses sustained by one hundred people working full-time for a year.

They use this indicator to make (often unreasonable) inferences about which factory is safer, which is getting safer, and which less safe.

Companies often offer prizes and bonuses to employees for good safety performance. For example, they may offer a new jacket to all employees within a factory whenever they collectively complete 500,000 hours of work without a work-related injury or illness that causes the victim to lose time at work. Imagine the poor fellow who cuts himself after 499,999 hours! If he reports it, his peers do not get the jacket! Better to hide it and drop into emergency on the way home from work.

Or imagine the no-nonsense plant manager who dishes out severe disciplinary measures whenever an injury can be remotely ascribed to non-respect of a procedure. With such an approach, all but the most severe injuries go unreported. In one plant I knew, within months after the tough guy retired and was replaced by a new plant manager, the accident rate shot up. His bosses concluded the safety performance of the new guy was not as good as the fellow he replaced. What had really happened was that the workers were no longer hiding their injuries.

One of the strangest sights I saw was a large room in the basement of a struggling pulp and paper mill. In it sat about twenty injured men, some with crutches leaning against their chairs and some in wheelchairs. Most of them were relaxing. Some were at small work stations making small signs such as "Caution: Hot Water" for use in the mill. They were still, technically, and with a bit of a stretch of the imagination, on the job—so there were no, ahem, lost time injuries.

FOUR PRINCIPLES FOR RELIABLE MEASUREMENTS

What is a measurement? In the traditional definition of the term, it means to ascertain some physical property by comparing it with a standard, such as comparing your weight with a standard kilogram.

There are two other ways to measure: one can count, the simplest form of measurement; or one can score or rank or grade, the sort of measurement one sees on customer satisfaction surveys, at Olympic figure skating events, in psychometric testing, and on school report cards.

The term *measurement* is used today somewhat loosely, often meaning to turn anything of interest into a number that purportedly purges judgment and emotion out of business, economic, social, and other events, with reference to neither a standard nor even a reasonable certainty that the thing being measured actually exists.

There is a large variety of ways to define and measure performance indicators based on physical properties, on counts, and on ratings. You will always face the challenge of determining what inferences you can reasonably draw from them.

In this book we will attempt to demonstrate four principles for making reasonable inferences using measurement. When you understand them, you will be able to ask the right questions and determine whether an indicator is misleading or not.

You need to ascertain that:

Principle 1: There is sufficient background information to define what you arc measuring.

Principle 2: There are measurement methods sufficiently accurate and precise for the inferences you would like to draw.

Principle 3: Sound reasoning is used to make reasonable inferences based on the measurements and the background information.

Principle 4: The inferences correspond with reality.

All four principles must be followed. If any are violated, chances are you have a misleading indicator.

Figure 1.1   The four principles of measurement.

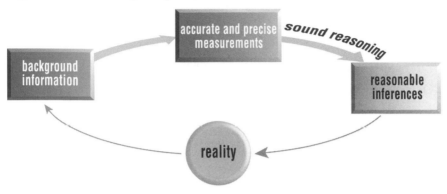

Measurement is a learning process. Your inferences will often conflict with your perception of reality in some way or another. This conflict should lead you to question the background information, the measurement method, your beliefs, your perception of reality, and the soundness of the reasoning you used to make the inference. The conflict should also lead you to ask whether the inference is right given the background information, the measurement method, and the logic.

It is only by fearlessly asking these questions that will you know whether the inference is reasonable and thus whether or not you have a *mis*Leading Indicator.

TOOL BOX

- Do not assume that a measurement or indicator measures what people say it measures.
- Don't believe the saying, "If you cannot measure it, you cannot manage it." There are many things at work and in life that you can manage without measuring them.
- Distinguish between things that can and should be measured versus vital but unmeasurable information.
- Be suspicious of any measurement that has not proven itself through experience.
- Apply the four principles to prevent your indicator from misleading you, or to prevent yourself being misled by someone else's.

TWO

Counting, Recounting, and Miscounting

Not everything that can be counted counts, and not everything that counts can be counted.

—Attributed to Albert Einstein

HOW MANY MANAGERS DOES IT TAKE TO COUNT THE LIGHT BULBS?

Many dozens of times in my management seminars I have conducted a little experiment that demonstrates the difficulties of the simple act of counting. It has, without fail, produced a successful demonstration. I ask the participants whether there is anyone in the room who cannot count, or who does not know what a light bulb is, or who does not know what a room is. I usually get some pretty strange looks. So I say, "Well in that case, I will take no questions. I would like you to work in silence and individually. Write your results down and keep them secret. Please count the number of light bulbs in this room."

Within a few seconds people start asking me questions: "Does the cupboard count as being part of the room?" Or, "Do the bulbs in the fire exit signs count?" I do not answer.

After a few minutes I ask them to report their results, one by one. In Table 2.1 you can see one set of results, typical for a group of twenty managers.

Table 2.1   Light Bulbs Counted by a Group of Managers

Number of light bulbs counted	Number of people who counted this number of bulbs
0	3
29	1
31	4
32	2
33	6
35	2
48	1
56	1
	20 people

The people who counted zero light bulbs said that all the bulbs in the room were actually fluorescent tubes, not light bulbs. The number thirty-two was derived from eight banks of fluorescent tubes with four tubes in each. The people that said thirty-one pointed out that one of the tubes no longer worked, so was no longer a light bulb. Those that counted above thirty-two counted the fire exit lights and other items that they surprisingly decided were light bulbs, because they emitted light, such as TV screens, laptop computers, and the little lights on wristwatches. Others made mistakes counting.

To demonstrate the difficulties in obtaining a consistent count of light bulbs in a room, I sometimes divide the participants into groups of managers and ask each group to define a light bulb and a room. They refine their definitions until everyone in their group counts the same number. They then give their definition to another group, and if the second group counts the same number, their definition is complete.

Each team will usually define light bulbs in a manner that produces a different count. So if there are four teams we now have four different counts of the number of light bulbs in a room. Some teams define them as the old-fashioned pear-shaped screw-in bulbs like the one shown in Figure 2.1.

Others will include these bulbous bulbs and the florescent tubes, and others will include any electrically powered device that produces light. All the definitions are arbitrary, as definitions are by definition, and most produce a different result. The definitions are less arbitrary and produce

Figure 2.1   One version of a light bulb.

Source: Image Copyright Zoran Vukmanov Simokov, 2010 Used under license from Shutterstock.com.

more consistent results if I provide a reason for the count, for example, so that maintenance can keep an adequate supply of spares on hand.

That's a new twist to an old joke. How many managers does it take to count the light bulbs in a room? Twenty: four to write operational definitions of rooms and light bulbs, six to test the definitions, and ten to practice counting with the definitions. Counting them is a lot harder than screwing them in. After forty-five minutes, twenty managers usually cannot agree on how many light bulbs are in the room.

Light bulbs don't move, they don't immigrate or emigrate, they are conceptually simple, they don't die or get born, they don't vote or have opinions, they are not consumers and don't spend money, and yet they are difficult to count, even when confined to a single room.

The counting of light bulbs in a room illustrates what happens when we do not follow the four principles described in the first chapter. In my seminar light bulb counting exercise I never provide any background information with which a reasonable definition of a light bulb can be made. Without that definition, there is no way to count accurately and precisely, and no way to make a reasonable inference.

Many people rely on accurate counts. Census and opinion polls are based on counts. Managers require accurate inventories, which are based on counting. Wildlife and fisheries managers rely on counts of animals and fish to decide on management policies, when seasons should be opened and

Figure 2.2   What happens when you violate principle one.

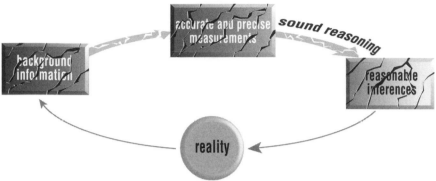

closed, and how much wildlife can be taken. Websites count clicks. Public health officials rely on counts of cases of disease to determine whether and when to institute drastic measures such as quarantines. Factory managers want to know how many injuries occur in a month, or how many defective widgets were produced, or how many environmental spills occurred.

If these counts are all done as poorly as the counting of light bulbs, we are in serious trouble.

There are two more things that complicate counting. The first is that people rarely have the time or resources to count or otherwise observe all the things they want to count. Just as you cannot see all the fish in a lake when you need to count the fish that live there, you cannot always physically count all the objects in an inventory, or the people in a town, or the cases of disease in a province or state or country. You cannot count them all because you have limited resources: a shortage of counters, or time, or the ability to observe the things you want to count.

The constraints of time and resources are usually severe and always present. These constraints may make it virtually impossible to get an accurate count in a full survey.

The second difficulty is that the things people count usually move or change while they are being counted. Inventory is only static for defunct companies. People move in and out of census areas, die, and are born. Fish and wildlife wander continuously.

If you can count quickly enough you can get a snapshot number that shows how many things there were at one brief moment of time. This is why the census is taken on a specific date. If you cannot take a snapshot, the number of things you are counting keeps changing while you are counting them.

COUNTING AN ENTIRE POPULATION

In a census the intention is to count everyone, not a sample of people. When they count inventory, managers want every item counted. This presents the difficulty of finding every item.

At one time, some scientists used a very direct approach to finding the fish in a lake. They take a pesticide called rotenone and pour it in. Perhaps after a couple of beers on the shore, they head back out and count the dead fish floating on the surface. It's a trick they learned from indigenous peoples who used rotenone, found naturally in plant roots, to fish. It gives a good estimate of how many fish were living in the lake before they were poisoned.

In the census it is impossible to count everyone, and certainly impossible to poison them in order to count them, so census agencies use a variety of methods and make a number of assumptions to come up with estimates of population size. A lot is at stake from their estimates, as different levels of government share tax revenues based on the number of people living in states, provinces, counties, and municipalities. The count of people also becomes the denominator in calculations of rates such as the birth rate, death rate, murder rate, and divorce rate.

The *Arizona Republic* once ran a story titled "Shortchanged? Census, State Differ on Pinal County's Headcount."[1] The article went on to say that "the short shrift on population estimates have hampered long-term planning and short-changed the county on state-shared revenue funding."

The US Bureau of the Census had estimated—or inferred—a population of 229,549. The Arizona Department of Economic Security estimated a population of 246,660, a difference of 17,111, or 7 percent, greater than the sampling error in most opinion polls—which are based on samples. The county officials, according to the report, were not to be outdone, and said that both estimates were "likely low-balled."

The US Bureau of the Census estimates the number of people in each county every year, even though the enumeration census—or full count—itself is only conducted every ten years. The methods used to develop an estimate of the size of a county population between census years must address such issues as people dying, being born, moving in or out, being hospitalized, and so on. The source of data is often administrative records such as birth and death records, drivers' licenses, federal income tax returns, Medicare enrollees, and military movement. Demographers assume that "the components of population change are closely approximated by measuring change in selected administrative or survey data sources";[2] in other words, they assume that the people match the records.

How many people live in a county? With all the paperwork we fill in for governments it is amazing that they cannot get a more accurate count of how many of us there are. It could be that in this highly mobile age, the concept of a population that can be precisely counted is somewhat antiquated compared to less mobile ages. Like the definitions of weight and light bulb, the definition of a population is a bit jelly-like when you take a very close look at it, even though we know what it means in a rough way.

The census has elements of both the light bulb problem and the fish counting problem. When counting light bulbs participants in my seminars struggle with definitions. When counting fish the challenge is that fish move, are born and die, and are hard to find. In the census, census takers want to count residents, whatever they are. The homeless, the transient and hospitalized people, people away for a few months or weeks, the newly arrived, the recently departed, the remote and inaccessible, refuseniks, those with multiple residences, the forgetful and many others complicate the definition of what we are counting and make it difficult to find and count them.

To overcome these difficulties, census takers go to great lengths to define who is to be counted, when they are to be counted, where they are to be counted, and the penalties for hiding from the counters. Statisticians write journals and books on methods to overcome these problems. There is still, as with any measurement, some residual uncertainty. Despite this uncertainty, there is no plus or minus number reported with the census estimates, as is done with surveys. We are given a fixed number, such as the number for Pinal County, and told that this is The Number. And in most cases we accept it at face value.

Censuses undertaken by reputable government statistical agencies are probably, in most cases, good enough for practical, general knowledge purposes. Yet almost every day in the press you can read other population counts conducted with much less rigorous methodology. The Moscow Bureau of Human Rights[3] reported in 2006 that the Russian skinhead movement numbers up to fifty thousand people. Try defining a skinhead, much less counting them in a census of some kind. I have trouble imagining a temporary female census worker going up to a group of tattooed and head-shaved muscular young men to ask, "'Scuse me. Are you skinheads?" These sorts of numbers should not be accepted at face value and are usually little more than guesses.

SAMPLING—REDUCING THE NUMBER OF THINGS TO COUNT

To overcome the constraints of time and resources, we can sample a population and draw an inference from the sample, such as a count. Sampling gives us a more manageable number of things. From some samples—and it is not obvious which ones—we can draw reasonable inferences about the whole. When we want to know whether a pot of soup needs more salt, we do not eat all the soup; we taste a sample spoonful. You could sample customers to count the number (or proportion) that like your company's service; or sample employees to find out how many are aware of a new policy. In all cases we wish to infer something about the population from the sample. If the spoonful needs more salt, we infer that so does the whole pot.

Opinion polls (dis)grace the pages of our newspapers almost every day. Almost all of them are based on samples. Suppose, for example, a pollster selected a sample of one thousand people, and found that one-third of them believe Elvis is alive. In reading that number, you might be inclined to infer that in the remainder of the population from which the pollster drew the sample, one-third of the people believe Elvis is alive.

One usually hears a plus or minus number in media reports of opinion surveys: "Thirty-one percent of people believe Elvis is alive, plus or minus 3 percent, 19 times out of 20." This means that in some *future* survey of the same population that uses the same survey method, there is a 95 percent probability (i.e., 19 out of 20) that the estimate from the survey will be within plus or minus 3 percent of the value in the whole population. Alternatively, it means that if you do a large number of surveys, and in each one you calculate the estimate, and then the average of these estimates, then there is a 95 percent probability that this average will be within plus or minus 3 percent of the value in the population.

But there is a snag. Once the survey has been completed and the data collected and analyzed, we cannot say whether an estimate from this *specific* sample is within 3 percent of the value in the population. The reason is that you rarely get a sample that is representative of the population as a whole. A particular sample might be 1 percent off, or 6 percent off. It is usually very hard, if not impossible, to know.

Many people explain, incorrectly, the plus-or-minus number as follows: "if we did this same survey a gazillion times, and nobody changed their mind while we did it, about 5 percent of the time (1 time out of 20) the proportion in the *population* and the proportion in the *sample* could differ by more than 3 percent."

Of course nobody ever repeats a survey a gazillion times, or even intends to, so this explanation of the plus-or-minus number is mostly nonsense. And even if you could repeat it, answers to survey questions are not constants—as we saw not even weight is constant.

This plus-or-minus number is based on an important assumption: that the survey method permits you to make reasonable inferences about the population as a whole.

Many things can make such inferences unwarranted. If your sampling method preferentially selected certain groups of people, the proportion in the sample who respond a certain way could be quite different than the proportion in the general population. Likewise, if you preferentially sampled bits of ham in your soup, the samples of soup would be saltier than the soup as a whole. In both these cases, the sample cannot be used to draw reliable conclusions about the whole.

A similar problem arises if the samples are self-selecting. A self-selecting sample is one in which the person doing the survey does not control who is included in the sample, rather, the people in the sample do. This is one of the big drawbacks of survey tools such as customer feedback cards. Are unsatisfied customers more inclined to fill them? Or satisfied ones?

Most people who read opinion polls unknowingly assume the survey method permits reasonable inferences. And some people who conduct opinion polls know that they assume this, and use that fact to their advantage. Polls can thus become, through devious intent or ineptitude, propaganda. Consider the following two pairs of fictitious questions:

FIRST PAIR

1. Since Toyota's recall of five million vehicles due to a faulty accelerator peddle, is your opinion of Toyota's quality better or worse?
2. How likely are you to buy a Toyota in the next year, on a scale of 1–5? (With 5 being the most likely.)

SECOND PAIR

1. As you may know, after General Motors' bankruptcy and government bailout, the US government became GM's largest shareholder. Do you agree that governments should bail out failing auto companies?
2. How likely are you to buy a Toyota in the next year, on a scale of 1–5? (With 5 being the most likely.)

An opinion is a lot more slippery than a fish and harder to define than a light bulb. The two sets of questions would likely produce different results. To understand the results of an opinion survey, you have to have some knowledge of how the questions were asked, and whether they were asked in a way that pushed the answers one way or another.

The different possible samples that can be drawn from the population with a particular sampling method is the source of what is called sampling error. It does not mean a mistake has been made. It means there is some uncertainty due to the luck (or bad luck) of who (or what) gets included in the sample.

Sometimes this has serious consequences, as in the case of several commercial fishermen from Nova Scotia who had been charged with catching too many undersized scallops. They faced huge fines or jail.

You cannot count every scallop in a large fishing boat, so the regulations stated that fisheries officers were to take eight representative samples. The regulators did not define the word "representative," but presumably they meant that the samples would be a miniature replica of the population with respect to the size of the scallops, or close to it.

The fishermen put the scallops in bags, which they stored in the hold of their boat. Fisheries officers had boarded the fishermen's vessel and taken eight bags of scallops. From each they took 500g samples of scallops. The regulation said that there could not be more than thirty-three scallops per 500g, on average, in eight samples. (If there are more than thirty-three scallops, it means they are too small.)

Other than the bags they saw and general knowledge of scallop fishing, the officers had no background information on what was in the boat. The defense was concerned that the officers could ascertain the size of the scallops by the impressions they made on the bags and sample accordingly. The judge took the whole court onto a scallop boat to see.

The defense asked me to testify as an expert witness. I told the court that with the officers' method of sampling you could not make a reliable inference about all the scallops in the boat. I said that what was needed was a sampling method from which a reliable inference could be made and the sampling error calculated, similar to the way people are sampled in opinion polls.

Given the limited background information and the concerns about cherry-picking, there is no sampling method that stands out. I told the court that the best available method, give the circumstances, would be for the officers to count bags as they came off the boat and select them from predetermined numbers, such as to randomly pick the first bag and every thirtieth bag thereafter, or from a list of randomly generated numbers. As an expert witness in court, you answer questions, not give lectures. I did not get a chance to explain that random sampling had serious problems of its own. Although it would protect the integrity of the sampling process and would enable the calculation of sampling error, it could not assure representative samples.

The prosecutor's cross-examination helps explain why. It went something like this.

Prosecutor: "Mr. Green, is it possible that if you used such a method, that you could pick the eight bags with the largest scallops or the smallest scallops from the boat?"

I had anticipated that someone with only a basic knowledge of statistics would ask this question and had prepared my answer: "Do you play bridge?"

"Yes," the prosecutor replied, now on the defensive.

"And have you ever dealt a hand where every player was served all the cards in a suit, in order, from a shuffled deck?"

"No," he replied.

"Well, the chance of drawing the eight largest or the eight smallest samples is about 100 million times less than the chance of dealing such a hand." I said this merely to illustrate the low probability of the specific unrepresentative sample he was talking about. I expected him to continue.

"I have no more questions, your Honor," he responded. And that was that—the fisherman was eventually acquitted.

Random sampling violates our first principle by throwing away all background information. Nonetheless, many people recommend it because they do not understand what "19 times out of 20" means. If the prosecutor knew more about sampling, and had continued to cross-examine me, he would have shown how this violation misleads. Let's imagine a fictitious continuation of the cross-examination.

Prosecutor: "If you used the random sampling method you are proposing, presumably you would claim that 19 times out of 20 the number of scallops per 500g in the sample will be within such and such a number from the average in the boat?"

Me: "Yes, I would be able to make that sort of statement."

Prosecutor: "And would you know whether a particular sample, once you had obtained it, was within the such-and-such amount of the boat average or not?"

Me: "No, that I would not know."

Prosecutor: "So you would not know whether a particular sample was the 20th time or one of the other 19 times?"

Me: "No, that I would not know either."

Prosecutor: "Would such a sample occur exactly every 20th time, or on average one time out of 20?"

Me: "It would occur on average one time out of 20."

Prosecutor: "And if you used that sampling method and obtained a sample where the scallops were remarkably small or remarkably large compared to the other scallops you saw about you in the boat, would you feel comfortable concluding that this was a representative sample with which you could determine the average number of scallops per 500 grams in the whole boat?"

Me: "No, I would not feel comfortable with such a sample."

Prosecutor: "So, after having looked at your scallops so far, and compared them to what you saw in bags in the boat, you would feel inclined to get some more samples that looked similar to the scallops you saw about you in the boat?"

Me: "Yes, I would."

Prosecutor: "Well, Mr. Green, that does not seem so very different from what the fisheries officers were doing, does it?"

Me: "There are some similarities."

Prosecutor: "So is it fair for me to say that with your method of sampling you can make general statements about future samples, but unless you already know a lot about the scallops in the boat, and you use that information, you would not know whether those same statements apply to a particular sample from a particular boat?"

I would have had to answer that I would not. It may not have gained the prosecutor a conviction but it would certainly have exposed the weakness of random sampling. It can produce a particular sample that does not even come close to resembling a miniature replica of the population. It can produce all sorts of samples, some good, and some bad. We don't know because we have thrown away our background information. Random selection in effect says: I choose not to know. So we don't know the inferential error either. The fictitious cross-examination also shows the common fallacy of mixing up the sampling error of the sampling method—which applies to future samples, or averages of estimates from such samples—with the inferential error of an actual sample.

In a court case, where what matters is the guilt or innocence of a particular man or woman, not of a fictitious future man or woman, this confusion could have serious consequences.

Unlike the fisheries officers, when you sample soup you usually know what is in it before you sample it. This means you are reliably able to pick samples that enable you to make an inference about the whole pot. Pollsters tackle the problem the same way by acquiring a tremendous amount of information about the populations from which they are sampling, and use it before each poll, so that they get good samples that they can trust to make inferences about the population. They have sampling schemes that allow them, in effect, to create near miniature replicas that closely resemble the population as a whole.

This was not always true. In the 1948 US presidential election, all the pollsters predicted that Thomas E. Dewey would defeat Harry S. Truman. In fact, Truman trounced Dewey by 5 percent. The pollsters had assumed the undecided voters would not vote. They also assumed that people had made up their minds ten days before the election, and stopped polling.

Now with call-display, public fatigue with telemarketing, and other unwanted phone calls, many people do not bother to answer the phone when pollsters call. Different pollsters have different ways of tackling these problems.

Background information is as important as measurements (or in this case counts) when making an inference. Frequently it is more important. The more we know about the population, the more you can design a sampling procedure that is likely to produce samples that mimic the population you are sampling. This will give you less inferential error—in other words, you are likely to make a smaller error with your inference. If you knew everything about the population, you would not need to sample, or measure, anything.

In chapter one we saw that people do not have an inherent property called weight, even though they weigh themselves regularly. Weight is a concept that is sharp enough that we all think objects have weights, and this is a very good and practical approximation to reality.

The opinion of a population is another matter. A population does not have a fixed opinion, or a fixed percentage of people with a certain opinion, not even for a moment. Not only does opinion change depending on the way the question is asked, it changes in reaction to events, and may even change in reaction to previous opinion polls. This shifting and drifting of opinions is not captured by the precision that is quoted with reputable polls; nor is the inferential error of the *actual* sample.

Does this mean we cannot trust the results of opinion polls and other samples? No, it means that before you trust them you need to determine whether you trust their sampling and surveying method. Have they refined it over time so that they can be reasonably sure that the sampling error is close to the inferential error? Opinion surveys on voting intentions have one tremendous advantage over most other surveys in this regard: they can—sometimes—be calibrated with actual voting results. The challenge is that those who do not vote often offer different answers to pollsters than those who do vote, according to Doug Anderson, a pollster at Harris Decima.[4] The (partial) ability to calibrate makes it possible for pollsters to refine their sampling methods for greater and greater precision so that they can have a fairly high degree of confidence that the errors of the actual samples are close to the sampling error. Even then, such polls can fail spectacularly during turbulent times or major upsets.

In the scallop example, there was almost no background information about what was in the boat before the sample, and the sample was static. Voting intentions are very fluid. Anderson says, "There are intense communications campaigns bombarding audiences with the explicit intent of ensuring a favorable intention turns into the actual behavior and convincing those with other intentions to either change their intention and instead take a favorable action, or at least not follow through on their unfavorable intention."

Market research is not so fluid. Purchasing behavior changes more slowly, making it easier to catch trends in opinion polls on purchasing habits. Purchasing happens continually, unlike voting, which is focused on a single day.

The chart in Figure 2.3 shows support for the governing party during the 2008 Canadian federal election. The chart shows the results of eighty opinion polls, from three different pollsters. Each line represents the results for a particular pollster, and shows the percentage of people who said they would vote for the governing party. The huge variation in the lines gives an idea of how much uncertainty there is in opinion polling. They all vary between 34 and 41 percent for the first half of the campaign. The spread of 7 percent is a bit bigger than the margin of error of plus or minus 3 percent. In the second half of the campaign the results of the three pollsters took a dip, suggesting the government was in trouble.

Figure 2.3   Governing party support during the 2008 Canadian election. Three pollsters.

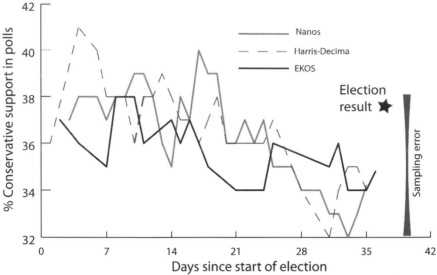

Source: Harris/Decima, Nanos Research, and EKOS. Used by permission.

The big dot at the end represents the percentage of voters who actually voted for the governing party in the election. It is similar to the results at the beginning of the campaign.

What inferences can we draw about the apparent shift in support at the end? Is it just sampling error we are seeing? Is it an inferential error? Or can we infer that something really happened to shift opinion in the second half of the campaign, and then again between the last poll and voting day? After the last poll, the leader of the opposition had given a disastrous and widely mocked interview. There was also a rally on the stock market. Did either of these affect voters' thinking? It is very difficult to make reasonable inferences to answer such questions from the polls, unless there are very large swings. (One pollster, Nanos, did a poll every day and calculated a three-day moving average, which is what is shown on the chart. The daily results have wider margins of error. On the last day daily his poll found 37.1 percent support—very close to the election result of 37 percent, but it did not show up in the three-day moving average.)

When you take a sample of soup, what you know about the soup beforehand (your background information) will help you figure out how to sample it. If it is a beef consommé you will probably be quite content to sample a single spoonful. Consommé is uniform. It has no chunks. If it is stirred, one spoonful will taste the same as another. Not so for chunky beef and vegetable stew. The broth may be warm and salty, but a spoonful of broth does not allow you to generalize about the whole pot of stew. The beef may still be frozen inside and the carrots may already be overcooked. Your sampling strategy for the stew will be quite different, and you will probably want to taste several of its components and from more than one part of the pot. Sampling the various components of a population like this is known as stratified sampling (from the Latin *stratum* or layer).

The same is true when sampling a large population of people. Pollsters have devoted tremendous resources to designing the best sampling methods. They use results of the census to break populations down by socioeconomic, ethnic, and age groups, and they break samples down geographically. Some have proprietary lists of a large number of people from which they repeatedly sample. Sampling plans, mostly built upon knowledge the pollsters have acquired about the population they are sampling from, have only a small component of randomness to them.

When companies want to know what people think of their products and services, they often make the mistake of only surveying their customers; they do not survey their noncustomers. A transit company that surveyed its passengers would not learn why the rest of the population does not take the bus. The British cleverly avoided this mistake in World War II when they were trying to determine where to reinforce their fighter planes. They reckoned that the aim of the German pilots was not good enough to fire at any specific parts of the British planes. They kept track of where the bullet holes were in the planes that returned to their bases and added armor plate to the areas where there were no holes. They reasoned that these were the spots where, when a bullet hit, the pilot was killed or the plane was disabled and could no longer fly.

COUNTING RARE EVENTS

Sometimes we need or want to count extremely rare events—events that occur so rarely we measure them in parts per million or hundred thousand or similar number rather than in percent. For example, "Six-Sigma" consultants and authors often use the term "defects per million opportunities." Another example could be rare forms of cancer that could occur if a new plant is built, or rare product defects that could harm consumers.

There are two ways to count these events. The first is to wait for them to happen and count occurrences. This would be a reasonable approach for a rare form of cancer, such as cancer of the ureter, that we can be fairly sure most doctors will diagnose properly. This approach is used because we cannot inspect every person, or even a sample of people, within a population to determine whether they have cancer of the ureter. The second way is to inspect very large samples to find occurrences of the event, and, based on the results of the sample, make an inference about the frequency in the entire population.

The Canadian Public Health Agency reports that the frequency of cancer of the ureter in males and females is about 4.6 cases per million people per year. This estimate also depends on the census takers having properly counted Canadians. If they were off by 7 percent, either high or low, the estimate could be somewhere between 4.3 per million and 4.9 per million, assuming the doctors diagnosed all cases correctly and reported them all, and that the patients with the disease went to their doctors for diagnosis.

The second method of counting rare events is often used in settings when some items are inspected or tested and those that have some property, such as a defect, are counted. Suppose, for example, that a large food manufacturer that makes millions of bottles of jam wants to know the frequency with which large insect bits or too many insect bits get into jars of jam. A few small insect bits are in virtually all jars of jam and virtually every other food type, but they are so small and few in number that nobody notices them or is harmed by them, unless they are too big or too numerous or both. When inspectors inspect jam jars for insect bits, they destroy the jam, so they cannot inspect all of the jars.

The United States Food and Drug Agency (FDA) has rules on this sort of thing for many foods, and it is in the interest of food manufacturers to comply. One of the rules states that chocolate is unsafe if "The chocolate in six (6) 100 gram subsamples contains an average of 60 or more insect fragments per 100 grams." For flour there is a different rule: 75 insect fragments per 50g (or 150 per 100g).

Suppose the food manufacturer has made some improvements to its process and, based on their hunches and background information about insects and their production lines, believes that the frequency with which its food products do not comply with these FDA rules is at most 20 jars in a million. They had an estimate from a few years earlier of 50 parts per million.

Leaving aside for a moment the problem of counting the insect bits within the food samples—a nonnegligible problem about which much has been written and tried—how many food samples will the factory have to inspect to be able to determine whether the frequency has decreased to 20 parts per million from 50 parts per million? It turns out it is an impractically large number.

We can calculate the probability of observing a contaminated jam jar, provided the jam jars become contaminated individually, and not in batches (much more background information is needed if they are contaminated in batches). If we inspect 1,000 jam jars, there is only a 2 percent chance of observing even a single contaminated jar, if the frequency in the population is 20 parts per million. We would have a 4.9 percent chance if the frequency is 50 parts per million. If we inspect 10,000, the chances are 18 percent and 39 percent respectively. At 50,000, they are 63 percent and 92 percent respectively. But inspecting food items for insect bits is a destructive, expensive, and time-consuming process. The cost of checking 50,000 jars for one food plant or even one food company puts it completely out of the question. Even a sample of 1,000 may be unreasonable.

This basically means that unless the cost of inspecting is incredibly low, a 20 or 50 parts or similar parts-per-million event that must be found through inspection is, for practical purposes, below the detection threshold.

Even if we were able to afford the inspection it would be very difficult to make an inference about the proportion of jars contaminated with too many insect bits. What inference could we draw if we inspected 10,000 and none were contaminated? What if we obtained one contaminated jar out of 10,000 sampled? Can we infer that there are one per 10,000, or 100 per million? Or should we infer 20 or 50 per million? The inferential errors for all these possibilities would be quite large.

The conclusion: counts of very rare events should be regarded with a skeptic's eye when they are based on inspection of a sample.

MAKING INFERENCES FROM COUNTS OF TRIGGERED EVENTS

We often count events that are triggered or spontaneously occur in some way and are then reported. The counts are typically described as rates, for example, the murder rate, the injury rate at factories, or the lost baggage rate for an airline.

Usually the purpose of these rates is to make an inference, although it is not stated as such. For example, people infer from the murder rate that their streets are more, or less, safe. They infer from the lost baggage rate that an airline is getting better or worse at baggage handling or that it is better or worse than a competitor.

These events are counted when they are triggered and observed. We do not inspect or sample people to determine who was murdered, nor do we inspect bags handled by an airline to see which were lost.

To compare counts of triggered events we must report them on a common scale, with a unit of a defined size. The unit could be, for example,

100,000 people in one year. We cannot compare cities if one city, the smaller of the two, reports that it had ten murders in the last six months and the big city reports that they had twenty murders in the last quarter. Although reporting the murder rate, for example, as 4.7 murders per 100,000 people per year makes it easier to compare the cities, it is not without difficulties of its own.

The problem with using a common scale is that it does strange things to the counts. Take a small town of 10,000 people for example. If it has no murders in a year its murder rate is 0 per 100,000 population per year. If it has a single murder, its murder rate is 1 per 10,000 population per year. When you scale this up you get 10 per 100,000 population per year. If we inferred from this that this city suddenly became twice as dangerous as a large city with a murder rate of 5 murders per 100,000 people per year, we would most likely be wrong.

The same situation occurs in industry when companies report lost time injuries per 200,000 man-hours worked. This is a typical way of reporting safety. A facility with 100 employees working 2,000 hours per year will have 200,000 man-hours of paid work per year, so the scale in the reporting of injuries and illnesses is meant to be equivalent to injuries and illnesses per 100 full-time employees per year. For a large company with thousands of employees, their safety "rate" will change very slowly with each incremental injury. A typical large company might have an injury rate of anywhere between zero and five injuries per 200,000 hours worked per year. For a company or factory with twenty employees the rate will increase in greater increments. The first injury will give it an injury rate of five, the second of ten, and so on.

People generally do not measure rates just because they are interested in the numbers they get by doing so. They want to make an inference from the rate. Consider an example. On a lovely clear lake two friends, Fred and Harry, own neighboring cottages with docks. If we counted the fish each friend caught every day, how could we infer who was the better fisherman? There will be days when Fred catches more than Harry and others when Harry catches more than Fred. It would be easy to infer who was better if one friend always caught his daily catch limit, and the other rarely caught anything. But what if their observed fishing success rates were not so obviously different?

To answer the question, it helps to think of two types of rates: the observed rate and the inferred rate. The observed rate is the number of fish each friend catches per day. The inferred rate represents the fishing prowess of each friend.

For a given and constant inferred rate, there is a particular pattern in the counts one expects to see. This pattern does not depend on what you are counting.

Figure 2.4 shows this pattern for two inferred rates. The number of fish each friend catches per day is on the bottom axis and the percentage of days you would expect each friend to catch that many fish on the vertical axis. It is based on Fred having a fishing prowess of one fish per day, and Harry having a fishing prowess of one and a half fish per day.

The pattern in Figure 2.4 follows what is called a Poisson distribution. It is named after Siméon-Denis Poisson (1781–1840), a Frenchman. Coincidentally, *poisson* is French for fish.

Figure 2.4 shows there is a lot of overlap in the patterns of counts for the two inferred rates, even though Harry's prowess, or inferred fishing success rate, is 50 percent higher than Fred's. For example, with these inferred rates, we would expect Fred to catch three fish on 6 percent of the days, and Harry to catch three fish on 13 percent of days. We would expect Fred to catch zero fish on 37 percent of days, and Harry to catch zero fish on 22 percent of the days.

What this pattern of expected counts means is that if they fish long enough, there could be days when Fred catches up to three fish and Harry catches none. Similarly there could be days when Fred catches four fish and Harry catches one. If we did not observe the two friends long enough, we could easily make the wrong inference about who was the better fisherman.

Figure 2.4   Number of fish Harry and Fred can expect to catch per day, given their average catches.

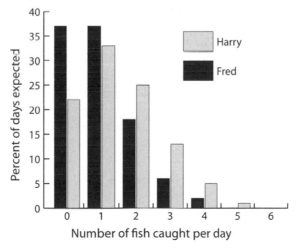

The upshot is that it is very difficult to make reasonable inferences about inferred rates on the basis of only one or a small number of observed rates because the large inferential errors would make them meaningless. To make an inference, you generally have to compare the counts over a long period with the expected pattern. Yet this is rarely done. It is typical to read a newspaper headline that says something like "Crime rate in Appleville rises" on the basis of a change in the observed crime rate. The headline seems to suggest that Appleville is a more dangerous place—that the inferred crime rate has risen—because the observed rate has risen. This is misleading. It is like inferring that Fred is a better fisherman than Harry because on Saturday he caught three fish and Harry only caught one.

In business unreasonable inferences are also made on the basis of rates for such things as customer complaints, work injuries, or production. For example, corporate bosses will often award plant managers for improved safety performance if their injury rate drops off. But this alone does not mean that the plant managers' safety *prowess* has improved even though his safety *record* temporarily did. You have to look at the whole pattern of injury rates. Often the rate will bounce right back up shortly afterward, leaving people scratching their heads, and wasting their time, trying to find an explanation.

IMPROVING THE ACCURACY OF COUNTS

To improve the speed and accuracy of counting, people are regularly inventing machines to aid in the task. If the resulting count is important to you, you should carefully check any claims of precision made by vendors, and check again once it is installed and operating.

A cookie manufacturer I once advised spent about $1 million on a cookie-counting machine. This manufacturer sold dry biscuits to customers who used them in their own plants to make into sandwiches with a sugary creamy stuffing between the biscuits. The biscuits are inexpensive compared to the stuffing. The customers needed to purchase exact quantities of the biscuits to match the expensive stuffing, and wanted my client to guarantee that they sold exactly the number of biscuits that they said they did.

The vendor of the cookie-counting machine guaranteed that it was "99.999 percent accurate." My client asked me to figure out whether their claim was correct. To me, "99.999 percent accurate" meant that the machine would only miscount by 1 cookie in 100,000, and my job was to verify the claim. No easy task. When I called the vendor he could not specify what he meant by his claim, other than to say "it is very, very accurate." Was his 99.999 percent just a figure of speech for "very, very," or was it meaningful?

Fortunately, we did not have to hand-count hundreds of thousands of biscuits. Not only would this have been time-consuming but just as inaccurate in itself. The biscuits were cellophane-wrapped in bundles. The counting machine was designed to take high-speed images of the bundles and count the biscuits by computer. We took several cartons of them and, in an elaborately designed experiment to control for the effects of handling the bundles, ran the bundles through the machine twice or more. If the machine was accurate at all, then in a small number of such runs we should have had identical results. The results made it perfectly obvious that "very, very" and "99.999 percent" were much too loosely applied terms. My client sent the machine back.

TOOL BOX

- Clearly define the things you want to count. You can test whether the definition is clear by asking several people to use it to count the same things. They should get the same counts.
- Describe the purpose of the count so that the counters understand the context of the definition. How will you use the count? Why are you counting?
- Use tools to reduce simple counting errors, such as hand-held counter clickers, tally sheets, turnstiles, electric eyes, and so on.
- Describe the population of things you are counting:

  - What are its physical or geographical boundaries?
  - Will you count objects that change, enter, or leave the population while you are counting? Or only those that were there at the beginning or end of the count?
  - How is this population different from similar or overlapping populations?

- Clearly state when counting begins and stops. Is this a snapshot or several counts over a longer period?

- Estimate how much effort will be required to count the objects in the time frame you have defined. Will you have enough people, time, and equipment to do the counting?
- If you are planning to sample from the population rather than count all objects in the population, you need a sampling plan. The sampling plan should:

  - Have a defined and published methodology that is subject to criticism and review by others
  - Have a good track record in allowing reasonably precise inference from a single sample
  - Have a sampling error that is acceptable for your purposes
  - Define the number of objects you must sample

- How will you determine whether your count is sufficiently precise and accurate for your needs? You should find ways to check whether the counters, definitions, tools, time frame, and sampling plan are working the way you expect them to work.

THREE

Measuring Accurately with Instruments

A perfect and just measure shalt thou have.

—Deuteronomy 25:14

Planes crash when their instruments fail. Businesses lose money when their instruments fail. Pilots constantly check whether their instruments work. Most managers just believe theirs do.

On the instrument panel of an aircraft such as a Boeing 727 there is a prominently displayed group of seven square lights called the "instrument comparator." Each light has an abbreviation on it to indicate what it is measuring. The instrument comparator compares the readings between seven pairs of vital instruments that are needed to fly the plane, usually the pilot's and copilot's.

When the difference between two instruments in a pair exceeds a certain predefined setting, the instrument comparator lights up. The pilot must then figure out, or guess, which of the two instruments (if any) is telling him the truth—or miss the runway. In the unlikely event that both instruments are off by a similar amount, the comparator may not light up.

The instrument comparator compares instruments for monitoring power supply, the heading the aircraft is flying on, the glide slope—or vertical position relative to runway approach—pitch and roll of the aircraft, the lateral position relative to runway approach, and the altitude. You don't need to be a pilot to see that these are critical measurements. Without them an instrument landing is impossible.

MEASUREMENTS QUANTIFY, BUT THEY DO NOT EXPLAIN

Sensors on aircraft provide information to the instruments, which then quantify it. Pilots are acutely aware of the limitations of the sensors on their instruments, and the biases they create in different conditions. The air speed indicator, for example, senses air speed by sensing the pressure of air outside the aircraft as it hits the inside of a pitot tube affixed to the fuselage. The instrument is calibrated to indicate a true air speed at a defined altitude, air pressure, and temperature. As the aircraft changes altitude, and as the outside temperature and air pressure change, the instrument develops a bias that changes with the altitude, pressure, and temperature. Pilots, out of necessity, know how to compensate for this bias in their interpretation of the instrument readings.

Like the sensors on the fuselage of aircraft, measurements extend the senses. We can tell by sticking our noses out our front doors whether the weather is warm or cool, sweltering or freezing; and we can look in the papers or the Internet to indirectly sense the temperature anywhere in the world.

It took many significant intellectual breakthroughs to develop instruments with sensors that quantify phenomena such as temperature, pressure, and many other physical properties. Until the end of the Middle Ages, people rarely used aids to improve upon their senses in the process of observation.[1] Measuring instruments for length, distance, time, level, angle, mass, and volume relied on sight without enhancement. The basic principles of many of these instruments have changed little since antiquity.

Sometime after AD 1600, clever people invented devices to observe facets of nature that had until then been unobserved, or observed only at the resolution provided by the naked eye. In 1609 Galilei Galileo made improvements that increased the power of the recently invented telescope to twenty, and for the first time saw new details on heavenly bodies that people had never seen despite watching them for millennia, such as sunspots and the moons of Jupiter. In 1655 Robert Hooke looked into slices of cork with his new microscope and was the first person to see cells.

From 1500 to 1900, instruments were invented to sense and quantify properties of electricity and magnetism, gravity, tension, pressure, sound, salinity, oxygen content of air, light intensity, acceleration, and many other things. Today it would be hard for us to imagine a world without volts, ohms, degrees, kilopascals, pH, calories, and so on, because they are part of our everyday reality. The measurement system humans have invented over the centuries has helped, in a very real sense, to shape our perceptions of the world around us. When we learn about distances, miles and kilometers become real for us. When we learn about temperature, degrees become real.

Our senses enable us to perceive the reality that surrounds us. Measurements, by extending the senses, extend our perception of our surroundings. We reflexively believe what our senses tell us, a habit illusionists and magicians exploit to entertain us. We are too readily inclined to believe what measurements tell us, a habit fraudsters use to exploit us. This ability of measurements and measurement units to make reality means measurements can be used as a tool to shape opinions.

The Greek engineer Philo of Byzantium invented the first thermoscope in 250 BC. The thermoscope did not measure temperature but created a visual display of changes in temperature—hence the term scope. It was made of a lead globe from which a tube carried air from the globe to a flask of water. When the globe heated, air came out of the tube, and when it cooled, air was sucked into the tube. Conceptually it was a breakthrough because it replaced the human sense of touch with a mechanical sensor based on the physical properties of lead and air and provided a visual display. Philo did not know why it worked.

Not until Galileo almost 1,900 years later was there an improvement. One version of Galileo's invention is a popular and attractive ornament today, with little glass bulbs that float up and down according to the temperature in a sealed glass tube filled with alcohol. The bulbs have labels on them indicating the temperature—by reading the number on the lowest floating bulb suspended in the middle of the device you obtain the temperature. (See Figure 3.1.) The other bulbs either float near the surface or lie at the bottom.

Galileo's original device did not have numbers. It sensed the temperature but did not quantify it. Like Philo's device, it used the physical properties of the materials the device was built from to sense and display temperature, although with greater clarity. As the density of the alcohol in Galileo's thermoscope changes with temperature, the floating glass bulbs float or sink, or, at the right temperature for a particular bulb, remain suspended. Philo's device could not distinguish between changes in atmospheric pressure and changes in temperature. Galileo, by sealing the tube, minimized the effect of atmospheric pressure changes, a principle still applied in the design of glass thermometers today. His application of the property of fluids to change density when the temperature changes is still in use.

Figure 3.1   A Galileo Thermometer.

The first attempt at quantifying temperature was in 1612 when the Italian doctor Santorio Santorio invented a scale for Galileo's device, which he used in his clinical work.

A doctor in another city who wanted to compare his temperatures with Santorio's would need to be able to recreate Santorio's scale on his own instrument, or to relate it mathematically to his own scale. But Santorio did not find a way to describe to someone else how to re-create the scale. He could thus use his thermometer to compare the temperatures of patients within his own practice to determine whether their temperature was going up or down, but the numbers would have little meaning anywhere else.

It took three and a half centuries to develop the standardized temperature scales, and the calibration criteria needed to recreate them, that we use today. Ole Christensen Rømer (1644–1710) took the next step and made up a particular mixture of salt and ice water. He used that to create and calibrate a scale in which water froze at 7 1/2 and boiled at 60. He filled his thermometer with red wine. In 1714 Daniel Gabriel Fahrenheit (1686–1736) switched from red wine to alcohol and then to mercury. Mercury gives greater accuracy because it expands at a more constant rate then alcohol. He invented the scale that bears his name. In his scale, zero was the temperature of a particular mixture of ice and water, and 96 was the temperature of horse blood, which he assumed was the same as human's.

In 1742, Anders Celsius (1701–1744) created an inverted centigrade temperature scale in which water boiled at zero and froze at 100. In 1744,

Carl Linnaeus (1707–1778) flipped the scale around to what is in use today, with 0 at freezing and 100 at boiling, and called it centigrade, with its unit or measurement designated (°C).[2]

In 1848, William Thomson, or Lord Kelvin (1824–1907) as he is more commonly known, proposed that 0 should be assigned to thermodynamic absolute zero and that we should use the degree centigrade as a unit, meaning that water froze at 273°K and boiled at 373°K. In 1954, 342 years after Santorio invented his scale, this scale became the Kelvin thermodynamic temperature scale and its unit of measurement was designated the degree Kelvin (°K) which at that time became the unit of temperature in the International System of Units.

From the time of Philo's thermoscope to the early 19th century there was little input from theory.[3] The builders of thermometers and the developers of temperature scales did not know precisely what temperature was. There is some confusion even today.

Many textbooks define temperature as the average velocity of molecules.[4] This is inaccurate. One definition of temperature says that it is the property that determines whether a system is in thermal equilibrium with another system.[5] When two systems, such as bars of metal, are in thermal equilibrium, they do not exchange heat with each other. They thus have the same temperature. But even this definition has problems. Temperatures can only be determined when a system, such as a pot of water, is, or is almost, in equilibrium. If you put the pot on the burner and crank up the heat, the different layers of water and the molecules of water within them dance a chaotic shuffle with each other, exchanging energy because they have different temperatures. The concept of temperature, that is, the sharp concept as physicists think of it, becomes meaningless in such a case.[6] So what is *the* temperature of the pot?

There are two important lessons here for business: First, to quantify physical properties there must be some way to calibrate the measurement device. Second, measurements quantify, but they do not explain. The ability to quantify and measure, while it may be very useful, does not necessarily grant fundamental knowledge and understanding of the phenomenon you are measuring. Some business writers claim that you can measure anything. You can certainly create numbers that look like measurements and call them anything you want, but they may or may not mean anything. When we say we are measuring some "thing," there will always be uncertainty about what that "thing" actually is. Defining "it" will often be difficult.

MEASUREMENT OBJECTS

In this book we will use the term "measurement object" to describe the thing you intend to measure. The word "object" means both a thing and a purpose or objective. This double meaning is appropriate because your objective is to measure some thing even if it is tough to define. It emphasizes that there could be a difference between what you intend to measure and what you actually measure.

Whatever temperature was, scientists throughout the centuries knew that they could measure it. They knew that liquids and metals changed density when they warmed and cooled, and that the density changed by the same extent under the same conditions. They used this principle to sense temperature and then create visual or electrical signals and quantify them.

The criteria for calibrating a thermometer, if its temperature range is within ordinary environmental conditions, can be fairly readily defined, are easily applied, and are not contentious. At sea level, distilled water freezes at 0°C or 32°F and boils at 100°C or 212°F. Metals are used for higher temperatures. And for greater accuracy the "triple point"[7] of water, rather than the freezing point, is used.

There can be more than one way to calibrate a measurement device. There are sometimes fortunes at stake in the choice. In the late 19th century, British and German scientists and politicians argued over two competing methods for calibrating instruments for measuring electrical resistance. Precise measurements, and thus calibrations, of electrical resistance were necessary to find faults in the telegraph cables, especially undersea cables. A single fault can render a cable that is thousands of miles long completely useless. The manufacture and laying of cables was a new and growing business at the time. The protagonists included Lord Kelvin and the German engineer Werner von Siemens (1816–1892). In 1847 Siemens and Johann Halske founded Telegraphen-Bauanstadt von Siemens & Halske, which grew into the modern multinational Siemens.

Siemens had invented a device that used mercury to calibrate electrical resistance measurements. In his autobiography he wrote that "the scales of resistance with the mercury unit, prepared by my firm, proved extremely useful in laying the cable from Suez to Aden, and for the first time made reliable determinations of fault possible."[8] He was able to pinpoint faults within meters, and then fish up the cable so that it could be repaired and transmit telegraphs. Siemens won contracts to lay thousands of miles of telegraph cables. Siemens's method, with some modifications, became the standard in the 1884 International Telegraph Conference.

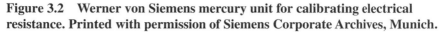

Figure 3.2   Werner von Siemens mercury unit for calibrating electrical resistance. Printed with permission of Siemens Corporate Archives, Munich.

TRUST IN MEASUREMENTS MUST BE EARNED

When consumers began switching from gas to electricity to light their homes in the late 19th century, there was no standard way to measure its consumption.[9] Consumers could not understand how such an intangible thing as electricity could be metered. They had difficulty trusting the entire measurement process in which unknown individuals used a mysterious device, to which they did not have access, to measure a quantity they did not understand based upon which they had to pay the bill. Consumers could not even read some of the first meters and relied entirely on the electricity companies to provide them with the readings.

They acquiesced in the belief, promoted by electricity suppliers, that a meter could measure the quantity of electricity passing through their meters as if it were a current of gas passing through a gas meter. But this was wrong. What matters when you measure power consumption is not the electric current itself, but the energy that passes through the meter. To measure energy you need to know both the current and the voltage. The same current with lower voltage provides less energy, and it is energy that people need to light their homes, not just current.

In 1889, none of the meters yielded equally accurate results over the full range of loads consumers used, from a single lamp to many. A British physicist, William Edward Ayrton (1847–1908), mounted a three-year campaign against the power companies and their meters, saying that "what was registered by the meter and what was charged to the consumer were two entirely different things."[10] He said that suppliers could cheat consumers by varying supply voltage.[11] He argued that if voltage dropped by 4 percent, consumers would get 12 percent less light, and it was light they were paying for. If it went too high, bulbs would burn out too quickly, forcing consumers to incur an additional expense. He won his campaign in 1892, and energy meters have been the standard technology ever since.

It strains belief today that so much mistrust could exist over an issue that is now mundane. Most of us never even bother to think about our electric meters and other measurement devices. Perhaps that has made people complacent.

Be careful before you trust measurements. Examples of measurement fraudsters exist in every field. Hwang Woo-Suk, the Korean stem cell researcher who had achieved heroic status for his research, admitted at his trial in July 2006 that he had fabricated data. In June 2006, University of Vermont researcher Eric Poehlman was sentenced to a year plus a day in prison for fabricating research data. He "admitted faking results in numerous studies and proposals for a decade beginning in 1992."[12] In 1997, an investigation showed that drilling data of the Canadian gold mining company Bre-X was fraudulent, causing a spectacular crash that wiped out $6 billion in market value and bilked thousands of investors of their money.

Untrustworthy measurements are not usually a result of fraud. It is not uncommon for any two people, be they nurses in a pediatric ward or pulp mill workers on the factory floor, to obtain different measurements of the same thing, or at least what appears superficially to be the same thing. Often there are slight, and usually unknown, changes in the object they measure and the conditions under which they measure it. In principle, if you measured an object that remained absolutely constant under precisely the same conditions you would get the same measurement every time. The practical problem is that objects and conditions change, so measurements vary. The challenge is to minimize those changes.

The chart below shows an example, taken from two pulp mill workers measuring something called "freeness" of pulp, which indicates how easily water flows through the pulp when it is on the paper machine. To get these measurements, a single bucket of pulp was given to two workers and they were each asked to measure freeness nine times, alternating between workers. They used the same instrument.

The average value of the data from worker A on the top line in Figure 3.3 was 98, and from the worker B on the bottom line, was 92. The dots show the individual measurements.

What is remarkable, and typical, about the data in Figure 3.3 is the extent of the variation for each tester measuring from a single bucket of pulp and using the same measuring instrument. One would hope, if they were measuring from a single bucket, that all the measurements would be very similar. The problem is that pulp is not uniform, and even though the workers use the same equipment, they use it differently and with different standards of care. So it turns out they are measuring different material in different ways, even though they think they are measuring the same pulp the same way, which is partly why they get different measurements. There is not a bucket of pulp; there is a bucket of lots of different pulps—another example of the difficulty of defining the measurement object. They do not use the background information about the pulp to take accurate and precise measurements, so the inferential chain breaks.

Figure 3.3   Measurement variability of two testers (A and B).

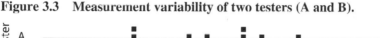
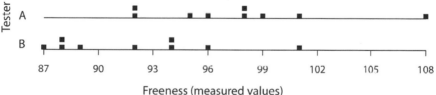

Freeness (measured values)

Figure 3.4   Inadequate use of background information.

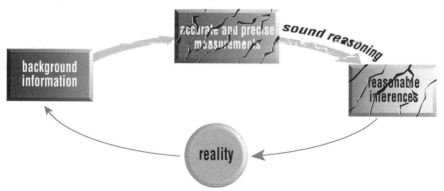

The variability of measurements of the same item or material is the *precision* of the measurement *process*. The *measurement process* includes the procedures, equipment, instruments, and steps to get a measurement.

The precision of a measuring process has a direct bearing on its trustworthiness. If a thermometer says it is 70°F outside you should be able to reasonably trust that the actual temperature is not far from the value you read on the thermometer. The difference between the value you read and the true value is what is typically called the measurement error. The difficulty, as we have seen, is that the notion of "true value" is a very slippery thing, and even if the true value were, for a moment, not too slippery to grab onto, we need some way of knowing what it is other than using the measurement instrument whose trustworthiness we are trying to establish. This knowledge is usually gained by trusting a set of standards, traceable back to something like *le grand K* under its glass bell in Paris.

When comparison with a standard shows that there is a discrepancy between the measured and the true value, the usual procedure is to calibrate the instrument so that it matches the standard. This procedure, however, can very easily add even more uncertainty to the values produced by a measurement device. For if a discrepancy is observed, and if we can believe that the calibrator—another thing or person we have to trust—took due care in the taking of the measurement and that it is not anomalous or fraudulent, how do we infer from that that the measurement process must be calibrated? With a single measurement we cannot make this inference if we do not know the precision of the measurement process.

Suppose, for example, that you weighed a standardized one-kilo weight, traceable back to *le Grand K*, and obtained a single reading of 1.01 kilograms. Is the measurement error of 0.01, or 1 percent, caused by a calibration problem, or by the precision of the measurement process? You cannot tell without more information.

The chart in Figure 3.5 shows twenty (simulated) measurements of a standard kilogram weight for each of two scales.

Scale two has a much lower precision, that is, higher variability. Scale one has far more precision, or less variability, than scale two. One could reasonably infer that a reading of 1.01 on scale one, with a standardized weight of 1.00 kilograms, indicated the scale was out of calibration by 0.01 kilograms, or 1 percent. An identical reading on scale two, which has a much lower precision, indicates no such thing. If a single measurement on scale two showed a .01 kilogram discrepancy between the measured and the true value, given the precision of this scale, the calibrator would be

Figure 3.5   Measurement variability of two scales.

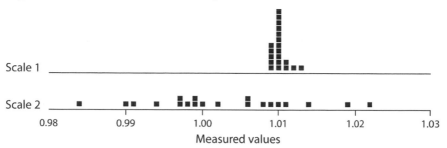

Figure 3.6   Measurement accuracy and precision.

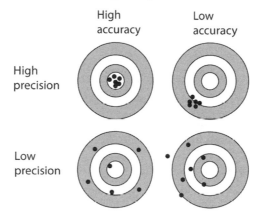

ill advised to make a calibration adjustment. To do so might in fact throw the scale *even more* out of calibration.

The "precision" of a measurement process may be defined as the closeness of a set of measurements of an identical item to each other. It is an intrinsic property of the measurement process and is unrelated to the measurement object. The "accuracy" is a relation between the measurement process and the measurement object. It is the closeness of the *average* of a set of similarly performed measurements to the value of the measurement object. (To the layman the terms "accuracy" and "precision" are synonymous. I confess it took me years to sort out their *statistical* meanings.) A lack of accuracy is often referred to as a bias. Another typical way to describe accuracy and precision is with rifle shots on a target, as seen in Figure 3.6.

DETERMINING MEASUREMENT ACCURACY

The accuracy of a measurement process often changes according to the value of the measurement object. For example, at 100 pounds the inaccuracy of a weigh scale could be 1 pound and at 200 pounds it could be 2 pounds. In this case, a simple 1-pound adjustment will not recalibrate the scale. The trustworthiness of a measurement process thus depends on its ability to measure accurately at all measured values within the range that the measurement process is used.

The charts in Figures 3.7 to 3.10 illustrate accuracy (they are constructed from simulated data). Figure 3.7 shows ten measurements of ten standards, whose values go from 1 to 10. The diagonal line indicates perfect correspondence between measurement and standard. The measurements fall on either side of the line with a band of roughly constant width and centered on the line, showing that both the precision and accuracy are about the same whatever standard is measured.

In Figure 3.8 the measurements lie above the line by a fixed amount, plus the jiggle on either side of the line resulting from the precision. A reasonable inference from this sort of pattern is that the measurement process is not accurate and that there is a discrepancy, or bias, which is constant at all measured values. This is called a constant measurement bias. (The

Figure 3.7   Measured versus standard values.

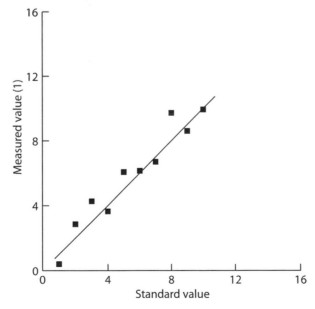

dashed line shows the trend of the measurements to make it easy to compare with the diagonal line.)

In Figure 3.9, there is no bias for small standards, but it grows as the standards get bigger. This generally means that the measurement bias is not constant, but increases as the value of the measurement object increases. This is called a nonconstant measurement bias.

Finally in Figure 3.10, there is a combination of the constant and nonconstant measurement bias.

Before you can make a proper calibration, you need to figure out whether there is a constant (Figure 3.8) or a nonconstant bias (Figures 3.9 and 3.10). You also need to know the precision of your measurement method. Before you infer that there is either a constant or a nonconstant bias, you need to compare the amount of the bias with the precision.

To use this terminology in a common situation, when someone says that his watch runs fast, the person usually means one of several things. Some people mean they have set their watches to run five minutes ahead so that they are not late for meetings. They know their watches stay on time otherwise; thus, they have built in a constant bias. Others mean that the watch speeds up over the course of the day, so that it tells the correct time if they set it in the morning, but by evening it is running ahead of the

Figure 3.8   Measured versus standard values showing constant bias.

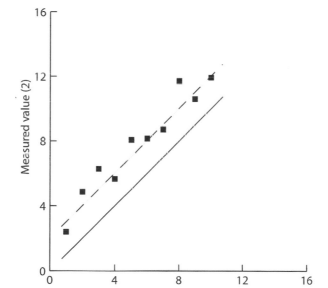

Figure 3.9   Measured versus standard values showing nonconstant bias.

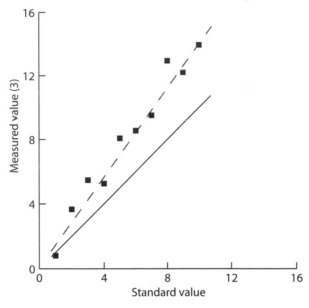

Figure 3.10   Measured versus standard values showing constant and non-constant bias.

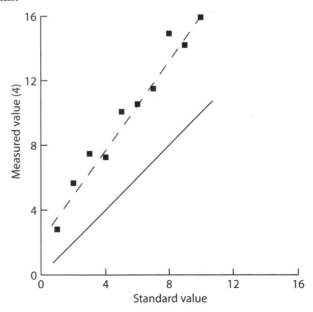

correct time. This is a nonconstant bias. And of course both situations can occur simultaneously.

Occasionally biases are built into gauges for a purpose. I suspect this might be the case with my car's gas gauge because of its rapid drop when it gets toward the bottom of the scale. I noticed that the speed at which the needle dropped between the 1/4 mark and the *empty* mark was much faster than at any other point in the scale. To figure out what was going on, I recorded how much fuel I added to the tank at each quarter of the tank, and calculated how much I should have added based on the capacity of the tank, as written in my owner's manual. The chart in Figure 3.11 suggests that there may be a nonconstant bias. When the gauge indicates Full, I could not any gas to the tank, so the tank really was full. When the gauge indicated 3/4, I could add 1/4 of a tank to it, so the 3/4 reading was also accurate. When it showed 1/2, I could add 1/2; and when it showed 1/4, I could add 3/4. But when it indicated Empty, I could not add a full tank of gas but only 7/8 of a tank—meaning there was still 1/8 of a tank of gas left even though the gauge said it was empty. Thus the needle drops the distance of 1/4 tank on the gauge in the time it takes to normally drop 1/8 of a tank, making it appear to drop quickly. Perhaps

Figure 3.11   Bias in gas gauge.

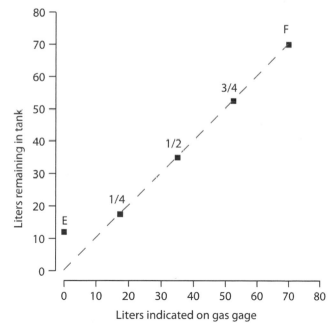

the idea is to create an impression that the car is rapidly running out of gas, an effect which the designers presumably knew would suitably alter our perception of reality because of our trust in their measurements. Or perhaps the irregular shape of the tank causes the rush into the gas gauge when tank is nearly empty, and the scale on the gas gauge does not account for it.

A gauge that is calibrated to fool people can cause them to begin to distrust the gauge once they catch on. It certainly has worked in the case of our car: my wife and I have had many discussions about how much farther we can drive once the gas gauge reads empty. We are missing this key piece of information, and are thus taking more risk than we would be taking if we knew the engine stopped dead when the gas gauge indicated empty. (Fortunately we have not overestimated yet. If we do, I suspect I will be doing the walking while my wife pulls out one of her ever-present paperback novels.)

Bias and calibration problems are not necessarily caused solely by instruments and their ability to sense natural phenomena. The measurement process itself, of which the instrument is merely one part, can introduce a bias. We saw in the example with the two pulp workers that on average they obtained different readings with the same instruments, so the measurement process used by at least one of them contains a bias.

For example, the managers of an ammonia plant were trying to reduce the number of rail cars that they had to downgrade every year. If the rail car contained more than 18 parts per million (ppm) of water in the ammonia, it was downgraded from industrial to agricultural grade, at a loss of about $1,000 per car depending on prices.

We designed a simple experiment in which a controlled set of sampling methods, collection flasks, laboratory technicians, and laboratory techniques were employed. The instruments were working fine, but the experiment showed that the sample collection process added a constant bias of up to 12 ppm of water. A tank car with 6 ppm of water in it would produce a reading of 18 ppm. It would therefore be downgraded unnecessarily. We experimented with different methods of cleaning and drying sampling flasks, taking samples from the rail cars, and preparing the samples in the laboratory. We also experimented in different weather conditions. The information helped us to develop a measurement process that eliminated the bias in the collection and preparation of the sample. After the first year there were five hundred fewer cars rejected—a savings of $500,000 per year.

CHARACTERIZING MEASUREMENT PRECISION

In practice, the determination of measurement precision is complicated by the difficulty in repeatedly measuring an item. This can only be done reliably when there is a standard item that is not destroyed in testing and whose properties do not change during the repeated measures. In the pulp example mentioned above, the two workers were each sampling from the same bucket of pulp. Pulp is lumpy stuff, and each sample they took from the bucket was a bit different from the others. Some of the observed precision was caused by these differences, and some was caused by slight changes in the measurement process and conditions. There are many similar situations where the short-range variations of the measurement objects are difficult to separate from the measurement precision.

When a constant (or virtually constant) standard is unavailable, measuring measurement system precision is problematic, especially if the measurement process is destructive. If you destroy an object when you measure it, you cannot measure it more than once, making it difficult to find the precision. What you can do instead is measure several very similar objects in close succession, and observe the variation among them. But then you cannot separate that part of the observed variation caused by differences in the objects, and that part caused by measurement system precision.

The only way out of this conundrum is to make educated guesses as to the relative contribution of the variation of the measurement object and the variation of the measurement process. Sometimes you may have background information that a measurement object is "smooth" over small scales of time and space, for example, "smooth" peanut butter. Or you might know that parts manufactured in very close succession and on the same machine are very similar. In such a case, if you measured several of these parts, you would be able to estimate the amount of observed variation that comes from the measurement process. Other times though, your background information could be that the measurement object is "rough" over small scales, like crunchy peanut butter. Then the variation caused by the precision is confounded with small differences in the measurement object. This makes it very hard to untangle the variation of the measurement object itself and the measurement variation.

Often people just assume (perhaps without knowing it) that the variation they observe in their measurements is caused almost entirely by the measurement object. In other words, they *assume* they have a measurement process with near-perfect precision. This assumption only makes sense if they have already taken great care to make the measurement precision very high, for it rarely is high unless such care has be taken to make it so.

In most cases, if the measurement is destructive, there is no easy way to separate the precision from short-range variation in the measurement object. In one pulp mill, I found that the variation within a single bucket of pulp was 75 percent as large as the variation observed in the pulp over the course of a whole day. Was this the result of poor precision of the measurement process, or high pulp variation within the bucket compared to variations over the course of a day?

The answer to that question mattered, because the mill manager had the habit of meeting with his superintendents every morning to review the pulp measurements from the previous day and decide whether the variation in the test results was sufficiently large to warrant making significant—and sometimes expensive—changes to the production process to compensate. He was (unknowingly) assuming that their measurement process was very precise and that virtually all observed variations were caused by perturbations and drift in the manufacturing process. If he was misled by the measurements he could unnecessarily perturb, or even upset, his operation.

I told them that it was possible that they were basing their decisions (upon which the quality of their newsprint and the profitability of their mill depended) on an unacceptably imprecise measurement process. Subsequent investigations gave credence to my suspicions. They were unnecessarily perturbing their process. Most of the variation they saw at their morning meetings probably came from a poorly controlled measurement process rather than a poorly controlled manufacturing process. Unfortunately this situation is all too common, because people trust their measurements just like they trust their electricity meters.

HOW COMMON OBJECTIVES BUILD TRUST IN MEASUREMENT

The managers of a global manufacturer of a specialty chemical used for coloring had designed a way to measure its brightness and implemented it in factories around the world. As the brightness of the colorant is a critical parameter for customers upon which large contracts were won or lost, top management had decreed that the variable pay of plant managers would depend significantly on satisfactorily attaining brightness targets.

The plants produced the chemical in the form of a powder and shipped it in quantities varying from pallets stacked with bags of colorant to entire trainloads. The quality assurance department took the samples and measured them.

The objective of the measurements, as the quality laboratories saw it, was to determine whether individual customer shipments met the brightness specification. The plant managers and production departments had a different objective: to determine whether the production process had drifted and therefore needed adjustment. In this way they could keep the colorant—and their bonuses—on target. These two objectives were not entirely incompatible, but neither were they identical. They ended up being competitive.

The plant managers wanted the labs to change the way they sampled powder and measured brightness. The quality assurance labs did not work for the plant managers, so they were not inclined to change. The frequency of their samples did not give the production managers the information they needed to determine whether to adjust the process. The process was quite variable and tricky to control. To the plant managers, it seemed that the quality assurance labs were just trying to catch their mistakes and cheat them of their bonuses, without giving them the information they needed to avoid off-spec product.

The production departments were constantly challenging the results from the laboratory. The laboratory managers felt their professional ethics were under attack. The plant managers felt their paychecks were under attack. Distrust and acrimony had grown to the point that in some plants they were barely on speaking terms.

The production process was difficult to maintain in a steady state. There was considerable variation in brightness within a single customer shipment. If the shipment was an entire rail car, how should they pick samples from the car to determine whether it met the customer's specification? What does it mean to say that the shipment met the customer specification? Does it mean that even if you tested all of the contents of the rail car (a practical impossibility not only because of time and resource constraints but because the test is destructive) *none* of it should be out of specification?

Or does it mean that if you take some samples, at times dictated by the sampling plan, that none of *them* are outside the specification? This definition would have no relevance if the samples were taken without regard to the actual variation within the shipment. It is the same problem we faced with the scallops in chapter two. Suppose it took three hours to fill the rail car and samples were taken at hourly intervals. Suppose the colorant in the samples was very bright and thus acceptable: we would still know very little about the composition of the whole rail car, because we know the process varies a lot. A plant could send garbage to the customer, even though the measurements were good.

Or does "on spec" mean that the average of the shipment, if it could be accurately determined through a clever sampling plan, should be within the specification? This would be a problematic definition for the customer given that the production process varies so much, because the average could be within specification while a large proportion of the powder could be out of specification. It could only be used if the variability within the entire load was understood well enough to determine how to sample it to obtain a reasonably representative sample.

Finally the company called a meeting of laboratory and production personnel from around the world to try and resolve the issue of trust over the measurement process. There were three main issues: first, what objectives should the measurements serve; second, whether the testing procedure itself was sufficiently accurate and precise for its objectives; and third, whether the method used to select samples provided a good representation of the material sent to customers.

The outcome of the meeting was a series of tests and trials at plants around the globe that produced a measurement process that, while not addressing all of these concerns, at least built up some trust and set production and laboratory managers on the course to resolving them over time.

HIDING AGENDAS BEHIND BAD MEASUREMENTS

Sometimes people are quite content with instrumental measurements that they do not trust because it serves their purposes.

Most industrialized countries require companies to report their pollutants. In Canada, for example, the government requires many companies to report the quantity of pollutants they discharge. The measurements are recorded in the National Pollutants Release Inventory, which is available to the public.

The government says nothing about how these pollutants are to be measured or what steps are to be taken to ensure the accuracy and precision of the discharge measurements. It would require a massive social, bureaucratic, and legislative effort to do so.[13] Both industry and environmental groups take advantage of the resulting ambiguity. In commerce, the buyer and seller both have an interest in ensuring accuracy of measurement for each transaction, which builds in a minimal level of oversight of the measurement process. Bureaucracies, armed with regulations on weights and measures, provide a more general level of oversight. These levels of oversight are missing in the Canadian National Pollutants Release Inventory.

Their website gives several instructive examples.[14] A galvanizing factory that has to calculate its total annual discharges of zinc to its wastewater may take measurements of zinc concentration on any twelve days it chooses throughout the year. They then multiply the concentrations by the flow of water on those days to get daily average discharges. It may then multiply this average by the number of days it was operating in a year to get a number that is supposedly the total amount of zinc discharged in that year.

This method, of course, leaves open the possibility of measuring zinc concentrations on good discharge days. Let us be charitable, though, and assume that the galvanizing factory makes no such attempt. There are still plenty of ways the measurement process can be very inaccurate and imprecise, such as the way it measures water flow and zinc concentration and the way it selects water samples and calibration standards.

Rather than striving to develop trustworthy measurements, businesses and environmentalists can each use the inaccuracies of the measurement process to their own advantage. Industrialists can use the methods of estimation to their advantage to report at the lower end of the allowed range. Environmentalists take advantage of anomalies in the reporting system to stir up fear about increases in pollutants. For example, industries do not have to report if their discharges are below certain thresholds, such as a 10-ton limit. A small increase in emissions due to increased production can push plants over the threshold, leading to a proportionally much greater increase in pollutants reported to the inventory. The environmentalists then cry foul.

FINDING READING ERRORS

Reading errors occur when people or machines filter or round information. In a large clinical study of kidney disease in children in Nova Scotia, Canada, nurses across the province had taken blood pressure readings from about four thousand children with mercury sphygmomanometers (the manual blood pressure devices seen in doctors' offices). The doctor leading the study expected that the blood pressure data would be an important explanatory variable for kidney disease.

After a quick scan of the data, it became apparent that there was a higher proportion of blood pressure readings ending in zero than ending in any other number. Two's were also very frequent. The odd digits were rarely reported. What had happened was that most nurses had rounded each reading to the nearest value of ten. For example, a nurse might report a reading such as 123 millimeters of mercury (mm/Hg) over 77, as 120 over 80.

The doctor leading the study believed he needed a fairly fine resolution on the blood pressure measurements to find the effect he was looking for. He was shocked at this finding because his instructions had been to measure to the nearest mm/Hg. By rounding to the nearest 10 mm/Hg the nurses had in effect reduced the resolution ten times.

This phenomenon is known as terminal digit preference, and has been observed in clinical research. One study[15] found that terminal digit preference might affect the treatment of patients. In a clinical trial[16] studying the treatment of high blood pressure, the researchers found that 42 percent of the blood pressure readings ended in zero. It also found a preference for the blood pressure reading 148 mm/Hg. "This arose from the instruction to investigators to reduce blood pressure to below 150 mm/Hg," they reported.

Doctors and nurses are highly trained people who understand the relationship between blood pressure and their patients' health. Yet study after study has shown that we cannot assume that their blood pressure measurements are either sufficiently accurate or precise for either patient care or clinical research.

For a nurse taking a quick blood pressure test or for an emergency room physician examining a patient brought in by ambulance, a reading to the nearest 10 mm/Hg is quite adequate for making a fast, general medical judgment about a patient's condition. Habits develop accordingly, and are hard to change.

Scale reading errors are caused by inherent limitations in the resolution of measurement scales, whether analog or digital. Consider a digital pH meter that gives a reading of 6.2. We know the pH is not exactly 6.2. It could be somewhere between 6.15 and 6.25, but we do not know where. (This assumes that the people who built the pH meter designed it to round correctly.)

A digital stopwatch does not round. If it reads 6.2 seconds this means (if they built it correctly) that the time is *at least* 6.2 seconds. What we know, therefore, is that the measurement is greater or equal to 6.2 seconds but less than 6.3 seconds.

Scale reading errors on analog scales occur when the measurement object falls between the incremental lines on the scale. In Figure 3.12 a ruler

Figure 3.12   Scale reading error with a ruler.

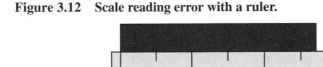

is used to measure a part. How long is the part? It seems it is almost 2.75 inches long, but not quite. Is it 2.73 inches long or 2.74? Different people give different answers. Some round up to 2.75 inches, others to 3 inches, and others still try to estimate between the lines and read 2.73 or 2.74.

There is no formal rule for determining the scale reading error on an analog scale. To find it, we must use our judgment and knowledge about the measurement process, and ask: What are the minimum and maximum values that the measurement object could have for which we will not see any difference with our instrument? Then it is up to you to decide whether such a reading error is acceptable.

TOOL BOX

Before trusting measurements of physical properties you should make a diligent and *ongoing* effort to determine whether:

- The measurement process is suitably accurate and precise to satisfy the purpose of the measurement over all ranges of the measurement objects
- The persons making the measurements can be trusted to report the measurements honestly
- The persons making the measurements have the necessary skills to consistently read instrument scales, select and prepare samples, and follow the steps of the measurement process and procedures
- The method of collecting samples is highly likely to produce representative samples, that is, samples that are a miniature replica of the population with respect to the measurement object
- The method of calibration only makes adjustments to the measurement process when there is sufficient evidence that it is inaccurate, as opposed to reacting to variations due to the precision of the measurement process
- The method of calibration uses a standard, if possible, that is traceable to an international standard (such as *le Grand K*)
- The sensors used in the measurement instrument are sensing the property you want them to sense
- There is a defined process for verifying and maintaining the quality of measurements that is implemented and itself tested

FOUR

Rating, Scoring, and Ranking Reliably

It explains everything, but predicts nothing.

—Pierre-Simon Laplace (1749–1827)

The way analysts rate stocks in the financial markets provides fertile ground for creating misleading indicators. One definition[1] of "stock rating" says

> A stock rating will usually tell the investor how well a stock's market value relates to what analysts believe is a fair value for the stock, based on an objective evaluation of the company.

Sounds like a solid, objective measurement process on which small investors can make informed decisions affecting their financial health.

Weiss Ratings, an independent company that issues ratings on financial institutions, analyzed "buy," "sell," and "hold" ratings issued to companies that had gone bankrupt. The company looked at a total of fifty investment banking and brokerage firms that had issued ratings to nineteen companies that filed for Chapter eleven in the first four months of 2002. Their study[2] found that:

1. Ratings publicly available from 94% of the 50 firms continued to indicate that investors should buy or hold shares in failing companies right up to the day these companies filed for bankruptcy.

2. Among the 19 bankrupt companies, 12 continued to receive strictly "buy" or "hold" ratings on the date of bankruptcy filing. (© Weiss Ratings, LLC. Used by permission.)

There can be little doubt that such ratings are meaningless.

Rating schemes can be useful when human senses work better than man-made sensors. There are many things for which we have not invented sensors. In good rating schemes, the rater follows well-defined rules and standards to arrive at a rating. The rater's personal opinions have little influence on the rating. This is achieved through blinding, training, calibrating, and so on. The result is that most ratings come from the rater's sensory experience of the measurement object and his consistent application of the rules and standards. In a bad rating scheme, such as the method used by stock analysts, most of the rating *is* the opinion of the rater, but it is disguised as an objective rating using standards. For this reason it is misleading.

One university introductory statistics course textbook[3] uses an example of rating that confuses opinions and ratings based on standards: "We might, for instance, measure the performance of the President by asking a registered voter[4] to rate it on a scale of 1 to 10."

What this registered voter would do is assign a number to their *opinion* of the president's performance. This is not the same as rating the president's performance. If it was some aspect of voter opinion we wanted, such as satisfaction with the president's performance, we would need to ask voters to rate their satisfaction with the president's performance on some scale, such as 1 to 10.

To rate the president's performance, rather than voter satisfaction of his performance, we would have to define what we meant by performance. If it was his actual success in reducing the deficit, we could measure his performance without asking registered voters to rate it: the deficit goes up or down with each president in each year by a published percentage and dollar amount (I will resist the temptation to delve into the problems of measuring the deficit, which are significant). The example described in the textbook does not measure the president's performance, as it claims to. It quantifies what people think about the president's performance.

In a rating scheme, as in any measurement, it is crucial to define the measurement object, and in particular whether the measurement object is the opinion of the rater or the quantification of the rater's sensory experience through precise rules and standards. For convenience, we will distinguish between the two by calling them the subjective and external measurement objects respectively.

Misleading rating schemes do not distinguish between external and subjective measurement objects. They are ambiguous about the measurement object: is it performance against some objectively evaluated standard, or it is an opinion? It cannot be both. There is often no recognition of this confusion.

Such confusion does not exist when we measure a physical parameter such as temperature. The motion of the molecules of the material around the thermometer's bulb changes the volume of the alcohol in the thermometer, creating a quantifiable signal. The thermometer does not have its own opinion about the temperature.

Ratings should be used when people want to quantify an external measurement object by asking trained people to use their sense of hearing, sight, smell, taste, or touch to compare it with a standard. If you want to quantify people's opinions you are doing opinion polling or research, not rating.

RATING SCALES SHOULD HAVE OBJECTIVE STANDARDS

Rating scales should be calibrated with an objective standard. This reduces the influence of the rater's opinion on the rating. In one industrial bakery, the managers had developed a 1 to 5 scale to rate how well the bread was baked. The reference scale had five photographs, each showing a loaf of bread. The first loaf was light brown, and the fifth loaf was dark brown, and the other three were somewhere in between. Quality checkers used the photographic scale to assign a score for each loaf. Litmus paper, used to measure the acidity, or pH, of water, also uses a color scale, with a number from 1 to 14 for each color. In rating scales such as these, we do not need to overly preoccupy ourselves with what is going on inside the rater's mind, so long as they have been trained to read the scale.

An elaborate rating standard has been developed for coffee cuppers. Cuppers are people who specialize in tasting and rating coffee. Although scientists continue to try and devise sensors and instruments for measuring chemicals in a good cup of coffee, all these devices can do is coarsely measure tastes such as sourness. Nothing competes with the trained nose and palate of a cupper.

Cupping is done in a room with a controlled environment so there are no distracting odors.

The room should have natural light since dim light is said to depress the sense of smell. Ideally the room would be between 20–25°C and have a humidity of 50–70% since excessive dryness depresses the sense of smell. The cupping environment should be quiet and no discussion should occur during the cupping process. The best time to cup is between late morning and late afternoon, when enough time has elapsed since the previous meal and before you are too hungry. Any mental distractions including sickness, lack of sleep, or stress can affect the cupping results.

© Coffee Research Institute. Used by permission.

Cups are arranged in a series of triangles laid out around a circular, rotating table. A jury of trained cuppers, usually three at least, taste the coffee with a special spoon in a loud slurping motion, and spit it out. Each cupper evaluates the coffee according to characteristics such as fragrance, aroma, flavor, aftertaste, acidity, and body. They score each of these characteristics on a scale which goes from –3 (very bad) through zero (uninspiring) to 3 (very good), and these numbers are sometimes added up to create an overall score.

The cuppers are occasionally "calibrated" by a master cupper whose sense of taste is presumed to be unimpeachable. The master cups with them and comments on their own scores until they match that of the master.

These techniques vary throughout the coffee industry but are similar in the basic premise that the numbers will only be meaningful if they are obtained through a standardized process with well-trained cuppers. At one coffee plant where I was consulting, the cuppers were all blind. Management believed that they would have a more acute sense of smell and taste. Similar rating procedures are used to taste other products, such as whisky, including the spitting out of each sample.

Rating schemes such as coffee cupping work when the senses of the raters are highly refined through a long training process and a natural gift. Such training and gifts are common. A musician gifted with perfect pitch and sufficient training can, upon hearing a single note played on a piano keyboard, determine which of the eighty-eight keys was played. A musician without perfect pitch but with a good ear and sufficient training, can, after hearing a reference note, determine which note was played on the keyboard.

Reliable rating schemes thus rely on refining of the senses and extensive training of the rater. They have objective standards such as photos of bread color, master cuppers, and tuning forks. They are applied where mechanical sensors, if they can be made at all, do an inferior job compared with human senses. (Animal senses can also be used if the animal is well trained, as in sniffer dogs). For example, the human sense of smell can detect hydrogen sulfide, a malodorous compound that smells like rotten eggs, down to a concentration of 0.0005 parts per million. Typical instruments can only detect it down to 0.5 parts per million, a concentration one thousand times greater.

SUBJECTIVE RATING SCHEMES HAVE LIMITED USE

I once did an experiment to test the usefulness of the ratings I was getting from participants at my seminars. There were about forty people in one particular seminar, so I made up twenty copies each of two slightly different evaluation sheets, shuffled them together, and handed them out.

The difference between the two evaluations was in the descriptions of the ratings. The two rating schemes were similar to those shown in Table 4.1.

If the descriptions had an *objective* meaning to the participants, I would have expected a difference in the average rating of about one point. If on average the course participants thought the course was satisfactory, then I should have had an average of 3 from people who filled in the first evaluation and an average of 4 from people who filled in the second. The averages, however, were pretty much the same. Now I ask participants to provide me with written comments and observations without scores.

CUSTOMER SATISFACTION RATINGS

You have likely been to a restaurant or bar where you were handed a customer comment card such as the one reproduced in Table 4.2.

Such cards can provide a general picture of customer opinion: they are a crude form of opinion research. But they are not ratings. They do not

Table 4.1   Seminar Evaluation Ratings

Score	First evaluation form	Second evaluation form
5	The best course you have ever taken	Very good
4	Very good	Satisfactory
3	Satisfactory	Acceptable
2	Acceptable	Unacceptable
1	Unacceptable	Extremely poor

Table 4.2   Typical Restaurant Customer Comment Card

Quality	Excellent	Good	Fair	Poor
Quality of food	☐	☐	☐	☐
Value for money	☐	☐	☐	☐
Service	Excellent	Good	Fair	Poor
Speed of service	☐	☐	☐	☐
Courtesy of staff	☐	☐	☐	☐
Appearance of staff	☐	☐	☐	☐
Cleanliness	Excellent	Good	Fair	Poor
Inside store	☐	☐	☐	☐
Outside store	☐	☐	☐	☐

compare with defined standards, but with a collection of personal standards. How can one differentiate between excellent, good, and fair speed of service? If you order a beer, and a few minutes later the waiter brings you a beer, is that slow or fast, excellent or poor? Does it conform to your expectation of roughly how long it should take a waiter in a busy bar to deliver a beer? Are you in a rush or do you have a few hours to kill? If it conforms to your expectations, is that "excellent" or "fair"? A comment card such as the one in Table 4.2 could provide a rating in extreme cases where the restaurant's performance exceeded or violated almost all its customers' standards, such as food that tastes like five-star restaurant food but costs as much as fast food, or food that make patrons violently ill. But if you need a comment card to tell you that, you have more serious problems.

There is tremendous variability in the responses to customer rating cards, which makes it very difficult to identify trends over time or differences between restaurants in a chain. The variability in the answers comes from the variation in the food and service, and the variation in the personal standards of customers; from variation in the external measurement object and the subjective measurement object. It is impossible to differentiate between the two, except in extremes.

One of the most perfidious forms of opinion research masquerading as a rating are employee performance ratings that many companies use for job performance appraisals. How can a boss objectively evaluate traits—such as initiative, organizational ability, or creativity—the way coffee cuppers rate coffee or bakery workers rate bread—when one boss's view of what these traits are and what role they play in performance may widely differ from the next boss's view? How do you define a standard for these traits? How do you make sure that the relevant traits for a given job are assessed in the rating? How do you stop a boss from rating an employee to support their past judgments and previous opinion of an employee, rather than according to some standard? None of these are possible. If you need to rate employees, define the external measurement objects to which they contribute and measure them as accurately and precisely as you can.

FINANCIAL INCENTIVES DISTORT RATING SCHEMES

At one large training firm that delivered hundreds of courses across North America every year, trainers had to pass out evaluations to participants at the end of the course, and hand them back in a sealed envelope. The instructors could earn a bonus worth up to 25 percent of their training fee based if they received a high rating.

One clever trainer figured out a way to train the participants to give him high scores. Instead of handing out the evaluation only at the end of a four-day course, he handed them out every evening and reviewed the scores. The next day he would speak to people who had given him low scores in one area or another. Sometimes they would say such things as "I never give a 5 (out of 5) because nobody is perfect." The trainer would then patiently explain that a 5 did not mean perfect but excellent, and that the company really did want the participants to use the full range of scores. Bit by bit, the scores would creep up during the course and by the end of the week he would usually get his bonus.

Such inflation occurs in rating schemes such as internal company audits and school grades. In the United Kingdom, the percentage of students who obtain an A grade in their A-level tests (the final exams at the end of secondary school) doubled between 1991 and 2006.[5] Every year as the results come out there are scornful claims that the exams have grown easier, according to the *Economist* magazine, while the government claims that teaching methods have improved.

In 1999 the RAND Corporation[6] analyzed different types of tests schools in the State of Kentucky administered to their pupils. Kentucky had established a testing program known as KIRIS (Kentucky Instructional Results Information System). Schools received large cash rewards if their KIRIS scores increased to certain levels targeted by the state. Not surprisingly, the KIRIS scores increased rapidly. According to the RAND study, "they would be roughly equivalent to erasing about half the difference between

Japan (one of the highest scoring countries) and the U.S. (which ranked 18th out of 25 nations) on the recent Third International Mathematics and Science Study (TIMMS) in the space of only three years."

The researchers also looked at tests to which financial incentives were not tied and found, again unsurprisingly, that that there had been negligible inflation.

What are we measuring in evaluations of school or teacher performance? Are we measuring the performance of the schools or the pupils within them? Are we measuring the performance of the teachers? Or are we measuring the ability of the teachers to teach students to obtain high grades on tests ("teaching to the test")? We are measuring a mixture of all of these things.

The thermometer hanging outside your kitchen window does not read your mind before sensing the temperature, and does not display a temperature that is close to what you want and within a reasonable range of what the weather looks like through the window. But when incentives are tied to rating schemes, this is what happens. The incentives create a feedback loop within the rating system itself. These rating systems are neither an extension nor a refinement of the senses but a distortion of them, creating illusions rather than information. They cause the rater to push the ratings in the direction of the incentive, within some reasonable range of what is possible.

Companies often use rating scales to score internal audits of various aspects of their performance, such as quality control, health and safety, and environmental management. Personal bonuses are often tied to the results. They may, for example, set fifty expectations managers must meet and audit their operations against these expectations. The performance against each expectation is rated on a scale. Typically, managers' variable pay is tied to increases in their scores. These efforts are usually undertaken in good faith with a view to ensuring that managers are focusing on priorities.

Auditing is a matter of judgment. Imagine the auditor who, after answering dozens of questions about a plant, obtains a plant score of 50 percent in the first year of the new audit program. He discusses the results with the plant manager before finalizing his report. The plant manager objects strenuously—he wants a lower score. This is the first year of the new audit program after all, and his variable pay is tied to improvement, so better to start low. "Be tough on us," he says nobly. Within the maneuvering room available, the auditor makes a few protests to demonstrate his independence and knocks the score down a notch or two.

The next year the auditor returns and the plant manager boasts about all the things he has done to improve his plant's performance. Much of what he did was "teach to the test." The auditor sees some changes, and gives him a higher score.

The following year the plant manager again forcefully makes his case for the improvements he has made. The auditor is hard pressed to notice any. The choice, even for a different auditor, however, is stark. To grant the same score is to accuse the plant manager of incompetence at best and lying at worst. It is to ensure he does not receive his entire bonus. It is easier to push his score up a notch then risk creating an adversary within the company.

If the auditor had on the other hand noticed improvements, he could still have an incentive not to give a high score. If the plant really is exemplary, others will want to see what it is doing, thus exposing the auditor's score to greater scrutiny and possible ridicule. Better to play it safe and go up slowly, leaving room for future "improvements" down the road.

In a measurement system such as an audit scoring system, an auditors' direct sensory experience comes from the evidence he or she sees and hears during the audit. Their opinions, and thus their audit reports, are formed from this sensory experience, and shaped by the financial and other incentives of the audit program, their own views of what is good and bad, and the protests and boasts of the person being audited. All this gets processed in their minds and hearts, and then filtered through the scoring system to produce a number.

These problems could be avoided altogether by dropping the pretence that audits can quantify performance reliably and objectively, especially when their results are tied to financial incentives and when auditor and auditee have so much riding on the results. Findings should be descriptive, and compared against defined expectations, or at the very best broken down into a small number of very broad categories.

Coffee cuppers, especially blind ones, do not have these problems when they cup because they do not know which batch of coffee they are rating. Each cup is numbered, or otherwise made anonymous.

The same principle is applied in clinical research for testing drugs. In double-blind clinical trials that are properly done (many are not), neither the medical practitioners rating the efficacy of drugs, nor the patients who are taking the drugs, know whether the patient is taking a placebo or the experimental drug. The purpose is to reduce the signals influencing the measurement process to the one under study, by canceling the effect of the expectations of both the doctor and the participants about the experimental drug. The "blinding" precautions go further. The people designing the study, administering the drugs to patients, assessing the effect of the drugs, and analyzing the data must all work independently and may not come into contact with each other. And of course the people marketing and selling the drugs must have no say or part in the research.

RATING SCHEMES SHOULD PROVE THEMSELVES THROUGH EXPERIENCE

Some rating schemes do not use objective standards but have proven over time that they have practical value. For example, IQ tests are a highly developed and sophisticated rating scheme. Do they mean anything? What do they measure? We are told they measure intelligence. What is intelligence? There is no definition, let alone a consensus. Many definitions say it relates to the capacity or the ability of the mind to perform certain functions, such as reasoning, abstraction, learning, and so on. Others believe that there are many intelligences, that most intelligence tests only measure academic ability, and that the other types of intelligence are just as important outside of school.

As we saw in chapter three, when scientists were developing thermometers, they did not have a clear definition of what temperature was. But they measured it anyway and checked their measurements against reality, in accordance with the four principles of measurement. As ways of measuring temperature improved, and as their background information and understanding of physics improved, they improved the definition.

Perhaps we could define intelligence by saying it is what IQ tests measure. But we do not need to worry too much about defining intelligence perfectly because IQ test results correlate roughly with important aspects of reality. They correspond with abilities that are important for getting along in society, such as academic performance, getting and holding a job, and so on. This correlation with important things gives the IQ tests meaning, even if we do not have a precise definition of intelligence. It could be the same with the customer satisfaction rating card at the airport or the rating card for the trainer: if, through experience, the results of the ratings correlate with things that are important, the rating schemes can become meaningful. This correlation is, in effect, a sort of calibration to a standard that remains elusive to precise definition. But it would be a terrible mistake to assume that just because you have measured something you have meaningful data. Certainly in the case of the stock analysts' ratings the correlation with important things shows they are meaningless.

The Apgar score is a rating system that has proven itself through experience. Virginia Apgar was an American anesthesiologist who, throughout her career, which began in the 1930s, became increasingly appalled by the poor care given to many newborn babies. There was strong disagreement amongst medical practitioners in the delivery room on how to define a healthy baby, and when intervention or resuscitation was required. There were some rating scales to rate baby health, but they were open to considerable individual interpretation. As a result, babies who were born looking sickly, malformed, too small, blue, or who had trouble breathing were frequently classified as stillborn and left to die.[7]

Dr. Apgar devised a score, which became known as the Apgar score, and published it in 1952. Doctors and nurses would observe the condition of newborns at one minute and five minutes after birth. The score did not reduce a baby's condition to a measurement of a single component of health such as blood count, blood pressure, pulse, temperature, or electrolytes—rather it provided a quick and easy measure of the overall condition of the baby. The score is based on heart rate, breathing, skin color, reflexes, and muscle tone. Babies can get between 0 and 2 points for each of the five categories, for a total score of 0 to 10. For each category there were clearly defined criteria. For example, heart rate would score zero if absent, 1 if less than 100 beats per minute, and 2 if greater than 100.

Apgar proceeded very carefully before publishing her scale and recommending it to other doctors. She reviewed the records of 1,025 live born babies at the Columbia Presbyterian Medical Center who had been rated by her method. She found that infants with a score of two or less had a neonatal death rate of 14 percent; those with scores between three and seven had a death rate of 1.1 percent, and those with scores of eight to ten had the

Figure 4.1   The four principles of measurement.

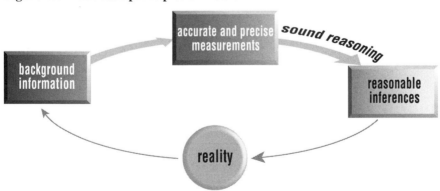

lowest death rate at 0.13 percent.[8] Similar results have been reproduced in more recent studies, and the score is still used half a century later.

Although there was not then a clear definition of neonatal health, Apgar went to great effort to obtain empirical evidence that her scale measured something that correlated well with health, that "something" being a baby's newborn condition and chance of short-term survival.

Similar diligence is warranted for any new rating system. Our third and fourth principles of measurement are that inferences should be reasonable and should correspond with reality. Apgar showed how this should be done.

We trust our senses, and have learned to trust measurements that extend our senses, such as measurements of temperature. Beware of rating schemes that have little to do with the sensory experience of the raters, and much to do with their opinion or motivation.

TOOL BOX

- Decide whether you wish to rate something against an objective standard or conduct opinion research. Do not confuse the two, even though sometimes they look similar.

- Develop an objective standard for the rating that uses one or more of the five senses, such as a color scale, sounds, a taste or smell, or a sensation to the touch.

- Develop a way to train raters to use the scale consistently

- Do not induce raters with incentives to change their ratings.

- Subject ratings, and your experience with them, to reality tests to make sure the ratings are meaningful and informative.

FIVE

How People React to Measurements

Thou art weighed on the balances, and art found wanting.

—Daniel 5:27

Our ideal of measurement is that it should produce objective information untrammeled by subjective judgment and insulated from unwanted influence. People and the way they react to measurements make this ideal very hard to achieve.

MEASUREMENTS DO STRANGE THINGS TO PEOPLE

When you see a police car sitting at the side of the highway, with a radar gun pointing at you, you will most likely brake or ease off the gas. The awareness of being measured affects your velocity and position. The observer affects the observed when people measure people. Even the fear of a hidden policeman measuring your speed will cause most drivers to moderate their speed—and increase their stress. Some communities put up electronic devices that measure motorists' speeds and display them on big electronic signs that everybody can see. They usually put these in sensitive areas, like around schools. They do it because they know many drivers will slow down when their speed becomes visible for all to see.

Measurement in social situations conveys intentions and goals; it defines priorities and values, and, like the police radar, is the basis of reward or punishment. It is thus neither objective nor neutral.[1] There is always an interaction between the observer and the observed, between the measurer and the measured.

Werner Heisenberg (1901–1976) was a German physicist who showed that it is physically impossible to measure the position and velocity of subatomic particles simultaneously and precisely. This is not because of imperfections in the measuring instruments. It is because there are inescapable uncertainties that arise from the quantum structure of matter. Light and matter interact: for example, light diffracts when going through small openings and the position of electrons changes when they are hit by photons.

Heisenberg described a thought experiment to explain this principle. Suppose you had a powerful microscope that allowed you to view an electron, and you wanted to measure both its position and velocity as accurately as possible. In order for you to see where the electron is, you need at least one photon to hit the electron and bounce off it through your microscope to your eyes. But by hitting the electron, the photon changes the velocity and position of the electron by an unknown amount. Thus you can know the position of the electron, but you have interacted with it and can no longer measure its velocity. The collision between the photon and electron changes both the position and velocity. This principle is known as the Heisenberg uncertainty principle. In a general sense it can be stated as "the observer affects the observed."

Physicists point out that when measuring physical quantities, the Heisenberg Uncertainty Principle only matters on subatomic scales. At bigger scales there are other types of interactions. For example, if you measure the temperature of a warm glass of water with a cold thermometer, the thermometer cools down the water in the glass, giving you a lower reading than you otherwise would have had. In a large pot of water this effect would be smaller. With careful design of the measurement instrument and the measurement process, these interactions can be insignificant. You should not, however, assume that they are.

THE HAWTHORNE EFFECT REVISITED

The Hawthorne effect is named after a series of experiments lasting several years between 1924 and 1932 from the Hawthorne plant, near Chicago, owned by the Western Electric Company. The plant manufactured relays for the Bell Telephone Company.

In the experiments the women working in the plant were given a variety of different working conditions and their output was measured.

Lighting was increased or decreased, rest pauses and duration of work were changed, and workers were assigned to either a test room or their regular department. The study's designers hypothesized that these were the variables of interest in this social-industrial productivity experiment.

The folklore that developed from these experiments, and that persists to this day, is that the performance of people who are singled out in a study of any kind improve, not because of the parameters or variables of the study under study, but because they are pleased with the attention they receive. According to the folklore, they worked harder because the lights were turned up, and then they worked harder because the lights were turned down, all because of the attention they received from managers changing the illumination and watching what would happen to their output.

This folklore was long ago shown to be bunk. In an article in *Science* magazine in 1974,[2] H. McIlvaine Parsons reviewed the original data and interviewed some of the women who were the subjects of the study. He refers to one of the myths, in which changes in illumination would cause the women working in the plant to work harder, regardless of what the changes were. "No report of the research that satisfied elementary requirements of scientific description . . . was ever issued."

Parson's review of the studies—almost fifty years later—reached a very different conclusion: "While this new look at Hawthorne has tried to rescue the reward factor from neglect, it has brought a new factor to light—information feedback." Parsons found that in one of the experiments, five women in a test room (he refers to them as "girls") received feedback every half hour on their production of relays. They also received a daily report that "specified the total number of relays each worker had completed, type of relay, total time for sets of 50, and time breaks." The experimenters had installed a separate counter for each operator.

"The girls kept setting higher goals of productivity because of the knowledge of results," he found. Parsons found comments made by the operators that the observer-supervisor recorded on his history sheets, such as, "I made 421 yesterday, and I am going to make better today." The earnings of each of the five women were based on the productivity of the five together.

What the Hawthorne experiments showed was that the productivity did not change because the lights were made brighter or dimmer. The productivity changed when the subjects of the study received measurements of their own productivity. If the measurements were tied to a financial reward for small groups of people, where one person's individual effort was more closely tied to their individual reward, it increased even more.

The study designers had thus missed the critical variable: the presence of (measured) information feedback, coupled with the ability for self-control and reward. The measurement *itself* was a variable in the experiment, rather than a neutral and objective means of assessing the other variables in the experiment.

(Unfortunately Parson's research had little effect on debunking the myths surrounding Hawthorne. In 2006 there were still five times more papers citing the original findings than citing Parson.[3])

The Apgar score (see chapter four) provides rapid and easy feedback to delivery room personnel, much like the rapid feedback received by the workers at the Hawthorne plant. It cut through the personal interpretations and conflicting expert opinions and provided a number that doctors and nurses could use to treat and save newborns, but, just as importantly, measure their own performance and compare it with other delivery rooms and medical personnel. It thus gave them a means to assess whether new practices and techniques worked. Within years, hospitals around the world had adopted the Apgar score. It drove rapid evolution in techniques to improve neonatal care. When Apgar published her seminal paper, neonatal mortality in the United States was around 1 in 30. It is now close to 1 in 500.[4] It was her measurement tool, and the feedback it provided, that prompted that improvement. The reason her score was so effective was because it gave doctors feedback that enabled them to improve the care they provided to newborn babies.

Measured feedback can enable people to improve control over their work—or over their own bodies. The Mayo Clinic, on its website, proclaims, "Using your mind to control your health." The clinic provides training on using biofeedback to control such things as brain activity, blood pressure, muscle tension, and heart rate, and, as patients progress, to reduce asthma, nausea, incontinence, and other ailments.

Biofeedback helps patients—or anyone for that matter—learn to use their own control systems to improve their condition. They do not need to know how the control system works, what parts of their bodies it involves, or why it works. Measurement is usually considered to be a tool to evaluate the efficacy of treatments for our ailments. It is also one of the treatments.

Similarly, measurement within an organization is one of the variables affecting behavior and self-control and should be considered as such, rather than just as a tool to measure the effect of the other variables.

HOW MEASUREMENTS CHANGE PEOPLE
AND ORGANIZATIONS

The Hawthorne experiments showed that measurement in organizational or social settings is itself a source of perturbation. In addition to providing feedback, the act of measuring also changes people's behavior by stating the intentions and priorities of the measurer. It thus implies the measurer's values. When a CEO rigorously measures variance from budget, people understand that sticking to budget is important, and act accordingly. When a plant manager measures and tracks the tons of product pushed out the shipping door every day, his employees understand that production quantity is what matters, and work to boost it. A CEO merely has to state that he wants reports on energy use, and people will know energy is now important to him. (When fisheries biologists pour rotenone into lakes to kill and count all the fish, they express their values too—and change the number of fish in the lake.)

In none of these measurements does the measurer measure his company's performance without significantly altering it, unlike the way one can measure the temperature of a pot of water. He is both measuring and changing it simultaneously. He cannot know the natural state of either budget variance or production tonnage, because by measuring them he changes their state.

Measurement is a behavior modification technique for subatomic particles as it is for people. The difference is that the subatomic particles do not think. They cannot know what measurement the observer expects, and the particle itself has no expectations. The particle's behavior is changed because it gets knocked by the photon, which is the means of observation. When measurement is used in social or organization settings, the objects of the measurement usually know or can guess the expectations plainly and react accordingly. This is why the driver slows down when he sees or suspects a speed trap and the patient's blood pressure increases when the doctor measures it—a phenomenon known as the white coat effect. It is a tight-knit interaction between measurement, intention, and reaction. Measurement in these settings could only be objective and neutral if there were no interaction, that is, if it were clandestine, which would be quite impractical.

When managers start measuring anything new in their organizations, they should ask three questions.

- First, what perturbations will the measurement, and the intention (or threat) to measure, cause?

- Second, will the perturbation be positive or negative?
- And third, will the measurement provide information that will enable people to improve control over their own work?

The perturbation begins with the choice and communication of measurement objects—what you choose to measure. Measurement objects reveal the values of the person who chooses them. Managers communicate their values explicitly when they say what they want to measure, irrespective of any objectives they set and track with the measurements.

This is often manifested in the frequently tense relationships between large industrial companies and their neighbors. When such a company wishes to expand or change its operations significantly, it is typical to hold public meetings to allay public fears about increased environmental and health impacts. Many well-meaning and diligent engineers and scientists have been floored by public anger before they even present their data. Stating something like, "We have measured the concentration of carcinogen X," whether that concentration is large or small, is equivalent to stating a belief in a right to increase their cancer risk, and the concentration of X, even slightly. The angry reaction from the members of the public subjected to a powerful neighbor who holds such a belief is understandable. The measurements themselves subsequently become irrelevant, much to the dismay of the diligent engineers and scientists who painstakingly obtained them.

The perturbation effect will be negative if the measurement is used—or if it is feared it will be used, like the police radar gun—as a policing tool, rather than as a feedback tool. Motorists flash their headlights to warn other motorists of speed traps, or buy radar detectors. Within organizations people adopt similar ruses to make it harder to get caught or to avoid the ignominy of "failure to meet target."

A consumer food products company I was advising on measurement issues decided that it had to improve service to its customers, who were distributors, grocery chains, and large restaurant chains. As a result of some bad customer experiences, plant managers were under tremendous personal pressure to show rapid improvements in customer service. Senior management told plant and distribution managers to measure customer service, which was defined simply as the percentage of orders filled as intended, and pressured them to get service up to a specified target level very quickly. Similar pressure was applied throughout the organization. A chart in one plant showed that the percentage of orders filled as intended was now bouncing along nicely in the high 90s.

But there was a radar detector built into these numbers. "Customer service" was more specifically defined as the proportion of cases of product over or under the ordered quantity, outside a range that someone in the company decided was acceptable. If a customer ordered 1,000 cases of some product, then any shipment between 980 and 1,020 cases that were shipped on schedule was deemed acceptable. This gave them a little more flexibility in meeting a high customer service standard. (It was a misnomer to call this measure "customer service" because it did not measure other components of service, such as timeliness of delivery, as opposed to timeliness of shipping).

But this performance indicator was very misleading. If those one thousand cases were composed of five different stock-keeping units, or product types, the shipping personnel did not determine whether the quantities for each of the individual stock-keeping units met their customer's order requirement. In other words, if the total order of one thousand cases was comprised of orders for five stock-keeping units of two hundred cases each, the shipping personnel only looked at the total order, not whether there were two hundred cases of each of the stock-keeping units. There could be one stock-keeping unit completely missing from the order, but the shipment was acceptable if there were the right total number of cases.

This of course rendered the measurement of customer service nearly useless and made it much easier to avoid reprimand (at least until the customers caught on). If they were short on one product they could add more of another, more than what the customer wanted, to meet their customer service target.

The perturbation effect was negative: customer service measurements improved while actual customer service declined. Instead of providing feedback that would enable managers to improve service, it encouraged them to play with numbers to meet target and keep their bosses off their backs. When I pointed out to the managers the weakness in their measurement tool, they started measuring the stock-keeping units individually.

PEOPLE DO STRANGE THINGS TO MEASUREMENTS

People like their measurements to confirm their beliefs, not contradict them. When people get a measurement that is very different than previous measurements, or from their expectations, they naturally worry that they have made a mistake. They are more likely to "correct" these measurements, or discard them. They do not worry so much when they get measurements that are close to, and thus confirm, previous measurements or their expectations.

A high-profile example of this involved the measurement of the ozone hole. The Total Ozone Mapping Spectrometer is an instrument on NASA's Nimbus-7 satellite that makes 140,000 measurements every day, or more than 50 million per year, of ozone concentrations in the upper atmosphere around the globe. The scientists originally designed their software to exclude any ozone measurements below 180 Dobson units in its analysis of ozone levels. Instead, it flagged them as possible instrument errors. The scientists had thought that 180 Dobson units was such a low concentration that it would probably be indicative of instrument or transmission errors rather than actual ozone levels. Before July 1983, no instrument reading of ozone had been below 180. With such a large volume of data the scientists had to have some automated method of sorting out real data from instrument error, and 180 seemed like a reasonable cutoff.[5]

In July 1984 NASA scientists were processing data from the previous autumn when they noticed a sharp increase in the number of flagged measurements. They compared their readings from the Amundsen-Scott ground station at the South Pole that was also measuring ozone. The ground station reported ozone levels around 300 Dobson units, while the flagged data the satellite was reporting was below 180 Dobson units. In other words, by setting the cutoff at 180, they did not see the low values of ozone.

It turns out that the wavelengths on the ground spectrometer were set to the wrong values—the ground station was giving incorrect readings and the satellite's readings were correct. The NASA scientists did not know that at the time, and worked on the possibility that their satellite was providing incorrect readings. They missed the ozone hole as a result.

In 1985, British scientists[6] published a report in *Nature* announcing the discovery of large losses in ozone in Antarctica, which came to be known as the ozone hole. The British scientists made their discovery on the basis of data from the British Antarctic Survey ground station at Halley Bay. Within a year, NASA scientists also published a report in *Nature,* which confirmed the British analysis and, by analyzing their own data, confirmed that the ozone hole covered the entire Antarctic continent and not just Halley Bay.

The British report had itself been delayed by a backlog of data that stretched back several years. When the possibility of lower ozone levels first came to light, Farman, the lead British scientist, was concerned that the American satellite had not detected it, and was also concerned, like the Americans, about the possibility of instrument errors. He proceeded very carefully before reporting. The combination of the backlog and the disbelief of their instrumental data meant that the ozone hole, although detected by instruments as far back as 1977, was not discovered and reported by atmospheric scientists until eight years later.[7]

The striking thing about this story is that despite a tremendous amount of brainpower, computing muscle, and scientific resources, the ozone hole was overlooked for several years longer than it could have been. These top scientists had, perhaps, preconceived beliefs about what the data should look like and what data should be, at least temporarily, not reported. Data that did not fit these beliefs they treated as suspect.

This informal culling of data happens in many different circumstances. One environmental consulting group was doing a study of heavy metal contamination in lobsters. They had amassed data from hundreds of lobsters. In each bay or cove or other bit of coastline they caught three lobsters and sent them back to the laboratory. The lab technicians ground them up in blenders to get a mush from which they measured the concentration of heavy metals.

The consultants took the lab data and "cleaned" it up: they took each triplet of data and threw out the measurement that was farthest from the mean. When you measure concentration you usually find most measurements piled up at the small end, as concentrations cannot go below zero. The mean is close to this pile. Higher concentrations can get quite far from this pile, although they typically get increasingly rare as you move farther away from it. Their data cleaning procedure meant, in practice, that they were throwing out the data that told them the most about heavy metal concentration in lobsters. They meant no malice: it was an innocent but misguided attempt to remove possible measurement errors or data that was causing an undue influence.

Their expensive study therefore turned out to be quite uninformative. It was as if the people doing the study had gone to a three-star restaurant with a blender. It's easier to both ingest and digest a ground-up hotdog than a finely honed meal made with distinct ingredients. In a hot dog you cannot see the interesting bits, and a good thing too. But with measurements it is the unusual bits that often tell you what is really going on.

Hot-dog making with data afflicts businesses from top to bottom. I once had a brief conversation with a poor soul at a jam-making factory. He sat on a stool beside a conveyor that carried thousands of bottles of strawberry jam everyday day. The bottles wiggled and jiggled their way along the conveyor like cars on a rush hour freeway. Occasionally they jammed. The jam man's job was to unjam the jam jam.

His foreman told him that he was also supposed to grab five bottles of jam every fifteen minutes and weigh them on a scale that he had conveniently placed near the jam man's stool. The foreman gave him a chart with three lines on it: one for the target weight, and two lines equidistant from the target, above and below it. "We want the jam weights to be between the top and bottom line," the foreman said, like so many others. If too many go below the lower line you cheat customers, and the government does not allow it. If too many go above the top line, we waste money because you are giving more jam to customers than they have paid for.

The jam man took his foreman at his word and grabbed five jam jars from the line every fifteen minutes. He weighed each one. If a jar's weight was between the top and bottom line he marked an X on the chart between the lines to indicate the weight. If it was not, he grabbed another jar and weighed it, and so on until he got one that was. He produced exactly the sort of chart the foreman hoped for, but to get it, had removed all the useful information and displayed all the hotdog mush.

At the top of the corporate hierarchy there is a more sophisticated way to make hot dogs—with financial information. It is called presenting the results *after* "extraordinary expenses," "special items," or "special charges." It is outside the ordinary, so don't worry about it, just eat our financial hot dog and leave us alone. Perhaps one could be charitable and assume that the people behind such moves are motivated by the same desire as the environmental consultants with their mashed lobsters. Or perhaps not.

These special items have a disturbing habit of not being so special. Benjamin Graham, in his classic book *The Intelligent Investor*,[8] described the case of Alcoa back in 1968. The company had a number of special charges in their annual report, including the building of a wall.

Graham says "the alert investor might ask himself how does it happen that there was a virtual epidemic of such special charge-offs appearing after the close of the 1970s, but not in previous years? In some case they might be availed of to make subsequent earnings appear nearly twice as large as in reality." This practice subsequently became known as the "big bath theory," in which executives cleanse a company of all its bad news in one year so they can boost earnings, and their bonuses, the next.

What defines a special item? In a large corporation there are so many special events occurring in any given year that they are part of the ordinary episodic life of the business. Like the lobster mashers, perhaps many business people believe they know what the True State of Their Business Affairs should look like, and any event that is not part of the True State should be cleansed like a contaminated lobster in a Big Bath so you can see how much money the business was supposed to make.

Accounting rules state that extraordinary items are supposed to be both unusual and infrequent. But they are now so frequent that accounting professors conduct large statistical studies of them. Deechow and Ge[9] analyzed 63,875 firm-years (one company for one year) between 1988 and 2002 and found that, on average, 19 percent reported special items, ranging from a high of 51 percent in low-accrual firms to 12 percent in high-accrual firms. They concluded that "special items reflect underlying economics and are indicative of firms that have over-invested in strategies that have not worked." They "did not attempt to distinguish between big baths and underlying economics: both scenarios predict lower earnings persistence."

If 19 percent of firms in a typical year report special items, which reflect underlying economics and strategies that have not worked, they are not very special. The September 11 attacks were extraordinary events, certainly unusual and hopefully infrequent, in the minds of most of us, yet the US Financial Accounting Standards Board did not allow companies to treat losses they incurred from these attacks as special items.

WHY PEOPLE FILTER MEASUREMENTS

The moral of Heisenberg's uncertainty principle is that the observer affects the observed. This moral applies to the way measurements affect people. But when people are involved, and not inanimate subatomic particles, the measurements pass through their hands and minds. They make decisions about what to report and what not to report, about what is a valid measurement and what is not. They filter the data.

Measuring instruments are extensions of the senses. Our senses receive far too many stimuli to process them all in our brains—we only respond to a small fraction of them. Our senses and brains naturally filter the information. When a frog sits on a lily pad waiting for a fly, it is not interested in the sounds of birds singing and leaves rustling, but in the sound of a fly buzzing. It is not interested in the sight of trees in the distance but of small dark blips flying close by. Its brain can only handle a fraction of the information coming from its sensory organs, and only needs a fraction of it. The brain and eyes and ears combine to filter the extraneous information. After millions of years, the sensory abilities have evolved to be more sensitive to some stimuli than others. A frog has a built-in template to define which sensory inputs are relevant. The frog filters out those sensory inputs that do not conform to the template. That's how it gets the information it needs to catch flies.

Our sensory organs filter information. Our eyes cannot see ultraviolet light and our ears cannot hear at frequencies above 20 kilohertz. Our brains filter the signals they get from our sensory organs. A noise that bothers us at first, like highway noise or trains passing in the night, we gradually stop noticing even though our ears can hear them.

Perhaps our desire to filter out measured data is related in part to our natural ability to filter sensory inputs. It is also related in part to shame, fear, and greed. But whatever the reason, the implication is that whenever and to the extent that people are involved in measurement, there will be filtering of information that does not conform to their preconceived notions about what information is relevant.

Measurements do strange things to people and people do strange things to measurements. And data, despite some famous claims[10] to the contrary, never speaks for itself. Never did, never will.

TOOL BOX

- If you throw out measurements that appear to be outliers or exceptions you may throw out the most useful information.

- Carefully think through what messages you send to an organization by what you measure. The message may be more important than the measurements.

- Ask these three questions before implementing new performance measurements in an organization:

    1. What perturbations will the measurement, and the intention (or threat) to measure, cause?

    2. Will the perturbation be positive or negative?

    3. Will the measurement provide information that will enable people to improve control over their own work?

- Once you start measuring, keep an eye on how organizational behavior changes as a result.

- Remember that people do strange things to measurements, and measurements do strange things to people.

SIX

Why Performance Dashboards Mislead

For every complex problem, there is a solution that is simple, neat, and wrong.

—H. L. Mencken

Ten years after two Harvard Business School professors, David Norton and Robert Kaplan, published the *Balanced Scorecard*[1] in 1996, more than half of global companies had implemented techniques similar to the ones they described. Many of these companies use performance measurement "dashboards." There are now dozens of enterprise software packages that collect business performance measurements and display them as dials on dashboards, and these software packages are proliferating (see example in Figure 6.1).

Norton and Kaplan advise managers to use performance measures that balance "results from past efforts and the measures that drive future performance."[2] These latter measures should cover three perspectives: customers, internal efficiency and effectiveness, and learning and growth of employees and capabilities, according to the authors. They claim that this approach "provides executives with a comprehensive framework that translates a company's vision and strategy into a coherent set of performance measures."

Would such advice work for doctors?

The emergency room nurse calling from the Royal Valley Hospital was obviously upset and hesitated to speak. A colleague and patient of

Figure 6.1   Display on typical dashboard software.

Dr. Crawford's had been brought into emergency late the night before and had died of massive heart failure during the night. The news was stunning. His patient had been competing in a 40-kilometer cross-country ski race.

Crawford occasionally freelanced as an expert witness in medical negligence cases. Not infrequently, the families of heart attack victims sued their doctors when they suddenly died. And of those, a disproportionate number were otherwise fit and often quite athletic.

Crawford could think of nothing in his patient's medical record that would have predicted heart failure. As far as Crawford could remember his friend's record, all the common measures used to predict and assess his health were exemplary. The patient's blood pressure, body mass index, cholesterol and so on were all fine, and he exercised vigorously, did not smoke, and drank only socially.

Why would a man suddenly die of a heart attack when all his "leading indicators" showed he was healthy?

Masaaki Imai, in his book *Kaizen*,[3] which describes Japanese management techniques, also emphasized the need to balance the past with drivers of the future. He described the measures of past performance as "R-criteria" (R is for Results), and the measures that drive future performance as "P-criteria," for Process.

The purpose of the routine medical examination, or physical, is to attempt to identify signs of risk factors for illness. If physicians spoke like Harvard Business School professors, they might also call the information they collect during a physical "measures that drive future performance," and call health "future performance." After thousands of years of trying, doctors still do not know all the measures that drive future performance of their patients. They know only that such measures can at best tell them that good health is likely. That is the best doctors can say: likely. A heart attack or some other catastrophe could be imminent and cannot be ruled out. The measures do not "drive" health. Unlike doctors, in business we normally do not have millions of chances to test the usefulness and predictive ability of our performance measures.

This does not make the measurements useless. It just makes it hard to figure out what to measure and how to interpret the measurements if you want to know whether you or your business are healthy or bound for disaster. This has not stopped many authors and business researchers from trying. Phil Rosenzweig elegantly explains the challenge in his book *The Halo Effect*. Often these researchers rely on interviews with managers from successful companies and press reports about these companies. This approach cannot identify drivers of performance. As Rosenzweig says, "Do these practices lead to high performance? Or do high-performing companies tend to be described in these terms?"[4]

THE CHALLENGE OF MEASURING COMPLEX SYSTEMS

Large businesses, economies, ecosystems, and human bodies are complex systems. A complex system[5] is a system "whose properties are not fully explained by an understanding of its component parts." From the interactions of the component parts new properties emerge that cannot be explained in terms of the properties of the components.

Yet normally people try to understand complex things by studying their component parts. To understand a business, it is reasonable to start by gaining an improved understanding of the business model, the production system, the marketing system, the financial system, human resource systems, information systems, and so on. These subsystems are the component parts. To make a medical diagnosis, a family practitioner will often send his patient to specialists who specialize in understanding the various physiological subsystems: the immune system, the circulatory system, the nervous system, the skeletal system, and so on.

This type of analysis is part and parcel of what is considered the scientific method. It is hard to see how science could abandon it. But complex systems do not yield easily to such treatments. Perhaps this is a limitation of the scientific method—a limitation that researchers on complexity are trying to overcome. One of science's solutions is to branch into specific investigative fields. Chemistry and biology are two examples of scientific fields with their own autonomous methods and terminology to study chemical and biological properties that emerge from complex physical systems.

There are in general four broad goals related to measuring complex systems. First, measurements help us understand the parts of the system—whether it is a patient, a large company, or an economy. Second, they help us make predictions about what is likely to happen in the future. Third, they help us determine the extent of control, influence, or alteration we should exert on the system in an attempt to produce a desired result or to avoid an undesired result. And fourth, measurements are used to evaluate performance, however defined, and to create incentives to improve it. The more complex the system we face, the more difficult it is to meet these goals.

The extent to which they can be met depends on whether we have measured the right things; whether we have obtained reliable data; and whether the things we believe will influence future performance actually do influence future performance. But it crucially depends on information that not only does *not* come from measurements, but is frequently difficult to articulate.

Crawford gulped down his coffee, shaved and dressed quickly, and rushed to his medical office, a small unit with two examining rooms in a strip mall medical arts building he shared with three other physicians. His 2,500 patient files were arranged in color-coded file folders on a wall unit behind his receptionist's desk. Crawford, being color blind, hated the system and usually swore under his breath on the rare occasions he had to find a file himself while patients waited on the other side of the receptionist's desk. But at six o'clock on a winter morning, in an empty office, having had only one cup of coffee and no shower, the usually polite doctor was anything but.

He found the file and flipped through his notes. The last physical was less than two months ago. Blood pressure was 120/70; body mass index 23.2; total cholesterol, 4.1 mmol/L; blood sugar, 4.2 mmol/L. All were at the lower, and healthier, end of the normal range. Crawford flipped though the chart and found similar results in previous years. Continuing backwards, he found his notes from an earlier physical during which he had taken a detailed family history. No known family history of heart attack, heart disease, or stroke. His friend and patient had a relaxed demeanor, was physically active, and rarely lost his temper.

A doctor knows that he cannot rely just on measurements. He needs to touch, poke, and feel his patients. He needs to look them over, inside and out. He has to listen to their stories and their family stories, otherwise known as their medical histories. A family history of heart attacks or heart disease is usually given in narrative form—as a story—rather than as measurements. But it tells a tremendous amount about a patient.

In a complex system, even measurements that indicate health can rarely predict sudden massive change or even catastrophe. There is no fundamental reason why measurements could not be found that would predict them. There are, however, costs of time, resources, and effort associated with acquiring and processing the measurements. These costs of knowledge, as economist Thomas Sowell calls them,[6] force managers to reduce what they measure to a manageable number of key indicators. By their very nature, key indicators cannot tell the whole story. It is also challenging to find measurements that can predict sudden change or catastrophe because of the way complex systems behave.

"Complex" is different from "complicated." A complicated system is a system with many parts driven by outside forces, such as a steam engine, an automobile, or an airplane.[7] The relationship between the inputs, those "measures that drive future performance," and the future performance, can be quite well understood, and in many cases is understood well enough to define mathematically in such a way as to allow control of the system. Engineers and scientists can calculate the relationship between the gas and air that goes into an internal combustion engine and the torque it generates. They have a good enough understanding of the way all the components of airplanes work in relation to each other, and to the airflow around the planes, that they can build simulators that simulate reality well enough that pilots can train on them. And yet, even with such understanding, these systems are also prone to catastrophic failure.

Some complex systems can also be described mathematically, sometimes surprisingly simply. In a complicated system, we can create predictions or control algorithms from a mathematical model of how it works. In a complex system even a working mathematical description does not usually give us a way to predict or control its future state, except in a very general way, and often incorrectly. Weather forecasts are a case in point.

THE FLAWS OF THE DASHBOARD-MACHINE METAPHOR

In automobiles the dashboard contains measures that indicate some aspect of future performance: if the gas gauge reads empty, if the engine temperature is in the red zone, or if the low oil light comes on, we can make a pretty good prediction about how much farther we will be able to drive. Engineers know how a car works from the way its component parts work.

That is perhaps why many people use the automobile, or other machines such as airplanes, as a metaphor for deciding how to measure complex businesses. Indeed, the first example in the Balanced Scorecard describes a pilot flying with only one instrument. Throughout the book, reference is made to "drivers" of performance or strategy. The authors speak repeatedly of "linked cause-and-effect relationships" suggesting the relationships were, firstly, known to be cause-and-effect relationships, and, secondly, tightly linked, as they would be in a complicated system such as an automobile or airplane but are not in a complex system. In many ways, the whole book is written as if top managers sat in a cockpit with a great instrument panel, scanning the instruments, and making adjustments to the controls as they flew through the clear blue sky toward their strategic objective. This language contrasts starkly with the passive grammatical sentence construction prevalent in science writing, which shows the author has not assigned causes to scientific phenomena where he has no business doing so. Business authors call something a "driver" and everyone assumes it must be, because that is what they call it.

Gareth Morgan[8] has extensively described how people use metaphors to understand organizations. He says, "We frequently talk about organizations as if they were machines designed to achieve predetermined goals and objectives, and which should operate smoothly and efficiently." Metaphors, he says, provide insights into people and organizations that we might otherwise not make. Morgan says, "When managers think of organizations as machines they tend to manage and design them as machines made up of interlocking parts that each play a clearly defined role in the functioning of the whole."

Metaphors similarly play a useful role in scientific discovery. Metaphors evoke ideas, stimulate the imagination, help distill information, and suggest promising channels for future investigation. The metaphor of nucleotide sequences in DNA as an encrypted language may have helped the research in the 1960s that cracked the genetic code. But metaphors can also mislead. "The metaphor of the genome as a well-crafted blueprint or a finely tuned machine may have blinded many biologists to genomic imperfections" and their causes, according to one scientist.[9] (Now the DNA blueprint metaphor is often used in business to describe the way a company operates, as in "it's in our DNA," as if it was hard-coded like a blueprint or specification.)

Morgan also warns against the downsides of metaphors in organizational management. Held too dearly, they can become an ideology in themselves. They can make it difficult for the organizations to adapt to new circumstances. They can cause one to ignore new problems and situations. Sowell says that metaphors provide useful shortcuts, but like other shortcuts can also take you further from your destination.[10]

The metaphors people use, and the vocabulary these metaphors engender, affect what people choose to measure, or not measure, and affects how they interpret measurements and the information they convey. In business, language suggesting that measurements are taken from machines being driven by top management predominates.

In the 16th century the word "manage" was derived from the Italian word *maneggiare,* which means to handle horses, and is itself derived from the word *mano,* or hand. Now we handle the steering wheel: the metaphor is embedded in the word "manage" itself. It is a vivid contrast with another metaphor business people like to use—Adam Smith's "invisible hand." Smith used the invisible hand metaphor to argue that natural and unbridled market forces produced a much more efficient use of resources and public welfare than state planning and direction—or "management." The knowledge required to run a business in a market economy is fragmented by necessity: every entrepreneur, customer, and consumer has knowledge specific to their circumstances. This crucial fact makes a mockery of any attempt of concentrated economic decision making. Fragmented knowledge also occurs within large organizations, yet this is harder for many business managers to see.

The dashboard of an automobile has two types of displays. Those that are needed for sequential decision making, such as deciding to adjust vehicle speed or to fill up within the next 30 miles, show instantaneous measurements. Those that are needed for binary decision making—such as deciding to take the car to the garage—report on an exception basis only, such as a low oil pressure warning light. They only show a signal when a measurement falls outside a predetermined range of acceptable values. In some vehicles, the dashboards only show vehicle speed and fuel level—everything else is reported on an exception basis. On other vehicles, to give greater control, there are also instantaneous gauges for engine speed, oil pressure, battery charge, battery voltage, and engine temperature. Exception reporting is left for things such as doors ajar and hand brake on.

Many managers construct their "dashboards" for their organizations along the same lines. The plant manager who was promoted up from the ranks and cannot let go of his previous responsibilities is likely to be found in his office browsing through computer screens displaying live charts of dozens of production parameters, closely tracking their ups and downs. His mental metaphor is that he is now responsible for the whole machine, and therefore needs a dashboard with all the gauges to keep it finely tuned.

People relate to machines differently. Some do not care what all the gauges mean because a vehicle is just a tool for reaching a destination. They only want to know their speed, and whether the vehicle is able to get there. A manager with such a view of a business is far more likely to rely on exception reporting and a few broad measurements, such as overall productivity.

The exception report is consistent with the machine metaphor. An exception is a deviation from a specified value. We build machines to specification.

The machine metaphors, especially the automobile and airplane metaphors, tend to make people think of their businesses as if they were traveling along roads or paths toward their chosen destination or goal, like a car traveling down a highway (or an airplane flying on a flight path) past milestones. They measure accordingly, using such measurements as year-to-date performance toward a goal. Failure to meet goals is unacceptable—an exception. Running a business by relying predominantly on measurements of past results rather than on drivers of future performance is likened to watching the rearview mirror rather than looking to the road ahead while driving.

To the extent that the machine metaphor stimulates managers to build measurement dashboards that display both what they think are "measures that drive future performance" and past performance, it may be useful. But it risks misleading them into managing as if their organizations behaved more like machines than complex systems. Complex systems are episodic: patients have heart attacks, businesses go bust, and economies crash with little or no warning. Although vehicles can break down, it is possible to maintain and monitor them sufficiently to make breakdowns rare, or at least predictable. Complex systems can flip into a new state very quickly. This is different than a breakdown—the system does not become static as a broken vehicle does. It has new emergent properties and the components interact in new ways—like an economy in depression or recession and a business in creditor protection.

The word "episode" comes from the Greek words for *epi* (in addition to, upon), *eísod* (entrance) and *hodos* (path). In other words, episodes are unusual things that get in the way along the path. They become mere exceptions, to be reported as exceptions that interfere with the measurable attainment of goals. But episodes are what make walking down paths more interesting than sitting in a room. It is in the nature of traveling along paths that they occur. Rather than seeing business life as episodic, and designing businesses, managing them, and measuring accordingly, the metaphor influences managers to build businesses and measure their performance as if they were "hodic," or travelling along a chosen path, and destined to get to the goal, come hell or high water.

The purpose of a vehicle is to travel along a chosen path to a goal. Morgan says "we typically take the goal-oriented strategy as a necessity of organizational life, it is in point of fact a socially constructed necessity, characteristic of a mechanical mentality."

MEASUREMENTS CANNOT REPLACE THE SENSES

The dashboard metaphor is taken to extremes by some management writers, persuasively misrepresenting the role of measurement in organizations. Here is one particularly heady example:

> We find the dashboard metaphor useful because running a team without a good, simple guidance system is like trying to drive a car without a dashboard. You might try it in a pinch, but not as a matter of practice, because you'd lack the necessary information—the speed, the amount of fuel, the engine temperature—to ensure that you reach your destination. The dashboard is a key feedback mechanism that makes you (as the driver) and the car part of the same transportation system. If that system broke down—if you no longer had the information you needed to drive it—then the car would crash, or roll to a halt, or simply run out of fuel.[11]

The dashboard on the Model-T Ford had no instruments. The word "dashboard" then would not even have conjured up images of measurement. It was a piece of wood. The first instruments were installed in 1919, about ten years after the Model T went into production, and only for cars with the optional starter. Eventually speedometers became optional and ammeters—needed for the starter—standard on all cars.

Imagine that you are given a can of black paint, and obliged to pick between painting either the dashboard or all the windows before you drive across town. You could not drive to the end of the street with blackened windows, yet you could drive for thousands of miles without a dashboard, provided you remembered to fill up with gas every few hours, check your oil level, not drive faster than the ambient traffic, and listen for strange noises from under the hood.

The key feedback mechanisms for driving a vehicle are sensory: what you see, hear, smell, and feel. You do not need the dashboard to drive the car. It is a secondary feedback system that helps you maintain the car, and it helps you refine your driving to precise speeds. Cars are constantly wearing out and consuming fluids. The dashboard gives you a broad overview of this process of deterioration and consumption. As such it is a risk management tool and a control tool that helps you control the process of deterioration and consumption.

The measurements in the dashboard are not *replacements* for but *extensions* and *refinements* of the senses. To save you from having to get out of your car to check the oil dipstick, there is an oil gauge—and it does not even tell you how dark and dirty the oil is. To save you from guessing the gas level, or estimating it with a siphon tube, there is a gas gauge. Other than speed and distance, all of the information on the dashboard is about the car and how well it is working. This is, of course, useful information— but it is not vital to the task of driving.

None of the information on a typical dashboard is about the environment through which you are driving the car. None of it serves as a "guidance system," as the above example claims. All of the information needed to guide the car is obtained through the senses. The external temperature display now common on many vehicles, and the electronic maps based on global positioning systems, are small steps in that direction. According to Microsoft Corporation boss Bill Gates, our inability to build instruments that can sense the surrounding environment as well as human or animal senses is the main technological limitation in the development of humanoid robots.[12]

The machine and dashboard metaphors can inculcate the false notion that measurement replaces the senses. The cliché, "If you cannot measure it, you cannot manage it," is a direct product of this metaphor. If measurements did replace the senses, the cliché would be true. Measurements enable managers to extend their senses to places they cannot go. It enables them to obtain information that cannot be sensed by their own sensory organs. It permits them to evaluate whether machine-like operations, such as factories, distribution systems, or order processing systems, conform to expectations, or whether they are deteriorating. But it does not and never will replace the information they obtain from their own senses, from looking around, or from a conversation with someone on the floor where the actual work is being done.

When people interpret the machine metaphor literally, they assume that cause and effect are closely linked, as they are in an automobile or airplane that is working normally. In most simple machines, they are. But as large human organizations become increasingly complex, the link between cause and effect becomes increasingly blurred. Their relationship becomes less linear, and more influenced by positive feedback loops.

POSITIVE FEEDBACK LOOPS LIMIT THE USE OF MEASUREMENTS

My grandparents once told a funny story that involved a positive feedback loop. They accidentally switched the temperature controllers around on their electric blanket. My grandfather got cold, so he turned up what he thought was his controller. But it was not his controller: it was my grandmother's. This made my grandmother warmer. She then turned what she thought was hers down. But of course it was not hers: it was my grandfather's, so he got colder and turned his up again. The more they kept adjusting their blanket controllers, the worse it got.

Positive feedback loops are found in many complex systems—but they are often missed until the system flips into a new state. Sowell points out the fundamental predicament of economies: there is not enough to go around. Ecosystems have the same predicament—critters fiercely compete for energy, nutrients, and space. Positive feedback loops can arise in these complex systems when constraints change—making some desirable resource or undesirable nuisance suddenly much more or less plentiful. In an economy the resource could be credit or confidence; in an ecosystem it could be a nutrient. The nuisance could be taxes or regulations; in an ecosystem it could be an invasive species.

Phosphates are an essential nutrient for plant life. When phosphates from soaps and detergents fed the growth of huge stinking mats of algae in lakes like Lake Ontario and Lake Erie, it was explained very mechanically: phosphates fertilize algae. Algae then grow and die and stink up the lake when they rot. If that is how it worked, you could measure phosphates and get a good idea of what the "future performance" of the lake would be. But that explanation leaves out the positive feedback loop.

Bottom-dwelling creatures keep mud at the bottom well oxygenated. As phosphates from detergents and agricultural run-offs first entered the lake, chemical reactions in the oxygen-rich mud deactivated the phosphates and kept them out of the water. The reactions require cool, well-oxygenated lakes, which the lakes were at that time. For a while, these reactions prevented a measurable increase in phosphates in the lake water, even though there was an increasing amount going in.

The oxygen content of the lakes decreases every spring when they warm up. This reactivates the phosphates. They fertilize planktonic plants. As the plants grew abundantly, so did the small fish that ate them. The fish burned up more oxygen. So do the plants when they die and rot. This reactivates more phosphates. The lakes flipped when there were enough phosphates to establish a positive feedback cycle: more phosphates cause more planktonic plants cause more fish cause less oxygen cause more phosphates.

A complex system such as the Great Lakes ecosystem is best described through a narrative—a story. Measurements play a role. Measurements can tell us the phosphate concentration in the water and in the mud. They can tell us the clarity of the water. They can tell us the relationship between fish size and how much oxygen fish burn up when studied closely in the laboratory. But a few measurements cannot tell the story of a complex system. Measurements tell us what is going on in small, linear, almost mechanical chunks of the system's structures and processes. They cannot tell us how much oxygen some particular fish consumed in some particular spot in the lake. To understand the system you need to know the structures, the processes, and how they interact. Measurements are useful and practical for understanding individual structures and processes. They are not well suited to understanding how they interact to create a complex system.

Problems like algae proliferation happen in business and economics too. Economies are complex systems that flip between various states like ecosystems—from boom to recession or depression, or from net exporter to net importer. They have structure similar to ecosystems—banks, consumers, companies of various types, and governments—and a variety of processes acting on those structures.

Credit is an important nutrient for business life. Before the 2008 economic crash, various fiscal, monetary, and government policies that were intended to encourage home ownership and stimulate growth had created cheap credit for several years. Encouraged by politicians, mortgages had been given to millions of people who could barely afford them. They were enticed with low teaser interest rates. When the teaser interest rates ended and higher interest rates kicked in, there was an increase in the number of defaults. This prompted a positive feedback. Complicated bonds that held bundles of billions of dollars of these mortgages were downgraded as the number of defaults grew, and many became worthless. The banks that had set up these bonds started running short of cash. Banks started to worry about the solvency of other banks, and some major banks failed or needed to be rescued by government. Banks became reluctant to lend to each other, sending the interbank lending rates soaring. This drove interest rates higher in the market, which in turn caused more mortgage defaults. As banks stopped lending and people became short of cash, they started selling assets, provoking a precipitous drop in the housing and stock markets.

When complex systems are stressed by some change in constraints, they do not seem to respond for a while, and then suddenly they flip into a new state with new emergent properties. Strong competition can put enough pressure on companies to push them into bankruptcy, even if they survive a long time beforehand. Sudden positive feedback loops can push businesses into a tailspin during which customers, suppliers, bankers, and investors lose confidence and withdraw relations, effectively killing the company. Enron is a perfect example.

There are positive feedback mechanisms that arise when there are increasing returns in the market. For example, when profitable Internet companies like eBay or Google grew in size, their returns grew. The companies ploughed their returns back into more growth, which increased their returns and so on. Suddenly little start-up companies had market capitalizations worth many billions, and bigger than some companies that were considered giants. Railroads in the late 19th century experienced similar feedback-induced growth. Runs on banks, too, are positive feedback loops.

WHY DO SO MANY BUSINESS IMPROVEMENT INITIATIVES (SUCH AS SIX-SIGMA) FAIL?

Business executives often implement various programs to try and improve business performance and profitability. Ironically they often precipitate the opposite and flip their business into a new state. One corporate change program is called "Six-Sigma." Viewing businesses as complex systems sheds some light into why this happens.

Six-Sigma involves a greatly expanded use of measurement and statistics, combined with teamwork, training, projects, acronyms, and hype to drive improvements. There are many stories about success, and many books and consultants promising it. Companies such as General Electric, Allied Signal, Raytheon, and American Express say Six-Sigma has saved billions and transformed their companies.

Despite that, research indicates that about half of all companies that try Six-Sigma do not succeed.[13] Often programs are just left to die when success is not forthcoming. Corporate executives often introduce it with flawed mechanical thinking: training + teams + measurable goals + incentives = improved productivity. Efforts to introduce it put stress on the complex corporate system. Such heavy-handed mechanistic thinking in business is not a recent phenomenon. John Bangs and Carlos Hart, in their 1942 book *Factory Management,* describe how, while the plant manager was away because of illness, the remaining managers installed a system to improve productivity. When the manager returned, he discovered, "A heavy volume of expense was incurred in operating the system, and instead of speeding up managerial returns, it was actually slowing them down. Its control was complete, but its action was subject to disastrous delay."[14]

Modern Six-Sigma programs (and their ilk) often slow down returns, despite claims to the contrary. Companies and executive that do not get returns are not likely to boast about their losses. The story might go like this: Massive training programs take employees away from their work for several weeks. During their absence the extra burden of putting out fires falls on those remaining at work. They work longer hours and under increasing stress. When the others return from their training, they are given projects to work on to improve productivity.

The projects, training, and meetings take up an increasing portion of people's time, giving them less time to spend on their regular jobs. Employees soon realize that they should call just about any improvement they make, and would make anyway, a Six-Sigma project. They set their goals for their projects very carefully. If their bosses demand a 10 percent improvement this year and they know of a 20 percent savings, they will aim for 10 percent the first year and defer the balance for the next year—thus slowing down improvement. They create misleading indicators of project success, for example by monkeying with a favorite Six-Sigma measure called "defects per million opportunities." Since the more "opportunities" for defects they can include in the calculation, the better they look, as it will make the defect rate per million opportunities go down, any imaginable way for a product to be considered defective becomes just another opportunity. In one business book the authors put it this way: "Being of high integrity, we don't want to 'pad' our opportunities just to boost our score."[15] Padding happened in the Soviet Union—a centrally planned economy—where factory managers limited the amount by which they exceeded production quotas, even if they were able to exceed them by more, because to do so would result in a bigger quota next year.[16] The behavior results from the separation of knowledge and power, as Sowell put it.

Six-Sigma dashboards are established that measure and display key performance indicators of Six-Sigma initiatives and projects. They look at small linear bits of corporate performance, such as successful projects, defects per million opportunities, cost savings from projects, percentage of people trained in Six-Sigma, and so on.

But measuring the parts does not explain the whole.

To speed up progress, various people are appointed such as "master black belts," "black belts," "green belts," and various coordinators. They busy themselves by getting in people's way and consolidating their control over the business. Soon people find that the only way to get through a day is to live a duplicitous life. In one life they fight fires to get the product out of the door, and in the other they support the demands of the increasingly authoritarian Six-Sigma program.

Convinced of the virtues of Six-Sigma, managers often do not ask for nor listen to people's stories. They believe their own story and the story told by consultants, while following the numbers closely. Gradually—or sometimes suddenly—internal resistance to Six-Sigma grows, often accompanied by the hasty departure of the vice president who promoted it.

In addition to measuring aspects of a business, it is vital to talk—and listen—to employees to identify the structures and processes within the company that contribute both negatively and positively to its productivity problems. These could include policies, procedures, habits, beliefs, incentives, rules, measurement systems, communication habits and methods, equipment, office and plant layout, and so on. Before implementing changes or solutions, you should have sought out opinions and modified the solutions to achieve a high degree of consensus. This will reduce the stress on the system. Changes should be made quickly but incrementally, rather than radically, like a series of nudges. With each nudge or change, measure improvements, and ask employees, customers, and suppliers to tell their stories, identifying the adaptations of the system and the new structures and processes that have emerged. This is the Toyota concept of *"Genchi genbutsu,"* which means "go and see for yourself." The idea is that decision makers cannot make a judgment about a situation based solely on measurements and the reports of subordinates. You need to see the conditions with your own eyes, and interact with workers.

There are linear cause-and-effect relationships within individual structures and processes of a complex system. But understanding their properties does not explain the whole system, nor how it reacts to "measures that drive future performance." The machine metaphor creates the false impression that the measurements will provide a guide to future performance.

LISTENING TO THE FISHERMEN

Some people understand the need for qualitative information and not just measurements to understand a complex system. One Great Lakes fisheries scientist, John Goodier, did his research by spending time traveling with fishermen on Lake Superior. They spoke about where the fish spawned, migrated, and fed. Goodier peered over historical accounts from the men who, centuries earlier, managed Hudson Bay Company trading posts and who had recorded their conversations with Indian fishermen. He was able to piece together a very intricate picture of the Lake Superior ecosystem[17] and its structures before the trout and other salmonids crashed—a change in state—in the 1950s. He also knew that the fisheries statistics on landed catches of fish—the only hard data he had available at the beginning of his research—were too biased to be useful. The fishermen would land the fish that would fetch the highest price and release the rest back in the lake.

Goodier wrote in the concluding remarks of one of his papers that "the primary and most valuable sources of information are the 'old-timers' themselves, fishermen who have repeatedly demonstrated an intimate awareness of lake conditions and fish habitats. Such knowledge develops only from years of observation, from the certainty that economic and physical security depends on its accurateness, and from a respect for, and desire to conserve, the environment which has lent them a livelihood."[18]

You could interpret the word "environment" in many ways: the workplace environment, the economic environment, or the business environment. The point remains the same. The most valuable sources of information about the structures and processes in a complex system come from people whose economic and physical security within that system depends on its accurateness, and who have spent years observing it. Ask them to tell you their stories before you start measuring anything. Measurement can help you characterize and monitor individual structures and processes once they are identified and their general relationship to each other is understood.

A negative feedback mechanism is what happens when the electric blanket controllers are on the correct side of the bed. When you are too hot, you turn it down, and it gets cooler. When you are too cool, you turn it up and you get warmer. The negative feedback mechanism prevents vicious circles from getting out of control. There are negative feedbacks in the economy that arise when there are decreasing returns, such as tighter price competition that arises when too many firms enter the same market. This pushes marginal firms under, and loosens competition on price.

There is an additional layer of complexity in economies, in that unlike fish and algae, the players within an economy can act with strategy and foresight, although they do not always do so.

The increased understanding that economies behave like complex systems has helped us understand why it is so enormously difficult to predict the outcomes of economic trends, business plans, and government intervention. Episodic events happen and affect the outcomes in surprising ways, and there are many plausible outcomes with many different equilibria or states.

Detailed measurements of all aspects of economic activity bombard us constantly in the business news, giving the appearance that economics is a quantitative field. Measurement is the foundation of econometrics, which seeks to understand and quantify the relationships between such things as income earned and education, or between inflation and unemployment. But economists are notoriously bad at predicting market crashes. We need the stories to understand economic complexity and the relationships and events that cause the major economic flips and even economic heart attacks. One quote variously attributed to both Joseph P. Kennedy (John F. Kennedy's father) and Bernard Baruch (a presidential advisor and financier) warns investors that informal information can tell them that the market is about to crash: "Taxi drivers told you what to buy. The shoe shine boy could give you a summary of the day's financial news," referring to the period shortly before the 1929 crash.

Many politicians are blinded by a mechanistic, cause-and-effect metaphor about the cause of unemployment or other economic problems. They simplistically claim that it is caused by a lack of government support.[19] Add more government support and create jobs. Then unemployment should go down, according to this simple view. Such thinking ignores the fragmented nature of knowledge and the folly of concentrated, third-party decision making from a distance, with little or no feedback. It ignores the way complex systems respond to changes in constraints—such as the way lakes respond to an influx of new algae-causing phosphates, or the US economy responded to cheap credit.

Many business and self-employed people deride such simple mechanistic thinking about economics. They are like the fishermen on Lake Superior, whose "economic and physical security depends" on the accurateness of their knowledge of the structures and processes with which they interact in the economy. It is surprising, then, that so many of them, and so many business writers, use the mechanistic metaphor to aid their understanding of their own organizations. It is easy for them to recognize the role of Adam Smith's invisible, self-organizing hand in the economy, but under their own noses they see—or think they see—highly tuned machines that respond to their every command the way a car responds to its driver.

The function of measurement in a large or complex business is similar to its function in any complex system. It permits quantification of small linear bits of the system. It helps people understand the relationships between such individual components such as how the moisture in timber changes after it has been cut from the stump, the location and type of an ore body and the cost of mining it, the relationship between inventory levels and the delays in the supply chain, or the time it takes to process various types of insurance forms.

What measurement will not do is describe the system's structures, processes and feedbacks, and their interactions, nor will it necessarily identify new structures, processes and feedbacks, and interactions that arise when a system is stressed.

INTEGRATIVE INDICATORS OF COMPLEX SYSTEMS

One way to get round the problem of just measuring the bits is to develop "integrative indicators" that measure the health of a system such as a business or a lake. An integrative indicator attempts to integrate many of the facets of the system into a single number. They are arbitrary, and their usefulness can only be tested through experience. The Apgar score is an example. It integrates useful information about newborns, and experience has shown that it integrates the information into a useful indicator.

Salmon, trout, and related fish, collectively known as salmonids, are used by fisheries biologists as live integrative indicators[20] for the "health"[21] of aquatic ecosystems. Different human activities affect fish: fishing, pollution, introduction of exotic species, and destruction of wetlands. The number of salmonids is thus considered to be a response to human activities. The salmonids represent what people consider healthy in a lake: clean, cool, and clear. The more harmful human activities in and around a lake, the fewer salmonids live in it. Over time, the salmonids have proven to be a useful indicator.

Not all fish would be as useful as indicators. Some fish families, such as the cyprinids, which includes the carps and minnows, increase in number (up to a point) as human activity increases and water gets dirtier and warmer. This, too, was learned only from experience.

Unemployment and inflation are economic indicators that serve a similar purpose. If they are high and increasing, we consider the economy to be less healthy than if they are low, but not if they are too low. They do not measure a single structure or process within the economy. They are not generally the result of any individual policies or actions, although we know that in general inflation is the result of increases in the money supply beyond the rate of increase of goods and services in the economy. They attempt to integrate or average in some way the overall structures, processes, and interactions within an economy. Stock market indices are integrative indicators of overall market performance. There are rival indices because there are competing views as to what constitutes the best measure of market health and a rising market. Traditional indices are based on the market value of businesses in an index. Newer indices are based on their "fundamentals." The problem is that people do not agree on what the fundamentals are.[22] This problem occurs with all integrative indicators.

In 1997, Robert Wells, chief financial officer at the Bank of Montreal, in a paper in *Sloan Management Review,* described how the bank developed an integrative indicator for an overall level of performance, whose purpose was to "maximize long-term return on investment for shareholders, which it achieves with a performance measurement system."[23] The basic idea of their performance measurement system is similar to the balanced scorecard, in that they measure primary objectives, which are usually financial, and secondary objectives, that "drive or cause performance on the primary objectives." The paper used the machine metaphor and alluded to complexity, referring both to performance *drivers* and describing the modern organization as a "complex web of contracts, both explicit and implicit, that specifies relationships between the company and its stakeholders." The paper said the bank's measurement system "supports the bank's learning by identifying and testing models of relationships between drivers and results."

The performance measurement system summarized performance into a single indicator. The scores for each stakeholder group were weighted and added to determine an overall score or index of performance.

Unlike Apgar's seminal paper in 1952, in which she provided empirical evidence that her indicator worked, Robert Wells and his coauthors proposed their indicator on purely theoretical grounds with no evidence in their paper that it indicated something useful. The onus on anyone developing an indicator or index is to prove it works before recommending it to others or making claims as to its effectiveness.

In the ten years after the bank developed this performance measurement tool, the Bank of Montreal had the lowest return of Canadian chartered banks (Table 6.1). Clearly many factors affect shareholder returns. Perhaps returns would have been lower without this indicator, but in any event it would be hard to argue that it maximized returns.

The bank continues to use a similar indicator and the measurement system, with some modifications to enable it to measure "performance against strategic priorities," and believes it is integral to achieving results.

Back to Dr. Crawford: Was there really nothing he could have foreseen about his patient and friend?

A couple of weeks later, after he had seen his last patient for the day, Dr. Crawford sat down at his desk with a tired sigh, and saw an autopsy report his receptionist had left on the top of his paperwork pile. It was about his friend.

He had died of acute myocardial infarction. The left anterior descending artery, one of the arteries that deliver blood to the heart muscle tissue, was blocked with a thrombus, or blood clot. The pathologist had examined heart muscle cells in the microscope and found necrotic myocardial cells—dead heart muscle cells. The blood clot was lodged in a part of the artery where enough plaque had grown to occlude, or plug up, about 20 percent of the artery.

Plaque is one of the body's ways of patching up damage in arterial walls. Medical science does not know why plaque starts growing in some spots but not others. Once plaque starts growing, it restricts the flow slightly inside the artery. This restriction creates turbulence downstream, like the waves below a rock in a river. The turbulence in turn encourages the formation of more plaque, and a positive feedback cycle begins, initiated by unknown events, even in a healthy person.

When a person is exercising vigorously, the blood pressure and heart rate increase. When these high-pressure surges hit unstable and relatively stiff plaque, they can, rarely, cause bits of plaque to break off, leaving a small

Table 6.1   Stock Market Returns of Canadian Chartered Banks, 1997–2007

Bank	Total increase in value of shares. March 1997–March 2007
Toronto Dominion	1140%
Bank of Nova Scotia	550%
Royal Bank	388%
Canadian Imperial Bank of Commerce	302%
Bank of Montreal	261%

wound. This causes bleeding on the inside of the arterial wall, and eventually a blood clot inside the artery.

Those heart muscles that are starved of oxygen and sugar by the clot soon stop working. The remaining muscles, thrown off balance and rhythm, send the heart into an erratic beat known as arrhythmia. This erratic beat is not strong or regular enough to supply the rest of the body with oxygenated blood, resulting, eventually, in death.

Crawford threw down the report and looked out the dark window at the shopping plaza lights across the parking lot. The loss of a patient to whom he had recently given a clean bill of health is tough enough. But to lose a friend and colleague too was really rough. Although he knew he had done everything by the book, he wondered for a moment whether there was not more he could have done, whether he had gone far enough to learn more about his patient's condition.

Crawford knew there was not. The only ways to have done so were too invasive, risky, and expensive. He flicked off the lights, locked his office, walked across the dark and wet parking lot to his car, and drove home.

It is a tough conclusion for a dedicated physician to reach. It is one we should all heed. Despite our intense desire to use measurements to know what is going on and what is going to happen, in complex systems there is an inherent limit to such knowledge. It is a mistake to ask measurements to do something they cannot do.

TOOL BOX

- Do not be blinded by the metaphors you use to describe your business. Businesses are not machines.
- Disaster can strike even if measurements look good, because measurements cannot tell you the whole picture: measuring the parts does not explain the whole.
- You can drive an automobile with no working instruments on the dashboard, but you cannot drive it blind. Remember that measurements extend the senses but do not replace them.
- The stories and observations of workers are as important as measurements. Their economic and physical security often depends on the accurateness of their observations.
- If you develop an integrative indicator for your business, make sure it is meaningful and useful before depending on it.

SEVEN

Focusing Employees with Measurements

What is to be sought in designs for the display of information is the clear portrayal of complexity. Not the complication of the simple.

—Jacques Bertin (1918–2010)

On September 3, 1939, a few hours after British prime minister Neville Chamberlain declared war on Germany in his historic BBC radio broadcast, he sent a note to Winston Churchill, who was in the House of Commons listening to speeches, summoning him to come to the prime minister's room as soon as the debate died down. There the prime minister offered Churchill the task of directing the Admiralty and a seat at the War Cabinet. In his history of the war, Churchill relates:

> One of the first steps I took on taking charge of the Admiralty and becoming a member of the War Cabinet was to form a statistical department of my own. For this purpose I relied on Professor Lindemann, my friend and confidant for many years. Together we had formed our views and estimates about the whole story. I now installed him at the Admiralty with half a dozen statisticians and economists whom we could trust to pay no attention to anything but realities. This group of capable men, with access to all official information, was able, under Lindemann's guidance, to present me continually with tables and diagrams, illustrating the whole war so far as it came within our knowledge.
>
> At this time there was no general Governmental statistical organisation. Each department presented its tale on its own figures and data. The Air

Ministry counted one way, the War Office another. The Ministry of Supply and the Board of Trade, though meaning the same thing, talked different dialects. This led sometimes to misunderstandings and waste of time when some point or another came to a crunch in the Cabinet. I had however from the beginning my sure source of information, every part of it which was integrally related to all the rest. Although at first this covered only a portion of the field, it was most helpful to me in forming a just and comprehensible view of the innumerable facts and figures which flowed out upon us.[1]

When Churchill became prime minister in May 1940, he kept Lindemann in charge of what Churchill now referred to as his "S" branch, which worked out of 10 Downing Street, the residence of the British P.M. The "S" branch, by reporting directly to the prime minister, bypassed the steps and sequence by which advice normally comes to a prime minister.[2] It did, however, give Churchill a tremendous grasp of facts and figures, of the war effort, and of the country's ability to produce armaments and fighting men.

Churchill made direct requests to Lindemann (who subsequently became Viscount Cherwell) for statistical information and charts. In the spring and summer of 1940, after the fall of France, the humiliating evacuation of British troops from Dunkirk, and before an anticipated German air attack on Britain, Churchill led the British in intensive preparations against a German invasion. The British were under-armed and alone: the democratic allies in Europe had fallen under the Nazi boot, and the Americans were not yet in the war. Churchill was marshalling all the resources at his disposal in a desperate attempt to prepare to fight the anticipated invaders. He knew his resources were thin, and he knew that he had to monitor his growing fighting capacity closely. He also knew the stakes:

Hitler knows that he will have to break us in this Island or lose the war. If we can stand up to him, all Europe may be free and the life of the world may move forward into broad, sunlit uplands. But if we fail, then the whole world, including the United States, including all that we have known and cared for, will sink into the abyss of a new Dark Age made more sinister, and perhaps more protracted, by the lights of perverted science.[3]

His requests to Lindemann for detailed information were eloquently stated and precisely described, to a degree I have rarely seen in private enterprise. Here is an example from a memo Churchill wrote to Lindemann on July 7, 1940, days before the Germans launched their massive air assault on the British Isles in what Churchill dubbed the Battle of Britain.

I want my "S" Branch to make a chart of all the thirty divisions, showing their progress towards complete equipment. Each division would be represented by a square divided into sections: officers and men, rifles, Bren guns, Bren-gun carriers, anti-tank-guns, field artillery, medium ditto (if any), transport sufficient to secure mobility of all three brigades simultaneously, etc. As and when a proportion of these subsidiary squares is completed a chart can be painted red. I should like to see this chart every week. A similar diagram can be prepared for the Home Guard. In this case it is only necessary to show rifles and uniforms.

Churchill's charts (Figures 7.1 and 7.2) clearly focused on measurements that were of vital national importance: readiness for invasion. They were focused on results that the leaders of the British Army had to produce successfully to repel a German invasion. In a single glance, Churchill, or any of his top advisers and staff, could see the state of their readiness. By comparing two charts for successive weeks—two glances—they could evaluate progress in thirty divisions, seven types of firearms or artillery, and personnel. The charts showed, for each division, for each type of weapon and personnel, when readiness was more than 50 percent complete, when it was greater than the previous report, and when the division had surpassed its targets for readiness (which Churchill called "establishment levels").

The charts provided the minimum amount of information the prime minister needed—Churchill did not need to know whether a division currently had 7,631 men or 374 light machine guns, but roughly how far along in their preparation each division was, and whether they were progressing from week to week and month to month. He needed qualitative but accurate answers as to the state of readiness: he was prime minister and minister of defense, not a weapons purchaser. With a single chart he could identify divisions or weapons that were not sufficiently ready, or less ready relative to others, and that therefore needed his attention. The charts prompted action, rather than cluttering up his desk with pretty but useless graphical displays. The charts therefore made extremely economical use of Churchill's time and mental effort.

Churchill's charts built several data components into a single graphical display. The components included personnel, weapons systems, divisions, time (with the lines that indicate previous level), and establishment level.

Jacques Bertin (1918–2010) was a French cartographer who said[4] that good graphical displays should prompt questions at three levels. At the overall level, one quickly sees the structure of the data, what it is all about. At the intermediate level, one can compare different parts of the same

Figure 7.1   Churchill's state of readiness chart for July 13, 1940.

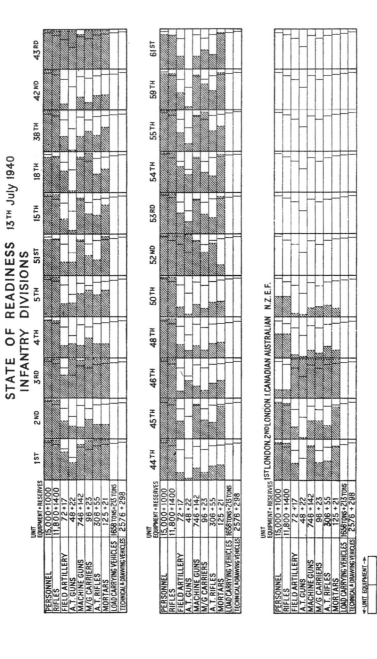

Source: Winston S. Churchill, *Their Finest Hour,* Book 1, *The Fall of France* (London: The Reprint Society, 1949; 9th impression, 1956), 226, 230.

Figure 7.2   Churchill's state of readiness chart for September 7, 1940.

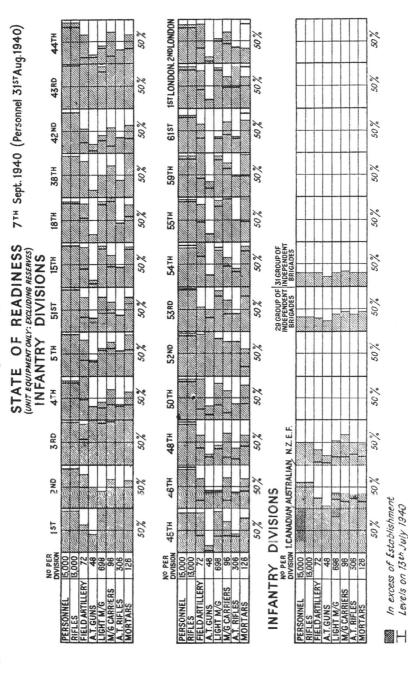

Source: Winston S. Churchill, *Their Finest Hour,* Book 1, *The Fall of France* (London: The Reprint Society, 1949; 9th impression, 1956), 226, 230.

structure, or different structures. At the most elementary level, one can directly compare any pair of numbers.

With his charts, Churchill could view the information at these three levels. At the highest level, he could see the overall state of readiness of the home defenses. At this overall level, the chart let him ask questions that dealt with an entire component, such as whether there were enough anti-tank guns.

At a more intermediate level, he could zero in on subsets of data components, such as assessing the provision of weapons for a single division, or comparing the state of readiness of one division with another. For example, the chart for September 7, 1940, shows that the readiness of the 1st Canadian Infantry Division was in excess of establishment levels in personnel and had reached it in everything else while the 42nd was below establishment levels in everything. Likewise he could compare the state of readiness of one weapons system with another. For example, the charts show that the troops were well supplied with rifles, but almost all divisions were behind in provisions of antitank guns. At the most elementary level of detail he could ask questions about single elements of data components. For example, he might have asked why the 53rd division was so far behind in field artillery. The charts enabled these questions because they preserved the structural integrity of the data.

The true value of well-defined graphics is that they enable the viewer to identify patterns, to turn data into knowledge, and most importantly, to help turn knowledge into action.

THE IMPORTANCE OF STRUCTURAL INFORMATION

Business writers and consultants today typically advise managers to calculate indices and percentages to measure the state of their enterprises. For example, Kaplan and Norton,[5] in *The Balanced Scorecard*, suggest measuring "strategic information availability" with the "percentage of processes with real-time quality, cycle time, and cost feedback available" and "percentage of customer-facing employees having on-line access to information about customers." Meyer and Ross, authors in Peter Senge's collaboration *The Dance of Change,* advise readers to develop similar measures, to strive for simplicity, and to display them on an "Operational Dashboard."

Many management writers advise their readers to limit the number of things they measure to some arbitrarily small number. Meyer and Ross,[6] for example, state, "If you could only track six or eight things, what would they be? The point is to avoid devising so many numbers and gauges that your dashboard looks like a 747 cockpit. Otherwise you'll spend all your time looking at the dashboard and forget to 'look out the windshield'—to actually implement the work."

I doubt many readers would disagree with their advice to "look out of the windshield," but it is not very helpful. As for the rest, you should measure what you need to measure to prompt timely and specific action, while preserving the structural integrity of the data. Every instrument on the 747 is there to help fly the plane. The instruments prompt the pilots to take specific actions. There is virtue in simplicity, but the number of things you should measure is dictated by the structure of the information and the actions that need to be taken, not by simplicity for simplicity's sake.

If Winston Churchill had taken the advice in *The Dance of Change*, he might have produced a silly "operational dashboard" that included a graphic such as the one below.

Simplicity is of course a desirable attribute of an information display. The operational dashboard in Figure 7.3, however, uses a lot of ink and space to display just two numbers. For Churchill such a display would have been almost totally useless. It only gives a broad measure of progress. By throwing out structural information, it would not have told him what corrective action to take. Furthermore, displaying the information in the form of a dial makes the display unnecessarily complicated.

Edward Tufte[7] said that graphical displays should "show the data; present many numbers in a small space; avoid distorting what the data have to say; induce the viewer to think about substance; reveal the data at several levels of detail, from a broad overview to the fine structure." The epilogue to his books states, "What is to be sought in designs for the display of information is the clear portrayal of complexity. Not the complication of the simple; rather the task of the designer is to give visual access to the subtle and the difficult—that is, the revelation of the complex."[8]

Figure 7.3   What Churchill's chart would look like today.

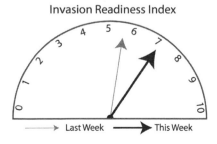

If Churchill had calculated an "invasion readiness index" instead of using his own brilliant charts, he would have been able to calculate it in many possible ways. They would all destroy structural information. A readiness of 97 percent sounds terrific, but if it resulted from one division not being ready at all, it would have offered a soft target for invasion. Likewise one could, with the right definition of readiness, calculate a readiness index of 99.8 percent, meaning that all equipment and personnel were in place except field artillery. Any representation of readiness had to preserve this structural information.

You may be able to calculate indices in a way that makes them mathematically valid, but by throwing out the structure of the data, they are not *structurally* valid. Peter Drucker, in his classic book *Management*,[9] wrote in 1973 that "to enable controls to give the right vision and to become the grounds for effective action, the measurement must also be appropriate. Thus, it must present the events measured in structurally true form. Formal validity is not enough." Yet the advice has not been heeded, and to a large extent, our creative and data crunching ability with computers has made it worse. Churchill was ahead of his time—his charts and his design of information displays for top executives applied principles introduced by such authors as Drucker and Tufte thirty years later.

HOW STRUCTURAL INFORMATION PROMPTS ACTION

When the structure of data is destroyed by calculating overall averages, percentages, and ratios, the resulting measurements merely provide information on general direction. General direction does not prompt specific and timely actions. Such measurements cannot be used for controlling processes or improving work. They can mask crucial information. They have, thus, perhaps more than any other type of measure, the potential to mislead.

To reveal structure the raw data must be reduced to something more intelligible. This usually requires calculating statistics such as averages, percentages, or sums for the main elements of the structure. Calculating overall statistics, as opposed to statistics for elements of the structure, destroys the structural information from the structural components that went into the average. Somewhere in the middle there is an optimum, as shown in Figure 7.4. We can avoid destroying structural information and find that optimum if we judiciously apply our background information about the existing structures we wish to preserve. Monthly averages destroy structural information *within* months, information that could be revealed by weekly and daily averages, but not *between* months.

Employee job satisfaction, or dissatisfaction, is rarely equal amongst groups of employees, and dissatisfaction does not have the same importance to the future of an enterprise for each group. Many companies measure it and report it as an overall number. In one remote pulp mill, the great majority of employees were reasonably satisfied with their jobs, or perhaps just glad to have them. They were amongst the highest paid in the region. The dissatisfied employees were concentrated among the bright young engineers that were being groomed for future leadership roles. Most of them were men, with wives who could not stand the isolation of the mill's site, or without wives and unable to find one. The top management, at head office, was quite dumbstruck when without forewarning and within a few months their best engineers quit, throwing to the winds their plans for the future management of the plant. The employee satisfaction measures had thrown out any structural information that might have given the management a hint about what was going on.

A measure of inventory turns for a consumer products manufacturer may suggest to management that there is too much inventory. "Twelve inventory turns per year" is how it is often reported. This gives the false impression that all inventory turns at the same rate. It ignores the structural

Figure 7.4   Reduce raw data to reveal, not destroy, structural information.

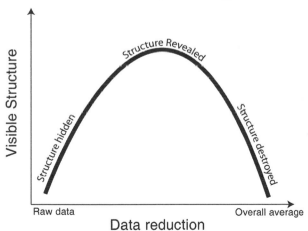

information. There is not an equal amount of inventory for every product. Nor is there an equal proportion of inventory for every unit of sales. Capturing, displaying, and acting on this structural information takes more effort than calculating overall averages and observing the overall direction they indicate. It also leads to greater improvements.

Both a logistics manager and a sales manager should know, for example, that the 2 percent of products that accounted for the top 20 percent of sales last year are currently taking up 28 percent of the inventory, and are thus turning relatively quickly. They might also find it useful to know that more than half their current product offerings account for less than 20 percent of sales, taking up 10 percent of inventory space. This information can prompt several specific actions: changing product mix, getting rid of slow-moving products, sourcing raw material differently, or changing manufacturing strategy based on the relative speeds at which various products turn. Figure 7.5 is derived from actual inventory and sales data from a consumer products manufacturer with close to 2,700 product stock keeping units (SKUs). (The smooth-looking lines are plots of the actual inventory data.)

A commonly used measure in industry is lost-time injuries per 200,000 hours worked. This measure scales the number of lost-time injuries in a year to an operation with one hundred full-time employees. It is used as a key performance indicator of safety performance, and is frequently

Figure 7.5   Relationship between sales, inventory, and number of products.

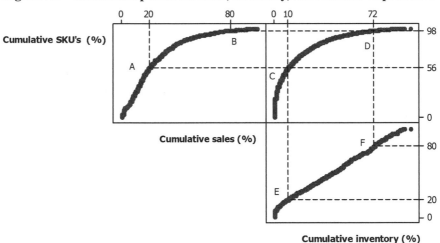

included on monthly tabular reports to management and occasionally on charts. When it goes down, congratulatory sentiments are expressed and awards are granted. When it goes up, a flurry of new programs, exhortations, and denunciations is launched. But it provides no information that can properly direct effort. All the structure in the data has been removed. To direct action, one must know what part of the body is being injured, what types of injuries are occurring, what departments they are occurring in, and whether the frequencies of these subcomponents are increasing or decreasing.

For example, in one company with a dozen plants, over the course of two years it was found that 55 percent of injuries, when classified by injury type, were sprains and lacerations, and 50 percent of injuries, when classified by part of body injured, were to hands and backs. The company kept track of 630 possible combinations of injury types and body parts. Directing effort to reducing sprains to the back and lacerations to hands, two combinations, would direct attention to 38 percent of all injuries.

The high-frequency injuries are summarized in Table 7.1. The table shows some structural information—the parts of the body and the injury types—but it makes it difficult to ask questions at Bertin's three levels.

By plotting the data in Table 7.1 in a graphical table such as the one in Figure 7.6, patterns emerge more clearly and the unique ways in which hands are injured is clearer. Bertin[10] calls this type of display a "reorderable" matrix.

This understanding of the structure shows clearly that the focus should not be solely on reducing injuries, but specifically on reducing sprains, especially to the back, and on reducing cuts to the hands.

Table 7.1   Injuries versus Parts of the Body

	Sprain	Surface wounds	Cut	Other	Burn
Hand	18	94	148	12	16
Arm	30	49	26	17	41
Back	121	18	3	4	4
Knee	47	47	2	7	0
Shoulder	62	11	1	2	0
Head	1	19	22	3	7

Figure 7.6   Injuries and parts of body, reordered.

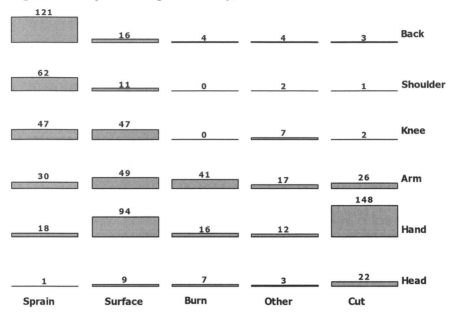

Sprain	Surface	Burn	Other	Cut	
121	16	4	4	3	Back
62	11	0	2	1	Shoulder
47	47	0	7	2	Knee
30	49	41	17	26	Arm
18	94	16	12	148	Hand
1	9	7	3	22	Head

The structure one sees in a set of data depends on the perspective from which one looks at it. A bricklayer sees a house at an elementary, or fundamental, level—the location of bricks and walls. An interior decorator sees it an intermediary level: the arrangement of rooms, windows, and living space. The real estate agent sees it at yet a higher level: its relationship to the neighborhood and how that affects its selling price.

When one is turning data into useful information, the person who needs the information must first understand the relevant levels and structures in the data. Removing all structures removes almost all information. A senior executive has as much a need to know the structures that are relevant to him as a worker. What differs is not the need for structure, but the structures of interest.

Consider a simple example: walking on ice. Clearly a useful measurement is the thickness of the ice. Without structural information, however, the average thickness is not very useful information. At our family cottage, we have played hockey on ice as thin as two and a half inches. And we have avoided ice one foot thick.

The thickness of the ice is a useful measure of safety only if you understand the structure of ice and how it changes. Some changes are almost instantaneous—such as when it breaks and you fall through. When it is freezing quickly, the ice expands and creates long hairline pressure cracks that sound like a rifle shot (creating a panicked response from the uninitiated). Water gushes out of the cracks and quickly freezes on the surface. If there is a layer of snow on the ice, this water often does not freeze, creating slush under the snow and on top of hard ice. Sometimes another ice crust forms on top of this layer of slush. You can fall through this thin layer onto the hard ice below.

It is crucial to know where the currents are; they cause lakes to freeze later and thinner. In places where the high sun beats down on rocks, it warms them up. The rocks radiate heat onto the ice, so it is thinner there too. When ice melts in the spring it does not melt like an ice cube, from the outside in, but from the inside out. When the sun has burned the snow off the ice, it begins to heat the dark water underneath, so the ice begins to melt from the bottom. When it gets to a foot or less thick, it turns into long, vertical crystals called candles that transmit more light to the water below, speeding up the melting. The water warms up in the sun, and then melts the ice. Melt water starts to fill in the spaces between the candles. On a windy day foot-thick ice breaks up and within a few hours it is all gone except for a few sheltered bays, with little candles floating in the water and quickly melting. You need to know how much the sun has warmed the ice recently.

At the most elementary level, we use measurement to interact with the physical world. The more we know about structure, the more we can refine our interactions and control the situations they present to us. The structures are mostly physical. When you know them you can design better ways to measure.

An engineer designing or improving a machine for soldering components, such as capacitors, onto a printed circuit board needs to know whether the differing heat capacities of these components will create thermal gradients across the board that prevent consistent solder quality within boards. The heat capacity of an object is its ability to hold heat. If components have high heat capacities they will act as heat sinks that remove heat needed to melt the solder. He also needs to know whether there are heat gradients within the oven that might affect the consistency of solder quality between boards in different parts of the oven. He can then control the process accordingly. Average temperature measurements destroy this structural information, and thereby prohibit more refined control. This may result in lower product quality. If he controlled the soldering process by only measuring average temperatures, the solder would be of much lower quality.

A municipality opening up a pond or canal for public skating does not want refined control, but a simple control that provides an adequate cushion for risk. The National Capital Commission in Ottawa does not open the Rideau Canal for public skating until the ice samples it takes are all between 10 and 12 inches thick. This "costs" the public opportunities to skate. There is thus a trade-off between simplicity of control, risk, and cost. Bureaucratic controls are often similarly simple, as opposed to refined, resulting in a higher convenience cost to the public—everybody waits in the same line-up.

STANDARDS, CONFORMANCE, AND MEASUREMENT

To control, you need standards. Every business needs standards. By creating these standards managers establish another and vitally important set of secondary structures. In the example of ice-skating, the elementary structure is the thickness at which ice will not hold an adult's weight. This is something over which we have no control—it is based on the laws of nature. The secondary structure is the standard—the rule, for example, that requires an ice thickness of 2.5 inches, 4 inches, or 12 inches. It is entirely the prerogative of management to decide whether a particular standard is needed, and if it is, what it should be.

It was a lack of standards, a heady sense of infallibility, and a reliance on talent and star power, mixed with a dose of criminal behavior fed by these failings, that contributed significantly to Enron's collapse. Enron had failed to implement standards on many of the most basic aspects of its business, such as trading strategies and cash management. When Greg Whalley took over as president, after convicted felon Jeffrey Skilling's ouster, he discovered Enron had no idea of its cash position.[11]

A class action lawsuit against Google, related to accusations of fraudulent click-throughs on their sponsored Web advertisements (a huge source of revenue for the company) forced the company to implement quality assurance standards to monitor clicks on sponsored ads.

Manufacturers that do not clearly define and adhere to standards for controlling their processes, soon find themselves awash in customer complaints, scrap, and possibly product liability lawsuits. Standards should prompt action to control processes. "Control" does not mean domination over people, but influence over work processes by those who operate them.

It is as important to measure conformance to standards, as it is to measure the elementary structures that give rise to the need for control. If a standard is worth having, management should measure conformance to it to determine whether it works, whether work conforms to it, and whether it is contributing to producing the desired results. This is a basic function of management oversight. This second level of measurement is performed poorly in most companies. A sure sign of this is the complaint that "after twelve months we seem to be solving the same problems all over again."

The director of a large portfolio sets a mandate for his investment managers, defined in such terms as asset mix, earnings quality, volatility, and so on. When the director measures the performance of his managers, he measures (or should) first the results: the return over various time frames and in comparison with benchmarks, and second, whether they are conforming with the mandate for the portfolio. In other words, it is not enough to get across the ice, you have to get across while conforming to standards designed to make sure you get there safely.

THREE LEVELS OF MEASUREMENT

The portfolio director thus measures at three levels. At the overall level, he is interested in results—the returns gained. At the intermediate level, he is interested in whether the managers have conformed to the mandate. At the elementary level, he is in interested in the fine details of individual investments or investment classes—although this level of measurement is of more interest to the investment manager.

The same three levels apply to my ice skating example. At the overall level, we are interested in results—how much skating we were able to do. At the intermediate level, we are interested in—and oversee, loosely, as it is a cottage—conformance to the standards we have established at our cottage for skating safely. And at the elementary level, we are interested in the thickness of the ice at the various locations and times, according to our understanding of the ice's structure.

These three levels of measurement are universal in character in organizations. At the overall level, managers measure results. At the intermediate level, and according to the structure they have established, they measure conformance to standards they have established. And at the elementary level, they measure the fine structure.

In manufacturing, the elementary measurements are used to control processes, according to the fine structures of the manufacturing process. The intermediate measurements are used to improve the process controls themselves. They can be obtained by computer—with online measurement devices comparing process data and sequencing steps with defined standards. The overall measurements are the entrepreneurial measures, such as quality, yield, and output. They are used to determine whether the entire enterprise is producing the desired results.

The elementary level of measurement provides workers (or skaters) with the feedback they need to perform their work. The intermediate level gives the feedback they need to refine controls. Yet it is the level that is most poorly performed and is regularly given short shrift. There are a number of reasons. Often management has not established standards against which they can readily measure performance. They leave the setting of standards to hope, and to the skill of employees. Or it is because they have not developed a means to measure conformance to standards.

There was a time when the manual collection of such data was an impediment. Today many variables are measured electronically, sometimes hundreds of times per second. With computers, it is a simple matter to compare these numbers with standards and find those cases where they do not conform. This can remove some of the burden of measurement at the intermediate level.

Managers often rely on auditors to determine conformance to standards. Audits are by their very nature infrequent and designed to identify gross failings of controls. They do not provide the feedback necessary to refine controls or standards.

Measuring conformance to standards provides important feedback both to workers and to managers. It helps continually refine and improve standards and the controls to achieve them. By comparing the conformance to the standards with results, you can determine where to look for the causes of unsatisfactory results. If the results are unsatisfactory and the conformance to standards is high, the standards are wrong or too loose and do not provide adequate direction (see box A in Table 7.2). If conformance to standards is low and results are poor, the process is not under adequate control or is incapable of achieving the standards (box B). Likewise if results are satisfactory but conformance to standards is poor, the standards are likely too tight and thereby adding unnecessary cost (box C).

Aggregating conformance to standards over various components of the organizational structure, such as business units, processes, or product technologies, directs management attention to improving the standards and controls themselves. It may also help them modify policies, cultural tendencies of the business, bad habits (usually their own), incentives, hiring and training practices, budgets, resources, and technology that may be preventing high conformance to standards.

I once worked with a commercial bakery that was implementing such a feedback method, based on the precepts of integrated process management (IPM) as described by Roger Slater.[12] A worker running an oven received high-frequency feedback with computer-generated charts on the quality of the cookies produced by the oven—measured on such finished attributes as humidity, color, and weight. They could also pull up trend charts and graphs that showed the conformance of the process to standards on such process variables as dough moisture, bake time, and temperature that affected the quality of the finished cookies. (See Figure 7.7 for a facsimile.)

Workers and managers alike could generate graphs to answer questions at different levels, such as the percentage conformance over selected time frames for an entire department or process, for subsets of variables within a process, for variables that affected specific attributes of the cookie, or for individual process variables. These graphs would prompt workers and managers to action. They could determine when they needed to improve the methods for controlling process variables to make them conform to standards, and when they needed to propose changes to the standards themselves. Managers were able quickly to identify processes, departments, and

Table 7.2 Comparison of Results and Process Conformance

		Results	
		Good results	**Poor results**
Conformance to standards	**Good**	Work conforms to standards; standards are effective. (e.g., people obey ice safety rules; no one falls through ice; plenty of days of skating)	A. Standards are too loose. Tighten standards. (e.g., rule says ice must be one inch think; someone falls through ice even though standard was followed)
	Poor	C. Standards are too tight. Loosen standards. (e.g., rule says ice must be two feet thick; people violate rule and no one falls through ice)	B. Work does not conform to standards; or standards are inadequate. (e.g., people fall through ice; they ignore ice safety rules)

Figure 7.7   Conformance chart.

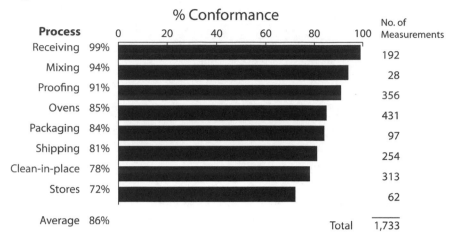

plants that were having difficulty achieving high conformance to standards and act accordingly. They could then offer technical assistance, training, new capital, and so on to help improve conformance. Within a year of implementing this system, quality and productivity increased significantly, and, most importantly, the workers knew how to maintain the gains.

STRUCTURE, STANDARDS, MEASUREMENT, AND ORGANIZATIONAL LEARNING

The elementary and intermediate levels of measurement inherent in the feedback loops I have described above make organizational learning easier. Consider a thermostat: it uses a single-loop "learning process, as shown in Figure 7.8." It senses the room temperature and compares it to the setting on the dial—the standard. If it "learns" that the temperature is lower than the setting by more than some threshold amount, it turns on the heater. If it learns the temperature is more than the threshold above the setting, it turns it off. The temperature range between the thresholds is the "dead zone."

For years my wife and I were stuck in a kind of single-loop learning on our thermostat. She likes it warmer than I do, so she would sneak the setting up and I would sneak it down. Eventually we admitted what we were doing and had a frank chat. She wanted warmth when she went to bed and got up in the morning, and I like it cool to sleep. So we bought a thermostat with a timer. Figure 7.9 illustrates single-loop and double-loop learning.

Figure 7.8   Single-loop learning.

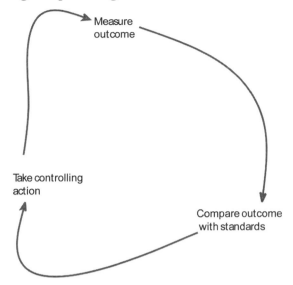

This questioning of the single-loop learning process and the measurements, actions, and learning that drive it are a second learning loop. Argyris and Schon[13] coined the terms single- and double-loop learning. In single-loop learning, we learn from feedback on outcomes to take control of actions that affect outcomes. In double-loop learning, we also learn to question our strategy for controlling processes that deliver outcomes, and the factors that govern those strategies.

Room temperature changes quickly when a heater comes on, so the temperature of the room is a useful indicator for the control loop. This is true in general when the response of the outcome to control action is quick. In many situations, the response to the control action is too slow for the outcomes to be a useful indicator for effective control action. Sometimes this is because it takes a long time to measure the outcome. In these cases the control action may amplify swings in the outcome. If you took a shower where there was an abnormal delay between turning the taps and receiving warmer or cooler water from the shower head, you would keep adjusting the taps until you got warm water, but the water would keep getting warmer—possibly uncomfortably so. You might then turn the taps the other way and chase the cold water too far the same way. A second loop soon would soon teach you about the problems in the first loop and how to compensate for the delay. Such delays are normal for overall business outcomes such as sales and customer retention.

Figure 7.9   Single- and double-loop learning.

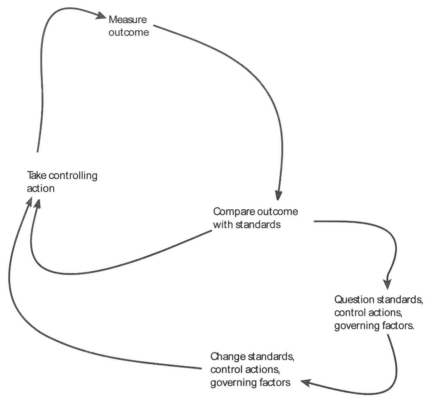

In such situations you should measure in-process variables (or "drivers") in addition to the outcomes. For example, in a cookie factory, oven temperature has an effect on the moisture of the finished cookies. But the effect is delayed. It is thus better to use oven temperature, rather than cookie moisture, as the control variable. Such a control scheme requires standards for both the outcome variable and the in-process variable. Each variable is independently measured and compared with its standards as part of the control strategy. Figure 7.10 below illustrates this for what can be called nested single-loop learning.

For such a control scheme to work, one has to know whether the in-process variable(s) has (have) an effect on the outcomes. In the case of the cookie factory, it is fairly obvious that it does. What is not obvious is how the in-process variable should be controlled and to what standard. In many

Figure 7.10   Nested single-loop learning on in-process and outcome measures.

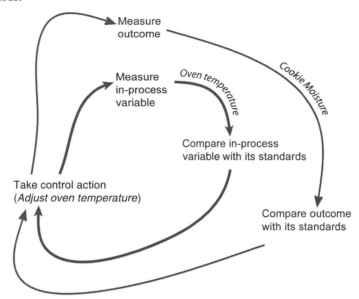

other cases sometimes what one thinks to be an in-process variable does not have the expected influence on outcomes.

In *The Balanced Scorecard*, Kaplan and Norton[14] state that measures should be selected from five perspectives—employee empowerment, learning and growth, internal business, customer, and financial. Executives should select these measures so that they are in a linking cause-and-effect chain, in which empowered employees develop new skills that lead to better internal business operations that create happy customers resulting in financial success. Kaplan and Norton go on to suggest that a "strategic feedback system" should be designed to test the hypothesized cause-and-effect relationships, and suggest using correlation analysis to do so.

Correlation analysis is a statistical technique to assess how two (or more) linked variables measured closely in time or space vary up or down together in a linear, or at least a predictable, manner. It cannot tell you which variable causes variation in which other variables, or if other variables drive them in tandem. As we saw in chapter six, in complex systems, as opposed to mechanistic systems, cause-and-effect variables are less linear, unlinked, and related through multiple layers and loops of feedback. Correlation analysis and its kindred statistical tools are of limited use in such circumstances. The lack of direct linkage and different frequencies of measurement between the variables make correlation analysis extremely difficult or impossible to perform. How then can the strategic feedback system be designed?

It can be designed using the same principles as a simple feedback system for the operator of the oven who is baking cookies. Every comparison of a variable—in-process or outcome—with its standard or expectation, is a measurable event. It either conforms or it does not conform to the standard. By aggregating these binary measurements over time and organizational structures, as percentages for example, new information emerges that enables a form of augmented, nested, double-loop learning. This principle is shown in Table 7.2 and graphically in Figure 7.11.

In such a feedback scheme, managers evaluate the conformance of in-process variables ("drivers of performance") to their standards, and the conformance of outcome measures to their standards, and compare the two (as in Table 7.2). Such a comparison enables one to question whether the in-process variables have an effect on the outcomes, whether the standards for the in-process variables are sufficiently high or indeed too high,

Figure 7.11   Nested double-looping learning with conformance feedback.

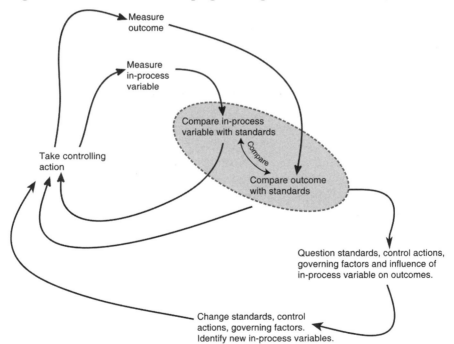

whether the control actions are adequate, and whether there are other governing factors that may be influencing outcomes. These governing factors could include dysfunctional corporate cultures, unidentified in-process variables, and anything in between. Phil Rosenzweig encourages managers to apply scientific principles to answering business questions, by asking, "If I do this, what will happen?"[15] A double-loop learning feedback mechanism enables managers to systematically answer this question.

The primary preoccupation of most businesses, as for Winston Churchill in the summer of 1940, is survival. The common term "firefighting," used in business to describe their never-ending stream of crises, is indicative of this struggle, as are allusions to Darwinian survival in the business world. Like the ice candles in melting lake ice, businesses that look normal from the outside suddenly collapse and disappear.

A person's health is primarily measured by comparing internal systems for homeostasis—or self-regulation—against what doctors believe are healthy standards. For example, doctors consider cholesterol, which is part of the body's system for self-healing and repair, to be unhealthy if it exceeds a certain level. Blood pressure should be neither too high nor low. Doctors do not control your blood pressure—your internal homeostatic systems control it. Doctors supplement these systems with additional control actions (usually in the form of drugs) when the systems are incapable of meeting healthy standards. Likewise, executives do not control the multiple processes within an organization: they control the control systems. They therefore need feedback that tells them whether the control systems are capable of meeting standards.

If the controls cannot meet internal standards, if there are no or inappropriate internal standards, or if there are few or poor controls, even organizations with tremendous capabilities may soon find themselves careening out of control.

TOOL BOX

To focus employee efforts:

- Create indicators that prompt specific action rather than just indicate general direction.
- Clearly and simply convey structural information in graphical displays of indicators.

- Create indicators that convey information at the three levels: fundamental, intermediate, and overall.
- Do not destroy structural information for the sake of simplicity.
- Use measurements to encourage organizational learning.
- Measure conformance to standards and show employees how to use conformance information to improve the way they control their work.
- To understand the relationship between in-process variables and results indicators, and to determine whether the control systems are working, compare the conformance to standards of each and create a feedback system that makes this easy to do.
- Use feedback systems to answer the question, "If I do this, what will happen?"

EIGHT

Going Against the Flow: Navigating Changing Data Streams

I, for one, believe that nothing continues the same for long.[1]

—Publius Ovidius Naso (Ovid), 43 BC–AD 17

When your pulse becomes irregular, it is reasonable to infer that you are ill, and when your employer's stock crashes, it is reasonable to predict that you will soon lose your job.

We measure streams of data to make inferences about the reasons they change, or to make predictions about the future. We would like to make reasonable inferences and predictions from data streams (based on background information and accurate and precise measurements) or we will be misled. The complication is that data streams are always changing. If they did not change, there would be no point in measuring them, which is why doctors unplug the heart monitors of dead people and stock exchanges delist the stocks of defunct companies.

Modern measurement and data dissemination techniques create thousands of streams of data that are reported to us in real time or at high frequency; data such as weather data, point-of-sales data from retailers, stock prices, market indices, production data from factories, shipping and sales data, inventory data, environmental data, Web traffic, employment, inflation and other economic indicators, and so on.

People pore over these data streams to determine if there has been some change in the fundamentals, and to make forecasts about the future. What do we mean by the "fundamentals" and how do we forecast? And how do we do it without being misled?

When you measure and "plot sea level" you get a data stream in a cyclical pattern showing the tides. This pattern is governed by the rotation of the Earth, of the Moon around the Earth, and the Earth around the Sun. These are well described by the laws of physics. The pattern of tides in any particular place, such as a harbor, can be analyzed mathematically to determine a specific law that governs the tides in that location. This is a *substantive* law because it is based on the essence of what is happening. Once you know this law you can make very accurate forecasts about the tides well into the future, which is how they make tide tables for mariners. When you compare measurements to the law, you can make inferences about change. If there is a large difference between the two, it is reasonable to infer that either the measurements are erroneous, or that the law does not apply to these measurements, so something *substantive* has changed.

There are many streams for which it is impossible to find a substantive law because we cannot readily understand the essence of what is happening. Data streams such as inflation, employment, market indices, and weekly sales of a business are examples. In these cases it is possible to use statistical techniques to find a *descriptive* law. The forecasts from a descriptive law are usually not as good as those from a substantive law, and reliable inferences are more difficult too.

There are five different types of laws governing the trends seen in data streams.

The most simple is a constant law. Here the underlying phenomenon or process remains in equilibrium around a constant mean level. Imagine a swimming pool. Normally the water level is held constant by pumps, valves, and drains, except for waves within the pool. If a drain plugs or a pipe leaks, you would see a big change in water level, and you would infer something was not working. It is easy to forecast a future level because it is constant. These are *stationary* streams.

Then there are the *nonstationary* streams. The nonstationary streams do not have a fixed mean. There are four types:

- Seasonal and cyclical data streams. In these streams the trends are composed of one or more cycles piled up on each other. The cycles can be hourly, daily, weekly, monthly, seasonal, and annual or longer. Examples are tides, daily deliveries of consumer goods to a large retailer, monthly employment figures, or daily water flow in a river.

- Stable trends. In these streams the rate of change is fairly stable. Many economic data streams exhibit this sort of behavior, such as stock markets for long periods, or inflation.

- Explosive trends. In these streams change is rapid and severe. An example is the explosive growth of bacteria in a piece of rotting food, or the implosion of Enron's stock price.

With the above three nonstationary streams there are ways to mathematically find the law, whether it is substantive or descriptive. It can then be removed from the measurements to see what else is going on in what remains. That is what the government does when it reports the "seasonally adjusted" inflation or job numbers. Once you know the underlying laws that make the stream vary, you can make inferences and predictions. But sometimes it is impossible to find any law, substantive or descriptive. In that case you have:

- Chaotic streams. These are totally unpredictable. You cannot learn from them, you cannot predict, you cannot infer.

STATISTICAL PROCESS CONTROL: MISLEADING INDUSTRY

Statistical process control (SPC) has been hugely promoted in industry by legions of consultants promoting Six-Sigma, its predecessor Total Quality Management, and related management fads. Six-Sigma is now pervasive in many industries, yet there is growing concern about the high rate of failures, which some surveys peg as high as 50 percent.[2]

The zealous promotion and application of SPC without regard to fundamental principles of measurement and inference has misled industry. The technique of SPC is used when there is a stream of measurements from some process, such as a manufacturing process, or sometimes administrative processes such as processing insurance claims. Its purpose is to make an inference about whether a process, which is supposed to remain at a constant mean level, has shifted. That is, the plug has been pulled from the pool to empty it.

I myself have trained thousands of people in SPC over two decades. All the books on the topic that I read explained it the same orthodox way, and it was consistent with my graduate training in statistics. Yet over the years, my doubts about it increased. Although the logic as explained to a nonstatistician seems unimpeachable, I noticed over and over again that my clients had trouble applying it except in the simplest applications. It contradicted their built-in cognitive processes and their knowledge of their processes. Orthodox practitioners of SPC accuse people who struggle with SPC of being statistical illiterates, rather than trying to understand why it contradicts their intuition.

In the late 1980s, I trained one group of process engineers at a metal refinery in SPC. The lead engineer had a PhD in metallurgical engineering, hardly an innumerate. Their efforts eventually dwindled and died. When I told him twenty years later about my owned changed views, he confessed that applying SPC at their refinery felt like smashing round pegs into square holes. It just did not apply to their processes, and contradicted what they knew about how to control them.

In an SPC chart, measurements are plotted on a chart with upper and lower "control limits," and the idea is to compare the plotted points with the limits. The control limits are supposed to indicate when action should be taken to bring the process back toward the mean. SPC is often used on both in-process and outcome variables (as discussed in chapter seven).

The statistical theory behind SPC imposes conditions that limits it proper use—that is, not misleading use—to stationary streams in which the variation around the mean is white noise. Physicists use the term "white noise" to describe variation from which you cannot extract any signal—like static you hear on your radio when it is not tuned into a station.

That does not mean that just because you can draw control limits, everything between them is white noise. But that is what people assume all the time. By doing this they deliberately *ignore* signals. And just because you can draw an average line does not mean that the process is governed by the constant law either, but people assume that too.

One of my first experiences with SPC was at a factory that manufactured mufflers. Within the plant, different machines cut up pipe into various lengths. A machine pushed each length of pipe against a stopper plate and clamped it in place. A saw blade then cut the pipe into the designated length. The machine removed the cut piece, released the clamp, and pushed the pipe forward to cut another piece. Based on that description, the substantive constant law applies.

Three times a day, the operator carefully measured a piece of pipe. The operator knew that vibrations and other wiggles in the position of the saw blade position, grit on the stopper plate, his measurement device, and so on, caused the pipe lengths themselves to vary slightly. Some measured pipes from this process are shown in a statistical process control chart in Figure 8.1. The control limits are calculated in the usual way.[3]

The SPC orthodoxy as misleadingly explained by legions of consultants—and by me earlier in my career—is as follows:

The control limits describe the bounds of variation above and below the mean within which the operator should *not* take any action to control the

Figure 8.1   Statistical process control chart of cut pipe lengths. UCL and LCL indicate upper and lower control limits.

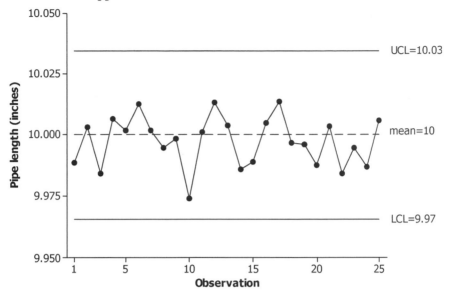

process. The statistical control chart shows which variations to ignore because they do not indicate any change in the underlying mean of the process—they are *common* causes and not *special* causes.

Clearly there are physical forces that explain each particular pipe length measurement. They do not vary "randomly," that is without any physical cause. The laws of physics are not suspended when control charts are plotted. According to the orthodoxy, the operator does not have enough information to assign a cause to explain measurements within the control limits with a reasonably high probability, and should therefore take no action.

Most people who hear an explanation such as this accept it, but many have reservations that grow over time. It is almost impossible for people who understand a process to accept that they cannot correctly determine the cause of variations *within the control limits* with a high probability of being right.

The concept that some variations on a control chart should be ignored because they do not contain useful information about underlying causes is counter-intuitive. Even when they are well trained in statistical process control techniques, people who have sufficient background information about a process cannot help assigning a special, and well understood, cause to at least some of the measurements from a stream of data from a process.

Usually Six-Sigma and statistical process control consultants have very little background information about their students' and clients' processes. The SPC orthodoxy makes sense to the consultants *because* of their lack of background information. These consultants instruct their clients to ignore their background information and the points between the control limits, but it rarely works and creates nothing but bewilderment. It does not work for an engineer with a PhD in metallurgical engineering, a very detailed knowledge of the chemistry and physics of his process, and more than a decade's worth of experience with the process; and it does not work for a machine operator who did not finish high school, but who has operated the same machine for twenty years and has a very good understanding of how it works, even if he is unable to articulate his understanding.

There is a good reason the consultants cannot train it out of them. It contradicts their built-in cognitive processes; and the background information they have about the process that the consultants lack. The orthodox application of SPC requires people to deliberately *ignore* background information, which leads to unsound reasoning and unreasonable inferences.

The orthodox courses and textbooks on statistical process control make another, related, fundamental error. They state that the probability that an observation will fall inside the control limits[4] is about 99 percent. This statement is based on the following premises:

a. the process mean has not changed;
b. there is no correlation between successive measurements; and
c. the measurements within the control limits are white noise whose variation is described by a Normal distribution.

Figure 8.2   Making unreasonable inferences.

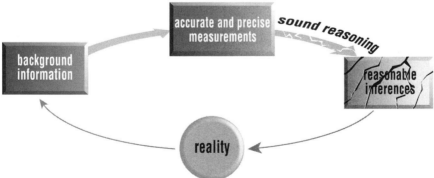

Therefore, according to this logic and these premises, if a measurement falls inside the control limits, the person observing the process should infer that the process mean has not changed. If some fall outside the control limits less than 1 percent of the time, so the (il)logic goes, they should make the same inference.

Put another way, this faulty reasoning is based on the following circular argument: "If the process mean does not change, then 99 percent of all future measurements can be expected to fall between the control limits. Therefore if a particular measurement falls between the control limits, or if 99 percent fall between the control limits, the mean has not changed."

This is like saying, "If there are no clouds, it is not raining. Therefore if it is not raining, there are no clouds."

This is unsound reasoning, which leads to misleading inferences, and makes the SPC chart a misleading indicator. By deliberately ignoring background information and using unsound reasoning, SPC violates our third principle for making reasonable inferences using measurement:

> Principle 3: Sound reasoning is used to make reasonable inferences based on the measurements and the background information.

Where does the 99 percent probability in the circular and thus faulty reasoning above come from? The control limits are based on the following premise:

> Consider all possible measurements that we could get from this process, including future measurements. The control limits indicate how far, over the long term (whatever that is), we would expect 99% of the measurements to wander away from the mean of the process if the process does not change, and if the Normal distribution adequately describes what we know about the distribution of the future measurements around the mean.

But this is not what the fellow controlling or observing a process wants to know. He is not interested in what all possible measurements might do over the long term if the process does not change. What he wants to know is how to interpret the specific measurement he has just taken *given his background information*. Now suppose he has plenty of past experience to give him strong reasons for believing that the process mean is constant most of the time, but sometimes it slips, which is why there is a control chart in the first place. He is on the lookout for signs of change. He wants to know:

The probability that the process mean has changed, given the measurement *he just took*, and given that the process mean sometimes slips (his background information).

The statistical process control dogma tells him:

The probability that *future* measurements will fall between the control limits given that there is no change in the process and that the operator willfully ignores whatever background information he has.

These are two very different probabilities. Yet in thousands of statistical process control courses and in fact in all textbooks on the topic that I have seen, the two probabilities are taught and explained as if they were equivalent. They are as different as the probability that an accused murderer is guilty given a DNA match and the probability of a DNA match given that he is guilty.

NOTHING COULD BE MORE MISLEADING

Consider an example to illustrate what I mean by "given the measurement." Instead of a measurement, I will illustrate with an observation: "given the observation." Once I read something along the lines of "the probability of being killed by a bear in North America is one in ten million per year, therefore don't worry about it." That's an inferential probability statement about what all possible bears might do next year. But what is the probability of being killed by a bear if you are wilderness camping and you observe one outside your tent? Inside your tent? Inside your tent chewing your foot? Clearly the probability, given the observation of the bear, must be increased.

People use background information to make inferences intuitively. It is part of our cognitive processes. It is the way we categorize groups of things or people into stereotypes based on our own experience, and then change our views on these stereotypes when the facts change and when we have new experiences with them.[5]

Stephen Pinker gives a simple example:

We perceive some traits of a new object, place it in a mental category, and infer that it is likely to have other traits typical of that category, ones we cannot perceive. If it walks like a duck and quacks like a duck, it probably is a duck. If it's a duck, it's likely to swim, fly, have a back off which water rolls, and contain meat that's tasty when wrapped in a pancake with scallions and hoisin sauce.[6]

The statistical control chart does not—usually—make use of any available background information about the process that generated the measurements. It treats all measurements within the control limits as being devoid of any useful information. It treats them as if they had the same information content as the infinite possible measurements that have *not yet been taken.* Yet the people who use the control charts on the factory floor *are* using—correctly—background information gleaned over much experience with the process. When you see something that looks like a duck and quacks like a duck—based on your past experience with ducks—you do not measure its legs, wings, beak, feathers, and DNA to figure out if it's a duck.

Suppose, to continue the pipe-cutting example, the operator had learned over many years that the saw blade has a tendency to suddenly loosen from its setting and drift out of position by up to about 0.02 inches to 10.02. This would cause a shift in the length of the pipe that he cut by about the same amount. (This is his background information about the actual pipe-cutting process he is observing.) As his job is to make pipes of constant length as best he can, he needs to know when the mean of the process is no longer equal to the desired lengths of the pipes. This is in fact the main purpose of the control chart.

He takes a measurement and observes a value of 10.02 inches, well within the control limits (see Figure 8.3). In his statistical process control

Figure 8.3   Pipe-cutting: new data.

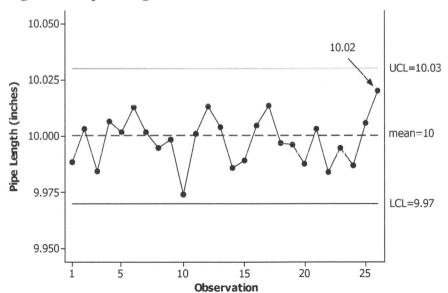

class he was told not to adjust the process, because 99 percent of the measurements will be within the control limits if the process has not changed, and 10.02 inches is within the control limits. But, as we saw above, he does not want to *assume* the process has not changed and calculate the probability of measuring a value of 10.02 inches if it has not. He wants to know whether the measured value of 10.02 inches indicates a high probability that the process mean *has* changed, using his background knowledge about drift in the process.

A logical rule found by Reverend Thomas Bayes (1702–1761) enables us to calculate probabilities by taking into account background information. By using the machine operator's background information, and applying Bayes's method (developed later into a sophisticated logic), we can calculate the probability of a shift in the blade, given the measurement of 10.02 inches.

We can try and quantify his background information. If the blade suddenly loosened about once every one hundred measurements, on average, his background information could be stated: There is a 1 percent probability that the saw blade *will shift* before the next measurement. If his background information was that the blade shifted every twenty-five measurements, we could say there is a 4 percent probability that it will shift before the next measurement. If he heard a noise that he usually hears just before the blade shifts, he might assign an even higher probability.

Once the operator gets the measurement of 10.02, he wants to assign the *new* probability that the blade has shifted, given the measurement. Using Bayes's method, we can use each measurement and the background information to calculate the probability that the blade has shifted. This is shown for various possible values of the operator's background information in Table 8.1.

You can see from the table that if his background information led him to assign a 4.4 percent probability that the blade could shift by up to 0.02 inches in the *next* measurement, once he *has* that measurement the probability that the blade *has* drifted is 50 percent, not 1 percent. Those are even odds! You can see from Table 8.1 that his instincts are right.

Although most people do not perform such calculations, people naturally, and correctly, make use of their background information. That is why they find the statistical process control dogma hard to swallow. (We will return to this idea in chapter eleven when we look at measurement and risk.)

If the results in Table 8.1 seem unbelievable, think of it this way. The control limits are placed three standard deviations away from the mean. A drift of 0.02 inches is a drift of about two standard deviations. The chance

Table 8.1   Background Information and Probability

Background information	Background and measurement
Probability that the blade will shift *before* he sees the measurement	Probability that the blade has shifted, now that he has *seen* the measurement of 10.02 inches.
10.0%	71%
9.0%	68%
8.0%	66%
7.0%	62%
6.0%	58%
5.0%	54%
4.4%	**50%**
4.0%	48%
3.0%	40%
2.0%	31%
1.0%	18%

of getting a *future* measurement two standard deviations or more from the mean, based on the Normal distribution alone, that is, if you ignore the operator's background information about the drift in the blade and pretend the blade and the mean are fixed, is about 2.3 percent.

The operator, though, has his background information about, or experience with, the blade (which SPC forces him to ignore). That is why his bosses gave him a control chart to use in the first place. They, and he, know the blade can shift. If they knew it could not shift they would not bother measuring the pipe lengths. Based on this he assigns a probability that the blade will shift by up to 0.02 inches in the next measurement.

He then gets a measurement of 10.02, or 0.02 inches above the mean. This is consistent with a shift in the blade. Should he assign a new probability to a shift in the blade? Surely the probability he had assigned before, whether it was 1 percent or 4 percent or 10 percent, is too low, given that he now has a measurement of 10.02 inches? And now that he actually *has* a measurement that *is* 2 standard deviations from the mean, the 2.3 percent probability of getting a *future* measurement two standard deviations or more from the mean is irrelevant.

The Westinghouse SPC decision rules are designed to help find out-of-control points or assignable causes within the control limits.

According to the rules, such events as two out of three points between two and three standard deviations from the mean, or seven points in a row on one side of the mean, indicate an out-of-control point. While it is true that these rules do require people to look at data within the control limits (which is good), the logic used to justify them is flawed. These rules are based on the following probability:

> The probability that *future* measurements will fall into a pattern defined by the rule given that there is no change in the process and that the operator willfully ignores whatever background information he has.

Whereas the probability of interest is:

> The probability that the process mean has changed, given the measurements the operator *just took*, and given his background information.

To further understand the importance of background information in interpreting the data, consider the data shown in Figure 8.4. The pattern of the data is exactly the same as the data in Figure 8.1, but the numbers themselves are different, and they have a different meaning. The background information is completely different. Now instead of measurements of pipes coming from a pipe-cutting machine with a mean determined mainly by the setting of the saw-blade position, they (let's pretend) represent the monthly efficiency of a factory.

In a situation such as this the statistical process control chart has little meaning.

For each wiggle in the monthly efficiency numbers, the plant manager knows what happened: over the course of a month there were maintenance problems, supplier problems, raw material problems, absenteeism, trials of new product, jams and blockages, and so on. In contrast, the operator of the pipe-cutting machine has less information about what causes each wiggle in his chart—not nil, though, as SPC would make you believe.

Statistical process control dogma would say to the plant manager, as one leading statistical process control guru put it, "This chart shows no clear-cut evidence of change. Some months appear to be better than others, but this chart indicates that it will be a waste to analyze any one month to see what is different from preceding months."[7] In other words, the dogma says, "Ignore all the measurements you obtained that fell within the control limits, which were designed to show the band within which future measurements would fall if the mean of the process, whatever that represents physically,

Figure 8.4   Same data, rescaled and different meaning. Now it's factory efficiency.

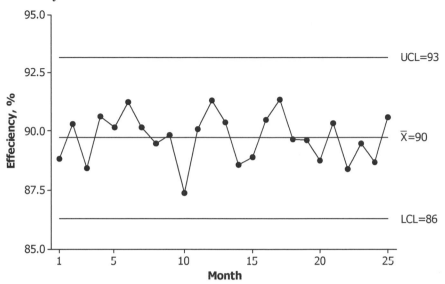

does not change. Ignore them even if you have substantial background information for each measurement." This is foolish advice.

The plant manager would be unwise to heed the statistical dogma because he has substantial background information. He knows that in the tenth month he had his worst result in two years. He knows that a drive shaft on the machine broke that month and caused several days of downtime. He knows most of what happened the other months too. I have met very few senior managers who are capable of following the SPC dogma when it is applied to their own measurements, precisely because they know the relevance of their own background information. They are less reluctant, and often quite enthusiastic, to ask their subordinates to follow SPC's dogmatic rules, because they do not know their subordinates' background information.

The only difference between the factory efficiency measurements and the pipe cutting measurements is thus the background information and the information about each measurement. The dogma makes some sense when the background information is limited to knowing only that you have a fixed process mean and constant range of variation around it.

The mean efficiency of the factory is not a measure of some single, concrete thing that determines the monthly efficiency, unlike the position of a saw blade or the depth of a pool. The efficiency is an integrative indicator of the combined effects of all the snafus and efforts over the course of two years and of the actions taken to overcome them. There would be no reason to believe that the mean or standard deviation of this "process" was fixed. Certainly the plant manager should be doing his best to improve it. (This does not necessarily mean it does not follow the constant law. Integrative indicators frequently do; for example, the mean height of a well-defined ethnic group can remain constant for long periods.)

The mean efficiency still conveys useful descriptive information—efficiency is an integrative measure that is useful for comparing a factory over time, or comparing separate factories. But it does not necessarily represent something tangible. It is much too elusive. The mean pipe length is tangible: it represents the distance between the stopper plate and the saw blade.

As an integrative indicator, mean efficiency is characteristic of a plant manager's normal operating regime. If he were able to maintain a constant degree of control over his factory, the efficiency measurements would bounce up and down in equilibrium on either side of it, commensurate to his degree of control. If he had such a degree of control, however, he would know much about why they bounced, since the process mean is not affixed to anything. Yet the premise behind a control chart is that you do not know what causes variations between the control limits. There would thus be no reason for *him* to use a control chart. A statistician, head office staff engineer, or senior executive with no knowledge of what's going on might resort to a control chart as a replacement for the plant manager's knowledge.

It is little wonder, then, that statistical process control has had such a rough ride. Yet legions of "Six-Sigma black belts" and assorted misinformed hobby statisticians have made millions of dollars telling their disciples to ignore the data between control limits and their background information in the name of "managing *with* data."

SPC AND PROCESS TINKERING

The hands-off approach promoted by statistical process control has at least had the benefit of preventing over-control, and getting people to get data where otherwise they would have had none. Over-control occurs when people adjust a process when it does not require it, or adjust it more than it needs to be adjusted. The action of over-controlling increases the overall variation in a process. Watch the wobbles of a child who is just learning to ride a bicycle.

Over-control occurs when adjustments are not proportional to changes in the substantive law of a process. To illustrate, I made some modifications to the original pipe length data. Instead of control limits at 9.97 and 10.03, I created imaginary specification limits at 9.99 and 10.01. These specification limits are the shortest and longest pipes that are acceptable. I then adjusted the data as if an imaginary and well-intentioned but over-tinkering operator were adjusting the process when he got a measurement that was below the lower specification or above the upper specification.

In each instance, where the measurements were above the upper specification limit of 10.01, my imaginary operator made an arbitrary downward adjustment of 0.01. For each instance where the measurement was below the lower specification limit of 9.99, the imaginary operator made an arbitrary upward adjustment of 0.01. I constructed Figure 8.5 by adding these adjustments to the measurements shown in Figure 8.1. There is an increase in variation. Such a method of control, which uses the specification limits without regard to background information and blindly calls for adjustments when measurements exceed the specifications, increases variation in a process. To the extent that statistical process control has reduced this common method of over-control, it has been beneficial.

This sort of poorly thought-out "tinkering," as statistician and quality guru W. Edwards Deming called it, does not justify automatically ignoring all data that lies within control limits. The feedback control loops used in everything from simple thermostats to complex chemical processes make use of measurements and background information from a process in carefully thought-out and tested controls, without ignoring measurements between some limits. They are based on the principle that the size of the adjustment is proportional to the size of the deviation from the target—the same principle we use when balancing a bicycle or driving a car within its lane on a highway.

Control limits should not be confused with the band within which no controlling action is taken on some devices. A thermostat could be set to turn the furnace on when room temperature cools down to 66°F and off when the room warms up to 72°F. This means that when the temperature is 70°F the furnace could be either on or off, depending on whether the room is warming or cooling. The thermostat's response (stay on or stay off) to a measurement of 70°F depends on recent history. This is not the case with a control chart.

Other process control devices make continual proportional adjustments. As a child learns to ride a bicycle through double-loop learning (and some bleeding knees) until the adjustments are correctly proportioned to the

Figure 8.5   Over-controlling the pipe-cutting process. Compare with Figure 8.3.

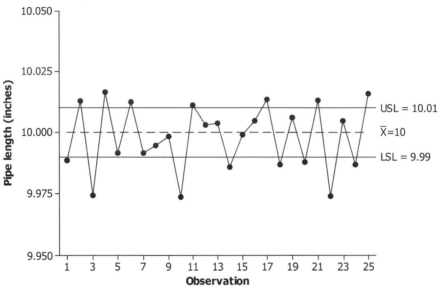

wobbles of the bike, similarly one learns to control a process. The first learning loop involves three measurements: the initial deviation of the process from its target, the size of the adjustment, and the resulting new deviation of the process (which then becomes the initial deviation for the next spin around the loop). The second loop involves studying the size of the adjustments relative to the resulting deviations, and adjusting the adjustments.[8]

NONSTATIONARY STREAMS: LEARNING FROM REAL STREAMS—OR RIVERS

Measurements and observations from real streams provide a useful vehicle for understanding how to make inferences and predictions from many data streams. To avoid being misled we need a method to interpret measurements from nonstationary streams that highlights changes that are greater than the underlying law, and that can help us forecast future measurements.

I occasionally enjoy the childish thrill of watching water flow down a river and bounce over rocks. From a distance, a standing wave in a set of rapids appears steady and constant, and of little interest. But from close-up, my eye is drawn to its continual dance up and down and back and forth, and is surprised by the drops of water it squirts hither and yon, out of step with its dance and out of line with the flow. A set of rapids, with hundreds of such waves, is a veritable Grand Ball of such movements and steps. At the end of the rapids, where the waves slowly disappear, the swirling eddies that shift and twist and gradually meld into each other and the dark, calm pool beyond relax the eye and the mind.

The US Geological Survey measures the levels and flows of thousands of rivers across the United States, and updates the data continually on their website. The chart in Figure 8.6 shows water levels measured every fifteen minutes in the Black River in upstate New York between the end of January and the beginning of March 2007. The levels are measured with a gauge located "on the right bank 200 feet downstream from Vanduzee Street Bridge at Watertown, and 3.5 mi upstream from Philomel Creek."[9] A gauge anywhere else would, of course, produce a slightly different chart.

The black line in the chart seems somewhat like a single wave in the rapids: dancing up and down with occasional measurements hither and yon.

In business it is typical to present this kind of data by showing a current result and comparing it to another result from a previous period. These

Figure 8.6   Gauge Height readings in fifteen-minute intervals, Black River.

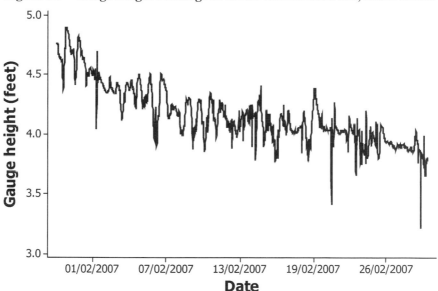

Source: Department of the Interior/USGS

Table 8.2   Typical Way of Reporting Data Streams

	This period	Last period	Change	Same period last year	Change
Production	121	118	3	134	(13)
On-time shipment	95	98	(3)	102	(7)

reports frequently look something like Table 8.2 (a period could be a week, a two-week interval, a four-week interval, a year, etc.).

In some conditions this can be useful way to present data. In others, it can be misleading. If there are cycles or periods in the data they should match the periods in the calculation and the report. Often there is enough background information to make a reasonable estimate of the length of the periods.

In the Black River data stream, there is a twenty-four-hour cycle to the data. In other words, the gauge height on a given day is strongly positively correlated to the data twenty-four hours before. "Positively correlated" means that if the gauge height twenty-four hours earlier was high, the current gauge height is likely to be high, and if the gauge height twenty-four hours earlier was low, the current gauge height is likely to be low. It would seem a logical choice to compare the current gauge height to the gauge height twenty-four hours earlier. This is what people are trying to do by comparing their results with results from the same time one period earlier.

To determine whether gauge heights are correlated with the gauge heights from the previous day, you can calculate what is known as an "autocorrelation" (this requires measurements that are taken at regular intervals). When there is an autocorrelation, a data stream is correlated with some other part of itself. There is a correlation between people's heights and their weights—people who are taller tend to be heavier. In an autocorrelation the correlation is not between two different variables, such as height and weight, but between the same data stream at different points in time. The measure of correlation, and autocorrelation, is a number between 1 and −1. A positive number in our gauge height data indicates that two gauge height measurements, separated by a constant time apart, go up or down together. A negative value indicates they move in opposite directions: as one goes up, the other goes down, and vice versa. A value of zero indicates that there is no correlation. The numbers 1 and −1 indicate perfect correlation, together or in opposite directions.

The chart in Figure 8.7 shows the autocorrelation for the Black River gauge height, for the same time period as the previous graph. What it shows is that there is a very strong—almost 1—correlation between adjacent readings of gauge height. In other words, not much changes in fifteen minutes. This can be seen because the autocorrelation at the left side of the Figure 8.7 is near 1. If the gauge height is high at any time, it is also likely to be high fifteen minutes later.

The autocorrelation eight days apart is much lower. If the gauge height is high one day, that does not tell you much about what it will be exactly eight days later. That is why the overall slope of the autocorrelation graph is gradually downward.

The series of waves along the slope results from the autocorrelation at twenty-four hours apart. The gauge height one day is more strongly correlated with the gauge height exactly one day later than with the gauge half a day, or one and a half days later. The half days are the trough; the full days are the peaks. The autocorrelation chart tells us that there is some basis for comparing the gauge height at any given time with the gauge height twenty-four hours earlier, to determine if it has changed.

If you wish to report your measurements as a change from the last period, it is important to get the period right. If you do not, the resulting numbers could be quite meaningless or worse. Figure 8.8 shows us the

Figure 8.7   Autocorrelation function for gauge height fifteen-minute readings from the Black River, February 2007.

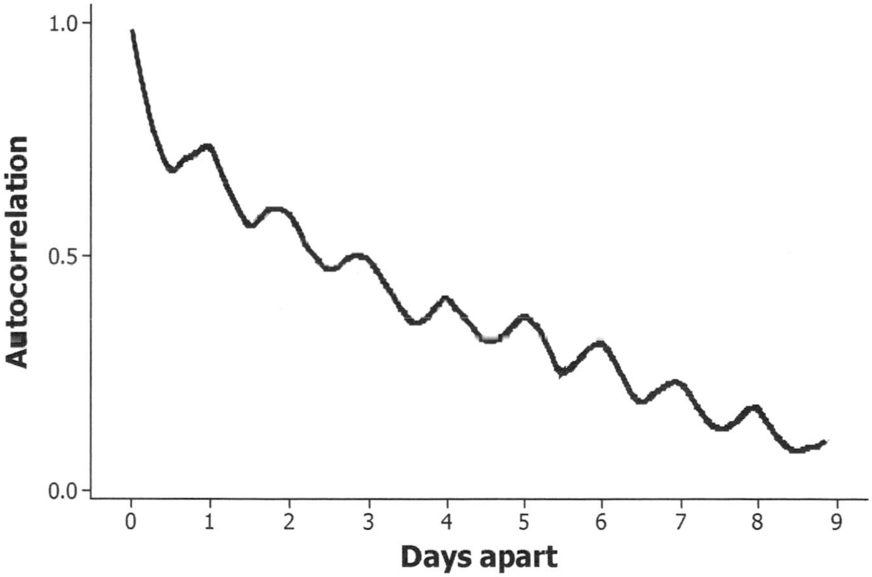

Source: Department of the Interior/USGS

Figure 8.8   Change in gauge height between fifteen-minute intervals. Black River, Waterdown, New York, February 2007.

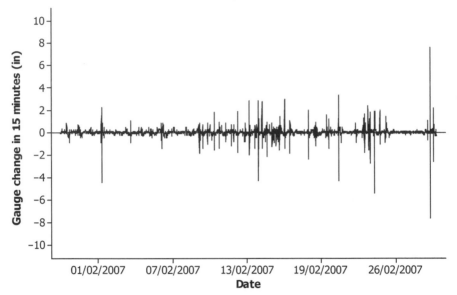

Source: Department of the Interior/USGS

successive increases (positive numbers) or decreases (negative numbers) between gauge height measurements that were fifteen minutes apart. It was calculated by subtracting each measurement from the measurement that preceded it fifteen minutes earlier. This is a comparison between *measurements*, but not between *periods* in the sense of periodic up-and-down cycles.

As expected, there is usually little change. On two occasions (the spike at the right of the graph near the first of March) in the data series, however, the river changed by slightly more than seven inches—first up, then down—in two successive fifteen-minute intervals. In both cases this was caused by a sudden drop in water level and an increase fifteen minutes later. These spikes could possibly also be caused by some kind of measurement error, or a data entry error, or perhaps by a rogue wave of some kind. On several more occasions it changed three inches, and on most of these occasions the same sort of thing happened.

It is pretty safe to say that the vast majority of times the change from one measurement to the next one fifteen minutes later is only a fraction of an inch. Another way of saying this is that because of the strong autocorrelation between successive measurements fifteen minutes apart, we really learn very little new incremental information with each new measurement, with the occasional exception.

(In the orthodox application of statistical process control, people rarely check for autocorrelation in measurements. It is hard to imagine many processes where measurements would not be more closely correlated with recent measurements than measurements that were taken a long time ago. If the measurements are autocorrelated, the arguments used to justify the use of the control limits are completely flawed.)

The change in water levels between measurements twenty-four hours apart, as expected from the autocorrelation graph, is much greater, and big changes are more frequent. The chart in Figure 8.9 is calculated by subtracting each measurement from the measurement that preceded it twenty-four hours earlier. In this instance we are taking the difference between periods, as we have seen a twenty-four-hour cycle to the measurements.

Figures 8.8 and 8.9 illustrate the problem we have when comparing a measurement with some previous measurement to evaluate the change. We wish to make an inference about whether there has been a change in the law, whether it is substantive or descriptive. But there is always going to be change in the measurements, like the dancing of a single wave

Figure 8.9   Change in gauge height in twenty-four-hour intervals, Black River. Black River, Waterdown, New York, February 2007.

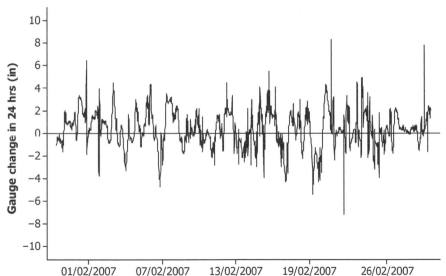

Source: Department of the Interior/USGS

in the rapids. A simple comparison with a previous measurement does not necessarily enable you to make a reasonable inference about the law behind the stream of measurements. If you make a comparison between measurements taken at the same time in the cycle, you get the change that is above and beyond that described by the law. But the ease with which you can make a reasonable inference about the law depends on how well the law describes the stream of measurements. If it describes it very well, as in tidal measurements, the inference is easy. If it describes it poorly, as in the Black River data and most business and economic indicators, it is more difficult.

Seasonal adjustments to economic indicators follow this principle. Seasonal adjustments remove the seasonal law. This way one can infer from a large change in the indicator, such as unemployment, that something other than seasonality is changing. Severe changes in economic activity, such as recessions or economic booms, can overwhelm traditional seasonal patterns.

Many streams of measurements have unusual spikes that are not readily describable by some law. These spikes can make it harder to identify fundamental changes in the underlying law. In 2008 there was a sudden surge in the price of oil to around $150 a barrel. It then just as quickly dropped back down to $50 a barrel. Economists forecasted in late 2008 that this rapid shift would cause inflation to turn negative in 2009, which it did, because the base period for the inflation calculation would include the high price of oil in 2008.

Investors had no way of knowing in March 2009 that the market had bottomed out and that it was about to turn into a bull market. Two years later it was easy to see that March 2009 was the change point. Sometimes you can tell right away that there is a change. Between September 30 and October 13, 2008, when the Dow dropped 2,272 points in thirteen trading days, it was easy to tell that the market was crashing. One of the biggest frustrations of investing is that changes in markets or individual equities are either obvious, or difficult to detect. That does not stop analysts and the financial press from offering explanations—or inferences—for every change in a market index: the market is down on fears of this; or up on news of that.

There are principles and methods to make detecting changes in data streams easier. But the lesson every seasoned investor has learned applies to inferences about most data streams: inferences about change in data streams, and the time of the change, are either very difficult, or very easy, and one is easily misled.

With data streams, the measurement object may be well defined, based on relevant background information. The measurements may be accurate and precise. But often measurements from data streams are used to make unreasonable inferences from reasoning that is not sound, or they are explained in a way that induces people to make unreasonable inferences. In that larger sense they are misleading indicators.

MAKING FORECASTS FROM STREAMS OF MEASUREMENTS

Nobel laureate Paul Samuelson once famously quipped, "To prove that Wall Street is an early omen of movements still to come in GNP, commentators quote economic studies alleging that market downturns predicted four out of the last five recessions. That is an understatement. Wall Street indexes predicted nine out of the last five recessions!"[10]

A forecast is an inference about the future. When unsound reasoning is consistently applied to an indicator to make forecasts, our third principle is violated. Even though the measurements may be accurate and precise, the inferences mislead if the reasoning is not sound. In this way the forecasts are misleading indicators.

The way we forecast and control depends on our knowledge of the input, the output, and the system, and on our ability to measure the input and the output. A microphone that a singer sings into sends a stream of information to the amplifier, that in turn transforms it into an electrical signal that it sends to a set of speakers. The speakers are another system that transforms the stream into sound waves—another stream—for our ears, which in turn transform the sound waves into electrical impulses for our brains. This is shown diagrammatically in Figure 8.10.

We understand how the amplifier, the speakers, and our ears transform the singer's voice into amplified music (or rather, the people that build them do). We can easily measure characteristics of each stream—unamplified

Figure 8.10   Input streams and output streams.

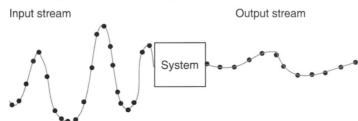

Input stream   Output stream

System

voice or amplified voice—and use it to figure out the other stream. We can forecast almost perfectly, in both directions. Typically, though, our knowledge about the input stream, the system, or the output stream is incomplete, especially if we are dealing with complex systems. It may be possible to measure only one or the other of the input and output, or we may have only a feeble understanding of the system that transforms inputs into outputs.

When the inputs are hard to measure, we may be able to use measurements of the outputs to forecast future values of the outputs. This is the principle behind some control schemes in industry, in which a recent measurement is used to predict the next one.

A sales executive may have thorough measurements on sales, his "output," for every product, for every store and every day—or even every hour. His goal is to forecast future sales so that his company can schedule production, raw materials, and shipping. His quantitative knowledge of the "inputs," however, is typically very sketchy. He typically has only a very general, qualitative understanding of the reasons people buy more of his product in some seasons and months than others—not enough to make detailed forecasts by week or day. His knowledge of the "system" is minimal. He must therefore rely strictly on measurement of sales—outputs—and his general knowledge to forecast sales in the near future.

Meteorologists use streams of data about air pressure, wind, temperature, and so on—the inputs—based on the laws of physics and their computer models of how they interact—the system—to forecast precipitation, one of the key outputs of their models.

Economists use measurements of input streams that they believe influence output streams, both of which they can measure. The trickier problem they face is trying to understand and quantify the system that changes inputs into outputs.

Sometimes we may not know which inputs cause changes in an output data stream, making it difficult to forecast. If we have data streams from several "candidate" input streams, we can try to find the best match between each candidate and the output data stream. But just because you find a match does not mean one causes the other. Many climate researchers have shown that increases in carbon dioxide match increases in temperature, and present this as evidence that carbon dioxide increases must be the force behind the warming. But others have matched streams of measurements from the sun to temperatures on the Earth, or variations in the Earth's orbit and wobble, and found a reasonable match, challenging the conclusion that atmospheric carbon dioxide concentrations are the main, or only, climate-changing force.

USING BACKGROUND INFORMATION TO MAKE FORECASTS

To make a forecast, you have to understand the law that governs the data stream, and you have to know how to incorporate background information into the forecast, such as the pipe-cutting operator's knowledge of saw blade drift, or the sales executive's knowledge of consumer tastes and habits.

In many cases, we may not know what kind of data stream we are dealing with. Our information comes from observing the data stream itself for a certain time. Over a short time, what looks like a stationary stream may turn out to be nonstationary, or even explosive nonstationary, if we observe it for a longer time. And what looks like a nonstationary data stream over a short time may appear stationary over longer periods. In other cases, we may know that a stream is nonstationary, but over the time interval we are interested in, it may behave reasonably closely to a stationary stream, and we can proceed to make not-too-extended forecasts as if it were one.

Forecasts for stationary data streams are the simplest. They are based on the successive differences between measurements and the mean of past measurements, which we calculate to estimate what we think is the underlying fixed mean. Statistical process control charts make forecasts using a simplified version of this approach that assumes there is no autocorrelation—a very limiting restriction.

In a nonstationary data stream, we know that the mean itself is changing, according to some law, which we may or may not know. It thus does not make sense to calculate differences from the mean of our measurements to make forecasts. Instead, given what appears to be a constant rate of change, forecasts are based on the successive differences between consecutive pairs of measurements. The successive differences are usually consistent over short intervals. The forecaster uses this consistency to make short-term forecasts.

In an explosive data stream, the successive differences between consecutive pairs of measurements continually increase (or decrease), resulting in an explosion (or implosion).

With a seasonal data stream, forecasts are made the same way as for stationary or nonstationary data streams. In addition, they are based on seasonal adjustments calculated from the differences between current measurements and measurements taken at the same point in earlier cycles.

A consumer products manufacturer I once advised had entered into a vendor-managed inventory contract with their customer. The vendor (i.e., the manufacturer) was responsible for keeping their customer's inventory stocked between targeted minimum and maximum levels. (This was a tall order, given the wild swings in demand over the course of the year.) The vendor had been experimenting with various methods of predicting sales. If they were short, they had to send product from their plants by truck rather than train, a far more expensive proposition, so that the distribution center would not run out. They were, therefore, searching for any method that would indicate a sudden change in sales pattern so that they could react to it without running below their minimum target level. The graph in Figure 8.11 shows weekly loads of their product that were shipped over seven years.

Although the data stream looks quite wild, the autocorrelation function shows some clear patterns. I calculated the autocorrelation the same way as I did for the Black River data earlier in the chapter, and plotted it in Figure 8.12. There is a strong correlation between the number of loads each week and the number of loads the week before and the immediately preceding weeks. There is also a strong correlation between the number of loads each week with the number of loads one year earlier. There is a slightly less strong correlation with the number of loads two years previously; suggesting that, as time wears on, the connection to the past weakens.

Figure 8.11   Consumer product loads shipped per week.

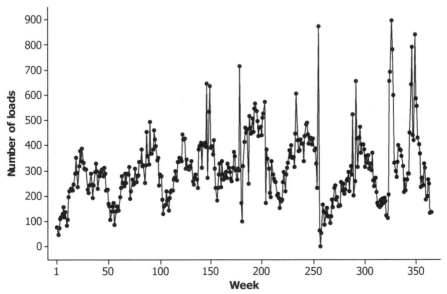

Figure 8.12   Autocorrelation function for weekly loads.

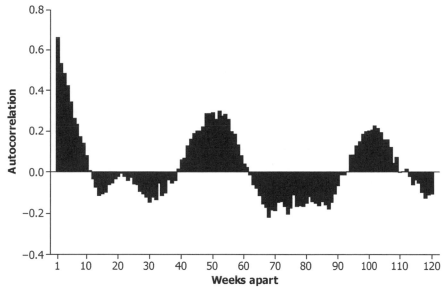

Source: Department of the Interior/USGS

The logistics managers at the consumer products company were using a six-week rolling average to predict the number of loads the distribution center would ship the next week. He had no basis for such a forecasting method other than its ease of computation. It can be seen from Figures 8.11 and 8.12 that there are large swings within less than six weeks. The method does not take advantage of information from cyclical variations in previous years. Nor does it take advantage of what the autocorrelation tells us: that the most recent week is the best predictor (with a correlation of 0.7), and that the farther back you go, the less value each week has as a predictor. Their method treated all six weeks as equivalent. I developed a forecasting tool that used the information from the autocorrelation. This reduced forecasting error by 40 percent. If I excluded large individual spikes in the number of loads, the forecasting error was 70 percent smaller. There is no way to forecast the spikes if you do not know the immediate cause—there is no substantive or descriptive law for them.

No mathematical way, that is. You cannot forecast future spikes from past data alone. But the logistics managers usually had good qualitative information about each spike. They knew as soon as their customer started promotional sales or got into price wars with their competitors, there would be a spike. They had a few days' warning before hurricanes struck, and of course they knew when they had struck. Their sales always went up before and after hurricanes as they prompted demand for their products. They also knew from experience that when the weather was unseasonably cold and crummy, sales dipped. The logistics managers naturally used this background information to forecast next week's deliveries. The background information gave them something of a descriptive law, even if in a qualitative, nonnumerical fashion. *The best forecast is one that uses both the background information and the measurements.*

The data stream from the loads of consumer products looks and behaves remarkably similarly to data from actual rivers. The US Geological Survey's data for the Black River goes back to 1920. Their long-term data is made up of average daily flow (in cubic feet per second), rather than measurements of gauge height taken every fifteen minutes, which is what we looked at earlier. (Gauge height is of course closely linked with flow, as the more flow there is, the higher the gauge). The US Geological Survey keeps the Black River measurements for a few months, and then calculates and stores daily averages, to save space. Eighty-seven years of daily averages are shown in Figure 8.13. The only constant is change.

Figure 8.13   Eighty-seven years of daily flow measurements, Black River, New York. Log scale.

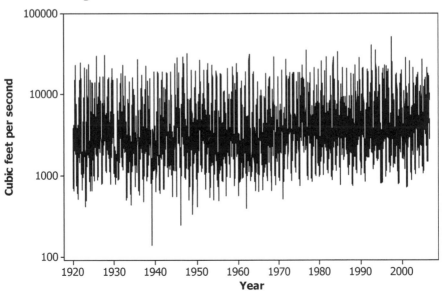

Source: Department of the Interior/USGS

Figure 8.14   Ten years of daily flow measurements, Black River. Log scale.

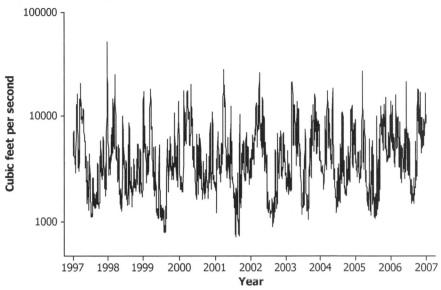

Source: Department of the Interior/USGS

It is hard to cram eighty-seven years of daily measurements into a single graph without making it look crowded, as it does in Figure 8.13. Figure 8.14 shows the last ten years of measurements, to give you a better picture of what is happening.

The autocorrelation function we saw in Figure 8.7 showed that there is a strong autocorrelation between measurements taken a few minutes apart and between measurements taken twenty-four hours apart.

The autocorrelation changes when we use daily averages. The autocorrelation function for the daily averages shows similar patterns (see Figure 8.15). There is a strong autocorrelation between measurements taken a few days apart and between measurements taken a year apart. The distance between the peaks in Figure 8.15 is 365 days, showing that the same underlying pattern repeats itself, year after year. Superimposed on this pattern are the daily and weekly dances of change, like dancing waves in a stream, that we saw in the autocorrelation of the measurements taken every fifteen minutes.

The autocorrelation for the daily averages does have one distinctive feature. The autocorrelation for daily averages 365 days apart is almost the same for daily averages two, three, and four years apart. But it is much smaller than the figure just a few days apart, which is above 0.6. In

Figure 8.15   Autocorrelation of Black River flow (log), twenty-four-hour daily averages (1997–2007).

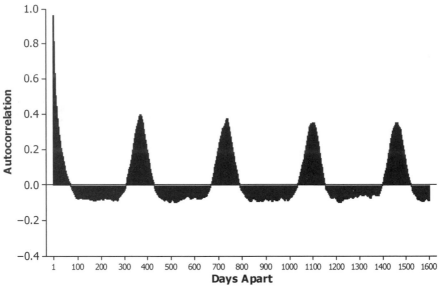

Source: Department of the Interior/USGS

comparison, the autocorrelation for the fifteen-minute measurements keeps decreasing the farther back you go.

We can use the autocorrelation function to figure out how useful a data stream will be in predicting future values of the stream. It can tell you how much common variation there is between different times in the data stream. To find out, you multiply the autocorrelation by itself. For example, in Figure 8.15 we see that the autocorrelation between measurements taken one, two, three, or four years apart is 0.4. Multiplied by itself, we get 0.2, or 20 percent. Thus 20 percent of the variation in daily average river flow is explained by the daily average river flow from one year earlier. The remaining 80 percent is explained by something else. So even on a river, with its predictable seasonal patterns that are as old as the ages, a simple comparison of what happened one day in one year with what happened a year earlier would only give a bit of information about whether some important change had occurred.

To make a forecast for the Black River, all the known cycles—daily, seasonal, and annual—should be included in the descriptive law for the river. Other background information can be included as it becomes available, such as predicted rainfall, recent rainfall, and so on.

A similar method should be used to make a forecast for the consumer products company. The forecast method should make use of the annual and seasonal cycles, and background information that is available at the time the forecast is made, such as sales promotions, unseasonal weather, or storms.

In a general sense, when you make use of the law governing or describing the data stream, and incorporate quantifiable and qualitative background information, you will make better forecasts.

TOOL BOX

- To make reasonable forecasts and inferences about data streams, you need to understand the law that governs or describes your data stream. There are five general laws:

  1. Stationary (flat)
  2. Nonstationary seasonal or cyclical
  3. Nonstationary trend (up or down)
  4. Stationary explosive trend
  5. Chaotic

- Do not apply the orthodox statistical process control methods (SPC) if the conditions do not apply. Instead, apply a method that incorporates background information and information about the law for that process.

- To make inferences about change in nonstationary streams, it is important to identify the various cycles that influence the data stream. There may be several.

- Data streams are always changing. If they were not, we would not measure them. Do not confuse a change in the data stream with a change in the law governing or describing the data stream.

NINE

How Averages Distort Indicators

The arithmetic mean occupies no unique position.

—John Maynard Keynes[1]

CLASS AVERAGES, POLITICAL PRESSURE

Rachel sat straight-lipped and looked across the cluttered desk with her steel-blue eyes at the vice principal, Melvyn Cunahan. "They're both so close to passing," Cunahan said. "I need you to boost the average."

Rachel, a high school physics teacher, had tabulated the final averages for her course. Two kids failed. Jessica was a weak student who would never study physics again and had an average of 47 percent. She needed the credit to graduate. Balpreet was a bright, lazy brat with an average of 48 percent. He wanted to go to engineering school. Rachel was not going to pass him: if he wanted to be an engineer, he had to know the material.

Normally when a teacher was asked to increase a class average at the end of the semester, he or she was expected to just add a certain constant percentage, say 5 percent, to everybody's grade. This was the preferred, and easiest, method. Or they could "bell curve" the grades, which meant they would both increase the average and change the range or spread of the grades. Neither of these ideas would achieve her goal of finding a defensible way to flunk Balpreet and pass Jessica, because Balpreet had a higher average.

Rachel, who had a master's degree in physics, had another idea.

After her meeting with Cunahan, she went to the staff room and opened her little cupboard, one of which was assigned to each teacher, and pulled down a red binder. She leafed through a few sheets and found the table she had made at the beginning of the school year. One showed how she was going to weight the different parts of the course in the calculation of the final average. The other was a similar table produced by the other grade 11 physics teacher, Andy (see Table 9.1).

At the beginning of the term, Cunahan had argued that Andy's weighting was better than hers. He had tried to convince Rachel, but she had said she needed a high weighting for class work to maintain class discipline. But now in hindsight she saw that with Andy's weighting, she could meet her goal. When she recalculated the course averages, she got the results shown in Table 9.2.

With Andy's weightings, Jessica passed with 50 percent and Balpreet failed with 48 percent.

She copied the grades for her other eleven students into the spreadsheet and checked that none of them got a lower mark with Andy's weightings.

Rachel had graphs that showed each student's class average over the semester (see Figures 9.1 and 9.2). Out of curiosity, she modified the graphs to show the averages with the two weighting schemes. During the year, she calculated and updated the students' grades once every three weeks, after each of the five large lab reports were finished. She was struck by the difference in the trends for Andy's weighting scheme and her own. Depending on whether she applied Andy's or her own weighting scheme, the grades either increased or decreased between updates. Between the fourth and the fifth update (Figure 9.1), Balpreet's average went up with Andy's weights and down with Rachel's. And between the first and second update, his average stayed flat with Rachel's scheme and went down with Andy's.

Table 9.1   Rachel's and Andy's Course Weightings

Course component	Rachel's weighting	Andy's weighting
Class work	30%	15%
Homework and lab reports	35%	55%
Final exam	35%	30%
Total	100%	100%

Table 9.2 Course Weightings and Grades with Rachel's Weighting and Andy's Weighting

Course component	Rachel's weighting	Andy's weighting	Balpreet's grades	Jessica's grades	Average of rest of class
Class work	30%	15%	30%	50%	70%
Homework and lab reports	35%	55%	40%	60%	80%
Final exam	35%	30%	70%	30%	60%
Total	100%	100%			
Average with Rachel's weighting			48%	47%	70%
Average with Andy's weighting			48%	50%	73%

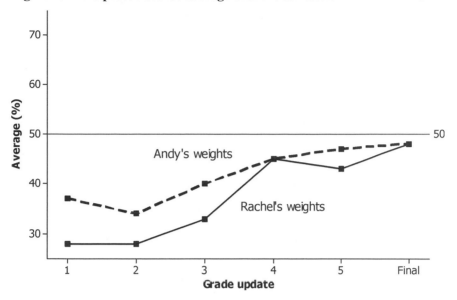

Figure 9.1   Balpreet's course average over the semester.

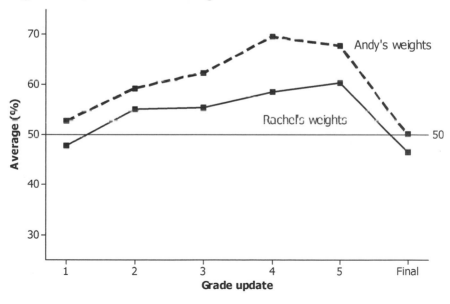

Figure 9.2   Jessica's course average over the semester.

Satisfied that she had found a solution to her dilemma, Rachel typed up a quick memo to Cunahan showing how she had met his request to increase the averages, and updated her final grade sheet. She added that she hoped he would be pleased that she had finally seen the merits of Andy's weighting scheme. She emailed it to Cunahan and went home feeling relieved.

ARE AVERAGES REPRESENTATIVE? STRUCTURE AND SIMPSON'S PARADOX

Why do people calculate averages of measurements? For convenience, we compress a lot of numbers into a single average. Consciously or not, we also use averages to make inferences about some underlying property of a population. For example, if Pine Crest School has higher averages than River Bank School, we infer that the typical student from Pine Crest is better than the typical student from River Bank, or that the teaching is better. How reasonable those inferences are depends on the circumstances.

What is an average? In common usage, the average is the arithmetic mean, a calculated value that, one hopes, comes close to being the most representative or most common value from a set of measurements, even though there may be no value in the set that is equal to the mean itself.

An average is an integrative indicator that boils down a large collection of measurements into a single number, or into a stream of such numbers, that, one hopes, is representative of the whole. The average grade of a class of students is supposed to represent the grade of the average student. A Belgian 19th-century scientist, who had the (above average length) name Lambert Adolphe Jacques Quetelet, collected social statistics on mortality by age, profession, weight, and many other variables, and, after averaging them, coined the term the "average man."[2] Some of Quetelet's contemporaries ridiculed the notion, saying there was no such man. Is there an average man?

Is there an average woman, for that matter? The *New York Times*[3] reported in 2007 that New York City women aged 21–30 earned on average 17 percent more than their male counterparts did. What would one infer about New York women and their socioeconomic success from this average? The article used an analysis of 2005 US Census data by Andrew A. Beveridge, a demographer at Queens College, and used median incomes. The *New York Times* used the term "average," suggesting the arithmetic mean, even though what was used was the median, the mid-value of the set.

A closer look at the data[4] shows that when the median incomes were broken down by different racial groups, the 17 percent advantage disappeared.

In none of the racial groups was the women's median income close to 17 percent greater than men's, and in whites it was 11 percent behind. The data from the article are reproduced in Table 9.3.

Table 9.3 clearly shows that the statement that women earn on average 17 percent more than men is not representative of the incomes in New York City. As a measure of income disparity it is not very useful.

Instead of breaking down the income data by sex or race, we could break it down by any number of factors that might cause differences in average incomes, factors such as neighborhood, education level, job type, marital status, number of children, age, and so on. We could break them down by one of these factors at a time or by several simultaneously. Incomes in a large city have *structure*, in the sense that we used the word earlier in this book. As we uncover this structure and break the income data into smaller and smaller subgroups, we may begin to wonder how far we have to break it down before we find no further structure in a group of people whose average income is, therefore, representative of that group.

Averages can mislead in situations with much simpler structure, such as baseball batting averages.

The batting average is the ratio of the number of times a player hits the ball and safely reaches first base or further, to the number of times he is at bat. It is an arithmetic mean of a sequence of zeroes and ones: one when he hits, and zero when he strikes out. If you multiply it by 100 percent, you get the average percentage of times a player hits the ball and gets at least to first base when he is at bat.

Consider the batting averages of players David Justice and Derek Jeter in the years 1995 to 1997 (see Table 9.4).

Table 9.3   Median Incomes of New York City Women and Men, Thousands of Dollars

	Men	Women	Excess of women's salaries over men's	
Asian	40.7	40.7	0.0	0%
Black	28.5	30.6	2.1	7%
Hispanic	25.5	27.5	2.0	8%
White	45.8	40.7	−5.1	−11%
All groups	30.6	35.7	5.1	17%

Source: Andrew A. Beveridge, Queen's College, Department of Sociology. Used with permission.

Table 9.4   Batting Averages of David Justice and Derek Jeter

	David Justice			Derek Jeter		
	Number of at bats	Number of hits	Batting average	Number of at bats	Number of hits	Batting average
1995	411	104	0.253	48	12	0.250
1996	140	45	0.321	582	183	0.314
1997	495	163	0.329	654	190	0.291
Total	1,046	312	0.298	1,284	385	0.300

In each of the three consecutive years, Justice had a higher batting average than Jeter. The apparently logical inference is that Justice is better than Jeter.

Overall, though, Jeter has the higher batting average (0.300 versus 0.298). How is this possible? This would suggest the opposite inference. It appears to defy both common sense and mathematical logic.

It is possible because the average of a set of *averages* is not equal to the overall average of the measurements on which all the averages are based. Consider the total number of at bats (1,046 for Justice and 1,284 for Jeter) and hits (312 and 385) in the three-year period. The overall batting average is the ratio of these totals (312/1,046 and 385/1,284). An annual batting average is the ratio of that year's hits to that year's at bats. A sum of ratios is not equal to the ratio of sums, unless the denominators are all equal, as grade school children learning fractions have found with much frustration,[5] and thus an average of the ratios is not the same as a ratio of the totals.

There is also some hidden structure in the annual batting averages. Jeter started playing professionally in 1995, and had only 48 at-bats that year. When a player first plays professionally, pitchers have not yet learned his strengths and weaknesses and how to pitch to him. Justice, whom the *New York Times* hailed as a "hero" in the 1995 World Series,[6] injured his shoulder in May 1996 and sat out most of the 1996 season. He only had 140 at-bats. If the two players had had close to the same number of at-bats in each season, their three-year averages would have told the same story as their annual averages.

The phenomenon we see in the baseball averages in known as Simpson's paradox. It manifests itself when averages of subsets show a different pattern than averages of the whole. In any large and complicated set of data there will be structure, and with the structure there will be subsets of measurements that are more similar to each other than to the whole. This means that the average of the whole may not be representative of any of the parts or even the individuals.

This paradox occurs regularly and can cause significant misunderstandings. It frequently occurs in cases where social researchers use means of various social groups to compare, say, differences between minority groups in social or economic matters, or to prove systemic bias. What looks like bias when the overall averages are compared frequently disappears when averages of smaller subgroups are calculated.

Averaging hides the underlying structure of the subsets of measurements. Consider the following set of measurements from a food products plant. It packed the food product into plastic tubs. The plant's goal was to make the product sufficiently viscous to stand up and not flow, but not so stiff that you could not apply it smoothly. Every hour the workers took a sample of five tubs, whipped them in mixers in a small lab beside the production line, and measured their viscosity. They averaged the measurements and plotted their averages. To speed up the whipping, there were two mixers. The chart in Figure 9.3 shows a control chart for twenty-six such sample means.

The young engineer in charge of the production line showed me the above chart with some pride. The chart showed the means comfortably moving along in a stable pattern. When plotted on a histogram (Figure 9.4), the twenty-six averages fall into a nice—almost—bell-shaped curve, centered on the grand mean of all the measurements.

Figure 9.3   Control chart of viscosity averages.

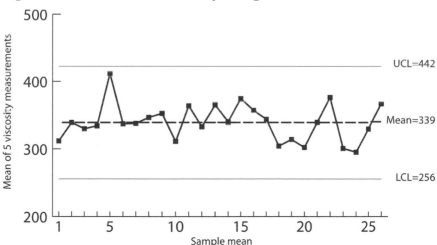

Figure 9.4   Histogram of viscosity averages.

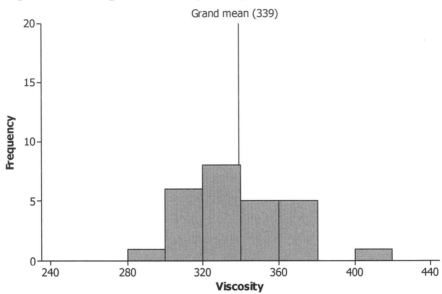

The inference that one could reasonably make from such charts is that the process is stable.

After I prodded him, the engineer then took the raw data and whipped up another histogram of the actual viscosity measurements, rather than averages of measurements. A new pattern emerged that shows two distinct humps, with the grand mean squarely in the middle (Figure 9.5).

The engineer was a little perplexed. Clearly, the grand mean of 339 is not representative of what is going on in the viscosity measurements. One can hardly say the measurements are centered on the mean.

The engineer did a little digging into the causes of this double-humped curve and quickly found out that the two humps resulted from the two different mixers the technicians used before measuring the velocity. It had never occurred to them that the mixers could have an effect on the measured value of viscosity. The average viscosity measurement from product whipped with one mixer was 281 and with the other, it was 399. The mixers were exerting a tremendous influence on the measurements, in addition to the influence of the underlying properties of the product. The measurements did not distinguish between the influence of the mixers and the properties of the product. The way they were averaging the measurements hid this vital fact, which, without averaging, was plainly visible.

Figure 9.5   Histogram of viscosity measurements.

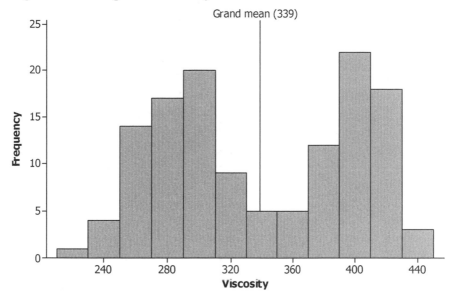

The viscosity example illustrates a central principle of averages: averages, when enough data is accumulated, tend to fall into a bell-shaped curve, centered on the grand mean. The reason for this is that averages throw away information—they forget. The more measurements you average, the more you information you lose about the original structural components of the data or any feature of them; that is, the more you forget about what you had averaged. All you are left with is a mean and standard deviation of the things you averaged. The more the original measurements are piled in a bell-shaped pile, the fewer measurements you will need to average to get a bell-shaped pile of averages. This is a ubiquitous tendency of averages with only a few exceptions.

Usually when you take groups of measurements and average them, you will get such a bell-shaped histogram. This is a useful property that allows us to predict, within certain levels of confidence, the boundaries within which future averages will fall if nothing changes in the process.

There is a bias in at least one of the two mixers, but we do not know which one. The engineer's averages gave him an average number for viscosity. Based on these averages, he inferred that his process was stable and in control. The averages he used were not, however, good representations of what was happening to viscous properties of the product in his process, because of the difference between the mixers. He averaged out measurement errors, and thus hid the errors caused by the mixers. He got averages whose connection to what is happening to the product is tenuous.

With this new information, it would be unreasonable to make the inference that the process is stable. The control chart (Figure 9.3) is misleading.

As we saw in chapter three, if you measure the same thing several times with the same measurement process, you will get a variation in the measurements. The greater control you exert over the measurement process, the less variation you will observe in the measurements.

The average of such a set of measurements provides a measure of the accuracy of the measurement process when you compare it to the "true" or standard value. The viscosity measurements were not from the same measurement process, but two processes. At most one of them could have been sufficiently accurate for the engineer's needs. The average of two measurements, one inaccurate and one accurate, is still inaccurate. Averaging measurements can be very useful, however, if the measurement process is sufficiently accurate for its intended purpose. Averaging increases the precision of such a measurement process. Averages of several measurements from such a measurement process vary less than individual measurements, and thus are, over the long haul, a safer way accurately to measure an underlying property of some kind.

WHY DO THE STOCK MARKET AVERAGES TELL DIFFERENT STORIES?

If stock market averages are averages of the same market, why are they different? The chart in Figure 9.6 shows the Dow Jones Industrial Average and the Standard & Poors 500 from 1990 to 2006, with 1990 set at 100 percent. After sixteen years, the DJIA was at 473 percent and the S&P500 at 429 percent. (The Value Line Arithmetic Average returned almost double, and the Value Line Geometric Average almost half as much. I have excluded them from the chart.)

In 1892, Charles Dow, Edward Jones, and Charles Bergstresser founded Dow Jones & Company. Their vision was to create a general indicator of market conditions. In the precursor to the Dow Jones Industrial Average, they added up the stock prices of the eleven companies in the index, and divided by eleven. Unlike the engineer and his average measures of viscosity, they were not averaging the stock prices to make an inference about some underlying property of the market—the average itself was the property that they thought would be useful, whatever it meant. Dow told it this way in a 1901 article in the *Wall Street Journal*:

Figure 9.6   Comparison of stock indexes.

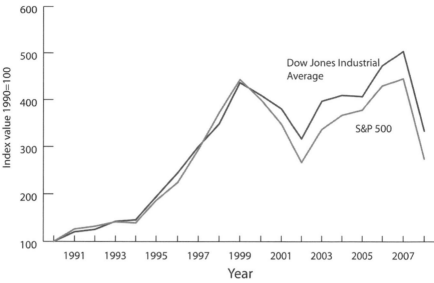

S&P 500 is a registered trademark of Standard & Poor's Financial Services LLC. Used by permission. The Dow Jones Industrial Average is published by and proprietary to Dow Jones Indexes, a licensed trademark and the marketing name of CME Group Index Services LLC, and has been licensed for use. "Dow Jones®," "Dow Jones Indexes," and "Dow Jones Industrial Average" are service marks of Dow Jones Trademark Holdings, LLC. "CME" is a trademark of Chicago Mercantile Exchange Inc. All content of the Dow Jones Industrial Average© CME Group Index Services LLC 2011.

A person watching the tide coming in, and who wishes to know the spot which marks the high tide, sets a stick in the sand at the points reached by the incoming waves until the stick reaches a position to where the waves do not come up to it, and finally recede enough to show that the tide has turned. This method holds good in watching and determining the flood tide of the stock market. The average of [stock prices] is the peg which marks the height of the waves. The price-waves, like those of the sea, do not recede all at once from the top. The force which moves them checks the inflow gradually, and time elapses before it can be told with certainty whether high tide has been seen or not.[7]

What does the Dow Jones Industrial Average measure? To answer that question you must know the definition and composition of the Industrial Average. What does a bathroom scale measure? It measures your weight, and you need know nothing about the measurement process, or how the scale works, to understand what "weight" is. With the Dow Jones Industrial

Average, the measurement process is itself the definition of the thing that is being measured. You cannot understand *what* is being measured unless you know *how* it is measured. The two are the same.

Today, the Dow Jones Industrial Average is an arithmetic mean of the prices of the stocks that make it up, but, instead of dividing by the number of stocks, as Dow originally did, Dow Jones & Co. divides by a number, called the divisor, that takes into account stock splits and other corporate actions that are unrelated to market action. As stocks split, Dow Jones revises the divisor downward so that the increased number of shares will not change the average. The Dow Jones is now made up of thirty large stocks.

The Dow Jones Industrial Average fails to enlighten as to what it is we are measuring and, therefore, it can be changed or modified at will without giving any grounds to accept or reject any new proposal. A stock is added if it has an "excellent reputation, demonstrates sustained growth, is of interest to a large number of investors and accurately represents the sector(s) covered by the average"[8] at the discretion of Dow Jones & Co.

The Dow Jones Industrial Average is what is known as an *instrumentalist* measure: it is not concerned with underlying truth or falsehood but merely practical value. In chapter three we saw another well-known instrumentalist measure: IQ tests. These have been shown to have some practical value even though intelligence cannot be defined so precisely that there is no dispute as to what it is. The same holds for stock market averages: it is hard to precisely define what we mean by a market average, even though we have a good general sense of what we are talking about when we say the "market is up" or the "market is crashing."

This of course means that anyone can define another measure of the market, such as the Standard & Poor's 500 index, to which we will turn our attention presently.

The Dow Jones Industrial Average is an integrative indicator that boils down a large collection of numbers into a single number, or into a stream of numbers, that, one hopes, is representative of the whole. As it is not measuring any specific underlying property, such as viscosity, it has itself become the property of interest because it has proven, in over a century, that it is useful as an indicator of what is going on in the stock market, or, at the very least, is a well-used indicator that correlates well with the fortunes of many companies and investors.

The Value Line Investment Survey produces a stock index based on the arithmetic mean and another using the geometric mean. Both indexes are unweighted, that is, they give equal weight to all stocks in the index. Value Line calculates the daily value of the indexes using means of the ratios of prices from one day to the next. The index based on the geometric mean systematically understates returns, according to Value Line.[9]

The Standard & Poor's 500 index, which was started in 1923, is a weighted average of 500 US stock prices, where the stocks are weighted by their market capitalization. Standard & Poor's claims that the index is "widely regarded as the best single gauge of the U.S. equities market."[10]

If the S&P 500 is a good gauge of the market, we should expect people who are paid to beat the market to do better. We can check to see if they do better by comparing the return of the S&P 500 to the return of mutual funds.

Figure 9.7 shows the year-to-year returns of the Standard & Poor's 500 index, from 1997 to 2006. The average return of the S&P 500 over the ten-year period 1997–2006 was 6.7 percent. The dotted line shows a return of 0 percent. Superimposed on the chart are the individual returns of sixty-three US equity mutual funds that invest broadly in US equities[11] over the same period (shown as little circles). The fund returns include reinvested dividends and exclude management expenses. Presumably, the fund managers were actively trying to beat the market. If we take Standard and Poor's claim at their word, the S&P 500 *is* what they should beat.

Figure 9.7   S&P 500 and sixty-three mutual funds.

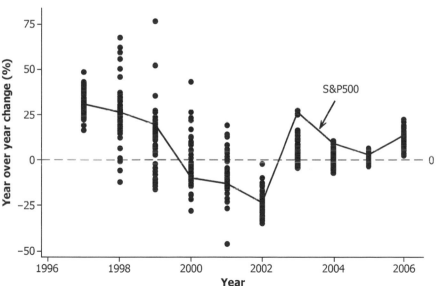

Mutual fund data from The Globe and Mail-GlobeFund Site www.globefund.com. S&P 500 is a registered trademark of Standard & Poor's Financial Services LLC. Used by permission.

The histogram in Figure 9.8 shows the ten-year average returns of the sixty-three funds. Once again, the averages fall into a bell-shaped curve. The average of all the average returns was 3.95 percent, and the average management expense ratio was 2.17 percent, for a total of 6.12 percent, about the same but slightly less than the S&P 500 return of 6.7 percent.

So far there is no evidence that the paid managers were able to beat the market average. Let's look at the mutual fund performance another way: how often they beat the market, rather than how much.

With sixty-three funds over ten years, there were 630 occasions in which the return of funds could exceed the return of the S&P 500. On only 210 occasions was a fund's annual return greater than the S&P 500's annual return, or one-third of the time. If we add the management expenses back into to the returns, there were 318 occasions on which funds exceeded the S&P 500, or 50.47 percent of the time. This method of calculation shows that the funds were ever so slightly better than the market average.

But 50.47 percent sounds suspiciously close to the percentage of time you would expect an imaginary fair coin (a tricky concept itself) to turn up heads if you flipped it hundreds of times, and you had no ability to control the outcome of the flips.

Figure 9.8   Histogram of sixty-three US equity fund returns, 1997–2006.

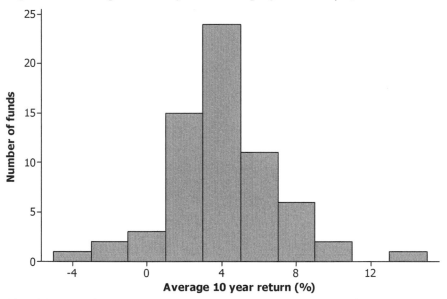

Mutual fund data from The Globe and Mail-GlobeFund Site www.globefund.com. Used with permission.

Consider a mind experiment with sixty-three coins and sixty-three coin flippers. The coin flippers vigorously flip their coins ten times, trying to get heads, like the mutual fund managers, who are trying to beat the market average. How do we determine whether there are really good coin flippers who can do better than imaginary fair coins?

When the coin flippers are finished flipping, we count the number of coins that never turned up heads, the number that turned up heads once, twice and so on up to ten heads in the ten flips. We can compare what we counted with what we would expect to get for sixty-three imaginary fair coins that have equal chances of turning up heads or tails. We can calculate the expected number of heads for the sixty-three imaginary fair coins using the binomial probability law.

If the flippers get significantly more heads than the imaginary fair coin, we might reasonably infer that some of the coin flippers are able to control the outcome of their flips, or that they have favorably loaded coins.

We can do the same comparison with the mutual fund managers and their ten-year experience with sixty-three mutual funds. If the annual return for a mutual fund is greater than the S&P 500, count it as a head. Now we expect heads more often than we would get with imaginary fair coins, because the customers of mutual fund managers pay the managers to come up heads as often as possible, and the imaginary fair coin cannot be influenced. Figure 9.9 compares the mutual fund "flips" with the imaginary fair coin flips. You can see that the coins and the mutual funds did about the same.

What does this tell us? The mutual fund results are very similar to the expected number of heads for imaginary fair coins. If the fund managers can perform consistently better than the S&P 500 average, there is little evidence of it here. The fund managers come up heads roughly as frequently as we would expect sixty-three imaginary fair coins to come up heads if tossed ten times, even if we do not deduct their management expenses.

The only fund that exceeded the S&P 500 ten times out of ten (after adding back in management expenses) was an index fund. The fund information stated that "the investment objective of the fund is to provide long-term growth of capital by primarily purchasing U.S. equity securities to track the performance of The Standard & Poor's 500 Total Return Index (S&P 500 Index)."[12]

As we saw earlier in this book, measurements do funny things to people. If managers who actively manage funds cannot on average do better than the "best single gauge of the U.S. equities market," what does this tell us about the S&P 500 as a gauge, and of the fund managers as managers?

Figure 9.9   Bar chart showing the number of funds with returns greater than the S&P 500 from 1997 to 2006.

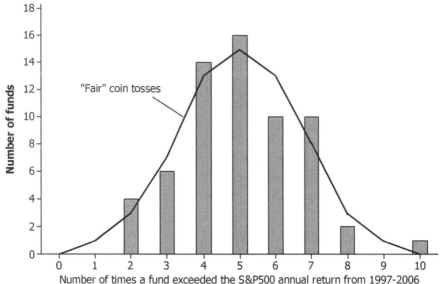

Mutual fund data from The Globe and Mail-GlobeFund Site www.globefund.com. S&P 500 is a registered trademark of Standard & Poor's Financial Services LLC. Used by permission.

There are several possibilities. The first is that the funds are centered on the S&P 500 because the managers aim for it, or at least close to it. They do this because the fund managers and their clients consider the S&P 500 to be the benchmark. They would be following John Maynard Keynes's admonition: "Worldly wisdom teaches us that it is better for reputation to fail conventionally than to succeed unconventionally."[13] If they stray too far from the index, their funds might tank while the S&P 500 increases. If they hug it, or if they fail, they will at least fail "conventionally."

This creates positive feedback. More than $100 trillion is managed by the global fund management industry. The choices the industry's agents make in investing their clients' funds will influence equity prices. This in turn will influence the averages they are trying to beat, which will again influence their choices. The S&P 500 thus becomes the average of the mutual funds, not because it passively mirrors their average performance, but because the index influences the decisions of the fund managers, who shoot for it, and, on average, hit it. If the index performs poorly and they perform poorly with it, they fail conventionally. They are paid a handsome 2–3 percent of their clients' capital for doing so.

The second possibility is that the S&P 500 is the best gauge, in the sense that it represents the average of the market. Over the long haul, the fund managers are incapable of doing better than the market average. They are paid a handsome 2–3 percent of their clients' capital for not doing so. The fortunes of any large group of mid-cap or larger stocks, like those groups of stocks found in mutual funds, are closely correlated to the S&P 500. The funds merely regress to the mean over time.

The third possibility is that the way Standard and Poor's calculates the index creates a combination of equities that is hard to beat. In that sense, it is not a fair representation of the average, but one of the best combinations of equities one could pick.

How do the funds compare with the Dow Jones Industrial Average? The sixty-three funds had higher returns than the Dow Jones Industrial Average 298 times out of a possible 630 times, or 47.3 percent of the time. The average return of the funds, calculated after adding management fees back in, was 6.2 percent versus 6.8 percent for the Dow Jones Industrial Average over the ten years. If we repeat the coin-tossing experiment with the Dow Jones Industrial Average, the funds do even worse.

Is the DJIA a better gauge of the average of the market than the S&P 500? All we can say is that it is a *different* way to measure the movement of the market, and a repeat of the coin-tossing experiment shows that the mutual funds had even more trouble beating it in 1997–2006.

This does not mean that the DJIA or S&P 500 cannot be beaten consistently by *any* mutual funds, or fund managers. For example, sector funds can consistently beat the general indices over lengthy periods, provided that the sector is picked well.

SIMPLICITY IS A DANGEROUS CRITERION

There is an infinite number of ways to calculate means. To make reasonable inferences from a mean, it must be justified on first principles, such as physics or economics, and be shown through practical experience to be meaningful.

In many circumstances, calculating an average is straightforward enough. You add up your measurements and divide the sum by the number of measurements. This is known as the arithmetic mean. But without knowing what the measurements represent, the arithmetic mean can be meaningless and misleading. Consider the following three pairs of numbers and their respective averages (Table 9.5).

Suppose each pair of numbers represents the lengths of the sides of a rectangle, such as the lengths of building lots for sale. The three rectangles are shown in Figure 9.10:

All three rectangles have the same area of 16, obtained by multiplying the two sides together. The average lengths of the sides of the rectangles, calculated from arithmetic means, are all different, going from 4 to 8.5. How well do the average lengths represent the *areas* of the rectangles? Figure 9.11 shows three squares constructed by using the average side lengths. Squares A, B, and C have areas of 16, 25, and 72 1/4 respectively. Clearly, the average lengths of the *sides* do not provide the information needed to obtain a fair representation of the *areas* of the rectangles from which they are derived.

The arithmetic mean is useful when our measurements relate to one another only through adding and subtracting. The arithmetic mean answers the question, "If all my measurements were the same, what value would they have to have, if I added them up, to produce the same total?" Its advantage, as John Maynard Keynes put it, "is that at all times the arithmetic mean has had simplicity to recommend it. It is easier to add than to multiply. But simplicity is a dangerous criterion."[14]

In the case of the area of a rectangle, the measurements are multiplied, rather than added, to obtain the areas. For such measurements the *geometric mean* is more appropriate. The geometric mean is calculated by multiplying the measurements together to obtain their product, and then, if there are *n* measurements, taking the *n*th root of the product. In the case of two measurements used to calculate an area, we obtain the geometric mean by multiplying them together and taking square root (Table 9.6).

Table 9.5   Three Pairs of Numbers

	Pair A	Pair B	Pair C
	4	8	16
	4	2	1
Average	4	5	8.5

Figure 9.10   Three rectangles with an area of 16.

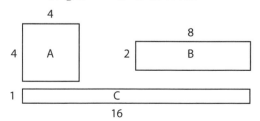

Figure 9.11   Areas derived from the arithmetic mean length of the sides of the rectangles.

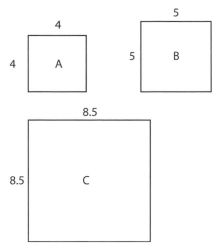

The geometric mean answers the question, "If all my measurements were the same, what value would they have, if I multiplied them together, to produce the same product?"

Consider the "average rate of return." Suppose a stock changes in five consecutive years by 15 percent, 12 percent, 8 percent, 11 percent, and –20 percent. The arithmetic mean of these changes is 5.2 percent. You cannot calculate a geometric mean when you have negative numbers. If you represent these numbers as 1.15, 1.12, 1.08, 1.11 and 0.8 (as I did in Table 9.7 with some other numbers) you can calculate the geometric mean, which is 4.3 percent.[15] The overall return after five years is the product of the returns in individual years. Only the geometric mean gives a proper representation of the overall five-year compound rate of return. The arithmetic mean will overestimate it.

An annual "return" is the ratio of the value one year over the value the previous year, less 1, times 100 percent. An annual return of 15 percent means that the value in year two, divided by the value in year one, is 1.15. To calculate the average return we must convert to ratios, calculate the mean, and convert back to returns.

Consider a stock that starts at $50, rises to $100 in the second year, and falls to $50 again in the third. It's clear the overall return over two years is 0 percent because the stock ended where it started, at $50. The annual average return is therefore also 0 percent. But what happens if we calculate the return by averaging the annual returns? The annual rates of return are 100 percent and −50 percent (ratios of 2 and 0.5). The arithmetic mean

Table 9.6   Comparison of Arithmetic and Geometric Means

	Set A	Set B	Set C
	4	8	16
	4	2	1
Total	8	10	17
Arithmetic mean	4	5	8.5
Product	16	16	16
Geometric mean	4	4	4

will produce an average rate of return of 25 percent,[16] whereas the geometric mean will properly give 0 percent[17] (Table 9.7).

The average returns of the mutual funds we looked at earlier were calculated with the geometric mean. The numbers in Table 9.8 represent the ratio of each year's closing value over the previous year's closing value. The three funds, from top to bottom, were better than the S&P 500, respectively, ten, three, and two years out of ten, before deducting management fees (the years in which they were better are shown in bold-face). They were better than the Dow Jones five, three, and two years out of ten.

To calculate the average return of several funds within a single year, the arithmetic mean is better. Remember that the geometric mean is used when the quantities we average are usually multiplied together, as returns are when calculating a compound return. The returns for several funds within a given year do not compound with each other. I have also shown the arithmetic mean of the annual returns of the three funds in Table 9.8.

The geometric mean is also used to dampen the effect of occasional extreme values. Suppose the following daily maximum temperatures (°C) were recorded from a weather station in November: 5, 4, 7, 3, and 25. The first four days were cool, followed by a freak warm pleasant day. The geometric mean is 6.4°C, compared to the arithmetic mean of 8.8°C. The geometric mean is a bit more representative of the temperatures most of the time.

Now consider the average of *rates*, such as speeds. What is the average speed of a car that travels 300 miles in five hours, partly on highways at 100 mph and partly on winding country roads at 50 mph? Table 9.9 shows how long it took the car to drive on three 100-mile segments of its trip:

In total, it travels 300 miles in five hours, giving it an average speed of 60 mph. The arithmetic mean of the three speeds, 50 mph, 100 mph,

Table 9.7   Stock Prices and the Geometric Mean

	Year end	Stock price	Ratio of prices	% return
	1	$50	–	–
	2	$100	2	100%
	3	$50	0.5	−50%
Arithmetic mean				25%
Geometric mean				0%

and 50 mph is 67 mph. It is clear though, that if a car travels 300 km in five hours, its average speed for the trip is 60 mph. This is the *harmonic mean*.[18] The arithmetic mean overestimates the average speed. Likewise, to calculate the average resistance of the components of an electric circuit of a certain overall resistance,[19] the harmonic mean must be used: the arithmetic mean also overestimates it. Resistance is the rate at which voltage is lost for a given amount of current, and is expressed as volts per current (volts per amp). Engineers use the harmonic mean and its related quantity, the equivalent resistance, when they design amplifiers and power applications.

The harmonic mean answers the question, "If all my rates were the same, what value would they have to have, to produce the same overall rate?"

The *weighted mean* is a variant on the arithmetic mean. The arithmetic mean places an equal weight on each number in the mean. If there are two numbers, each gets a weight of 1/2; if there are ten, each gets a weight of 1/10. In a weighted mean, each number gets an arbitrary weight, as Rachel showed. In some cases, the weights are pulled out of a hat, such as the calculation of a class average, where teachers assign weights of their choosing to each score. In others, they are picked with a bit of guesswork, and in other cases, the weights are themselves an average of some other numbers. In the calculation of the Consumer Price Index, for example, the prices of consumer products are weighted by the relative proportion of each product that consumers purchase in the total basket of consumer products that are included in the index. As we will see in chapter ten, this weighting scheme is still arbitrary, as the decision as to what goes into the basket and what stays out of it is arbitrary, even though economists and governments justify it with economic principles.

Some means are weighted unintentionally. Suppose, for example, that a quality control worker wanted carefully to measure the meat content of pans of frozen lasagna coming off a production line. She asks a worker to

Table 9.8 Returns of Some US Equity Funds 1997–2006 before Deducting Management Fees

	1997	1998	1999	2000	2001	2002	2003	2004	2005	2006	Geometric mean	Compound average return
TD U.S. Index	**1.323**	**1.277**	**1.199**	0.902	0.874	0.775	**1.276**	**1.099**	1.042	**1.149**	1.076	7.6%
Fidelity Growth America-A	**1.336**	1.222	1.130	0.897	**0.915**	0.759	1.073	1.003	**1.053**	1.072	1.034	3.4%
PH&N U.S. Equity	1.294	1.213	1.043	**0.933**	**0.926**	0.750	1.038	0.977	0.975	1.106	1.015	1.5%
Arithmetic mean	1.318	1.237	1.124	0.911	0.905	0.761	1.129	1.026	1.023	1.109	1.042	4.2%
S&P 500	1.310	1.267	1.195	0.899	0.870	0.766	1.264	1.090	1.030	1.136	1.067	6.7%
DJIA	1.226	1.161	1.252	0.938	0.929	0.832	1.253	1.031	0.994	1.163	1.068	6.8%

Source: S&P 500 is a registered trademark of Standard & Poor's Financial Services. LLC. Mutual fund data from The Globe and Mail-GlobeFund Site www.globefund.com. The Dow Jones Industrial Average is published by and proprietary to Dow Jones Indexes, a licensed trademark and the marketing name of CME Group Index Services. LLC, and has been licensed for use. "Dow Jones®," "Dow Jones Indexes," and "Dow Jones Industrial Average" are service marks of Dow Jones Trademark Holdings, LLC. "CME" is a trademark of Chicago Mercantile Exchange Inc. All content of the Dow Jones Industrial Average© CME Group Index Services LLC 2011. Used by permission.

Table 9.9   Miles Driven and the Harmonic Mean

	Miles driven	Hours	mph
	100	2	50
	100	1	100
	100	2	50
Total	300	5	–
Arithmetic mean			67
Harmonic mean			60

collect fifty samples. The production line has two heads that fill the pans with cooked, ground meat. The pans come down the line on two parallel conveyors, side by side. Suppose that to save the effort of leaning over the conveyors, and because he was not told otherwise, the worker takes most of the samples from the closest conveyor, with a few from the farther conveyor for good measure. The arithmetic mean of the meat content of these lasagna pans will be weighted toward the mean of the head feeding the close conveyor. If the worker picks ten samples from the farthest panel, or 20 percent of the samples, the average of the fifty pans is basically a weighted average of the averages of the two filling heads, with weights of 20 percent and 80 percent for the farthest and closest heads respectively. Similarly, if the worker whipped 20 percent of the tubs of product with one mixer and 80 percent with the other, the resulting average would be weighted toward the second mixer.

The *median* is special case of a mean that only uses the middle one or the average of the middle two values (trimming off the rest). It serves a similar purpose to the arithmetic mean, which is to find the middle point of a set of numbers. The median is the number in a set of numbers that divides the top half of the set from the bottom half; in other words, it is the middle number of a set of numbers sorted in order.

With three or more measurements, the median is unaffected by the largest and smallest values. I only have one nose, but I have more than the average number of noses per person. A small number of unfortunate people lose their noses through radical cancer surgery or through trauma, and have zero noses. If all people had one nose, the arithmetic mean number of noses would be one. If only one person has a nose amputation, and thus zero noses, the mean is less than one. Unless 50 percent or more people lose their noses, the median will remain one even if some people lose theirs. I am not alone in having an above-average number of noses. The vast majority of people also have an above-average number of noses, possibly more than 99.9 percent of people.

Like the geometric mean, the median is useful for sets of measurements where there are occasional extreme measurements, such as household income. For example, consider the following three household incomes: $50,000, $50,000, and $100,000. The median income is $50,000, while the arithmetic mean income is $366,667 and the geometric mean $135,721. Suppose that in a larger population, where the vast majority of households had incomes of less than $100,000, and a small number of households had incomes over $10 million, the median income would not be affected by the small number of very large incomes, while the arithmetic mean would.

Take the example of a small community with 1,000 households. The median income of the bottom 950 households is $50,000. There is a new part of town with 50 beautiful homes owned by wealthy business executives and sports stars, with large waterfront lots. The median household income of this part of town is $1,000,000. The median household income for the entire town is still $50,000. The (arithmetic) mean household income, however, for the whole town would be closer to $100,000, because a small number of high incomes bump up the average of the whole. For this reason, the US Bureau of the Census and other government statistical agencies usually use the median when referring to average incomes.

A lot of people confuse average with median. The Canadian Broadcasting Corporation runs a show called "Cross Country Check Up," in which people from across the country call in to voice their opinion on national issues. Usually there is an expert or two in the studio to provide commentary. In one show, the expert cited a survey of student opinions about themselves. The survey showed that 70 percent of students believed they were above average. The expert claimed that it was statistically impossible to have 70 percent of the student population be above average. Some expert. It is of course impossible for 70 percent of students to be above the median. By definition, only 50 percent are above the median. As with noses, however, it is quite possible for 70 percent of students to be above the arithmetic mean. If 999 students in a small college had final marks of 100 percent and one had a mark of 90 percent, than 99.9 percent of students would have average marks above the arithmetic mean.

The *root mean square* is used when the arithmetic mean is physically constrained to zero. Consider a set of measurements of an alternating electrical current. Because it is alternating back and forth on either side of zero, from positive to negative current, the positive and negative values cancel each other out. The arithmetic mean over a sufficient length of time will thus be zero, or very close to it. This will be true no matter how strong the current is. For this reason, you cannot compare the intensities of different currents with the arithmetic mean. The root mean square of the current does the trick. It takes the arithmetic mean of the *squares* of the measurements, and then takes the square root of the mean. In this way, it turns all measurements into positive values that no longer cancel each other out.

Although it is called a mean, the root mean square differs from all other means in an important way. The other means all try to find, in one way or another, the most central and common value in a set of measurements. The most central value, in those situations where the root mean square is useful, is zero. What it measures instead is the *dispersion* of the measurements around their central value of zero. It is thus the standard deviation, which measures dispersion around the mean, rather than a mean.

CLASS AVERAGES: INGENUITY

Cunahan read Rachel's memo and called her back to his office the next day. "Listen," he said, "I appreciate your mathematical ingenuity and your sudden conversion to Andy's weighting scheme, but I can't let you change the course weightings after the course is finished."

Cunahan saw the stress flow over Rachel's brow. "Look," he said, "you yourself argued the purpose of your weights was to get kids to allocate their efforts more in some areas than others. You can't now turn around and put more weight in areas where they put less effort and less weight in areas where they put more effort."

Rachel knew he was right. She looked at the floor, quietly, thinking. Cunahan knew she needed a moment to collect her thoughts and remained silent. "Give me a couple of hours," she said.

Rachel had not weighted the scores for the questions in the final exam. She had not indicated on the exam sheet how much each question was worth. There were five questions, and she had taken the arithmetic mean of the five questions using her usual score of 0 to 10 for each question. This is the same as giving each question a weight of 20 percent.

Back at her desk, she reviewed the spreadsheet where she had recorded the grades and confirmed that most kids had struggled to answer the first and second questions. She had put the most difficult questions at the beginning of the exam so that her students would attempt them first, before they ran out of time.

Rachel changed the weights for the questions in the exam (Table 9.11) and recalculated the exam scores. She plugged the new final exam scores into her previous spreadsheet. Balpreet's overall course average stayed the same at 48 percent. He failed. Jessica's went up to 50.4 percent. She passed. The grades of the rest of the class went up slightly too. She printed off the spreadsheet and updated her memo and grade sheet, and emailed it to Cunahan.

As he drove home that evening Cunahan thought about how much most of the kids in his school worried about their averages. The teachers whined that they got phone calls and emails from parents when the averages of their little darlings dipped slightly below what they thought their extraordinary talents entitled them to. Both parents and children tried to negotiate their marks and their averages, as he had done with Rachel.

There was political pressure too. If he let the hard-nosed teachers get their way, those that wanted to prepare their students for the university courses they themselves had taken decades ago, the school's average would be so low he would get rapped on the knuckles by the inspector. And if he let the touchy feely ones hold sway, those that did not want to hurt their students' self-esteem, the averages would inflate so high the school would lose all credibility with the universities.

There was an infinite number of ways of calculating averages; Rachel had pulled another one out of her hat today. The teachers' ingenuity in devising ways to calculate averages was a response to all the pressures. His sad duty was to make sure that whatever averages came out of that pressure cooker were defensible to all parties.

Table 9.10   Grade 11 Physics Final Exam Grades

Exam question	Original weighting	New-weighting	Balpreet's scores	Jessica'sscores
Question 1	20%	10%	10	1
Question 2	20%	10%	10	1
Question 3	20%	30%	10	4
Question 4	20%	40%	5	6
Question 5	20%	10%	0	3
Total	100%	100%		
	Average with equal weighting		70%	30%
	Average with new weighting		70%	41%

TOOL BOX

- There are an infinite number of ways to calculate an average. Don't be fooled when someone says they have calculated "the" average. Make sure it is the most reasonable average for summarizing the data or making an inference.

- Understand how the structure in the data influences the average. The structure may create subsets of data whose averages are very different than the overall average. The overall average will not be representative of the typical case in such situations, and you cannot make reasonable inferences with it.

- Be careful with bell-shaped curves. Often they are bell-shaped because there is some averaging going on that hides the key and informative structure.

- Stock market indices should be viewed as practical indicators rather than averages of some specific underlying property, even though they are called averages. To understand what inferences you can draw from such indicators, you must understand how they are calculated.

- In general, use:

  - Arithmetic means when measurements relate to each other through addition and subtraction.
  - Geometric means when the measurements relate to each other through multiplication.
  - Harmonic means when the measurements are rates.
  - Medians when there are extreme values or a very skewed distribution of measurements.

- Weighted averages are often useful, but they open the door to manipulation. Make sure you understand why and how the weights were chosen.

TEN

Opposing Views: Are You Being Misled?

We are trying to prove ourselves wrong as quickly as possible, because only in that way can we find progress.

—Physicist Richard Feynman, Nobel Prize winner

Can measurements resolve opposing views or controversial claims? That indeed is one of the most important purposes of measurement. We would hope and expect that people with opposing views, faced with new measurements and facts, would come to agreement about a claim. What often happens is the opposite—people react to new measurements by hardening their opinions and becoming increasingly polarized, because they think they are being misled.

One of the clearest examples is the measurement of global climatic temperature. Surely, one would think, scientists should be able to measure the global temperature and determine whether or not the planet is warming. Indeed many scientists, working under the auspices of the International Panel on Climate Change (IPCC), say that this has been done and that consensus has been reached. Yet there are a number of scientists, working for respected universities, who have measured the Earth's temperature differently and reached different conclusions. Rather than quietly resolving these differences through arcane technical discussions in the halls of academia, opposing opinions have hardened and reputations have been attacked.

Most governments are quite open about the methods and data they use to measure inflation. This has not brought together opposing camps whose views about inflation show no sign of converging.

In chapter three I described a chemical company at which plant managers and laboratory staff around the world were at loggerheads over measurements of product brightness. The plant managers were paid bonuses for producing bright (i.e., good) product, while the laboratory workers had incentives to catch bad product. The lab took the measurements. The plant managers did not trust their measurements.

Why do measurements often harden opposing views? It comes down to a logical fallacy in our reasoning: that a new measurement unequivocally either supports or opposes a claim. Whether it does or not depends on the background information of the person who hears the claim, and the probability that person assigns to being misled by those who take the measurement and make the claim. It may support the claim for one person and refute it for another if the probabilities they assign to being misled differ.

Suppose a lab worker named Fred measures a day's worth of production and says, "The measurement shows the product is no good and must be scrapped."

Mr. Smith, the plant manager, believes Fred is out to screw him. He reasons as follows: "The product is probably good. Fred is a quality zealot who has no regard for practical realities. He wants to prove production workers don't give a damn about quality. His measurement has no effect on my opinion of the product. I'll tell them to ship it anyway."

At another plant a lab worker named Freda takes a measurement and also concludes the product is defective. The plant manager at her plant, Mr. Wilson, believes Freda is a conscientious woman who is dedicated to the good of the company and the satisfaction of its customers. He reasons as follows: "Freda is a competent, diligent, and honest employee. I thought the product was good, but seeing this measurement compels me to change my mind. Scrap the product."

Finally, at a third plant, lab worker Fritz takes his measurement and finds defective product. Mr. Taylor is Fritz's plant manager. Taylor believes Fritz is not careful with his measurement devices and in the preparation of samples. He reasons as follows: "Fritz is ready for retirement and has lost his edge. The accuracy and precision of his measurements are generally poor. He does not have rigorous lab standards. His measurements are likely to be wrong and this new measurement just confirms it. I know that's good product. Ship it."

Each of the three plant managers receives new information from the lab workers. The information is *not* that the measurement shows the product is no good. It is the *claim* by the lab worker that the measurement shows the product is no good. Whether or not the managers believe that claim depends on their background information about the lab workers and the probability they assign to the truth of their claims. Each plant manager had different background information and assigned different probabilities to being misled. Personal beliefs and emotions may also affect the probability people assign to the truth of a claim. For example, someone may assign a low probability that a disastrous event such as a flu pandemic will occur because it scares them.[1]

Why does such background information matter? In well-established areas of physics it matters very little. Through previous successes, physicists can earn credibility, but it does not count for much. Even Einstein was wrong sometimes. Physicists are by nature skeptical. They do not believe any claim: it does not matter what people say about their research and what they found. Physicists will only believe something when a very high standard of proof is attained, and after they have carefully reviewed the experimental methods, the equipment, the measurements, and the calculations. And even then, that only makes it worth trying to replicate the experiment somewhere else to confirm the results. Background information about people matters less in physics because things lend themselves to clear definition and measurement. Variables can be isolated and carefully controlled. A physical constant is a physical constant—it does not change, and can be very clearly and precisely defined and measured.

The rest of us do not have the time or resources to recheck the measurements, methods, and calculations behind every claim we hear. We rely on the credibility of the person who makes the claim, and so the background information we have about that person matters.

Things like product quality, inflation, and global climatic temperature are not easily defined and, consequently, there are huge uncertainties about the meaning of the numbers. This naturally leads to a greater—and justified—suspicion of being misled. Often there are many or even innumerable possible definitions and as many ways to measure. Suspicions of being misled are the highest when there are competing definitions of the measurement object. As we have seen throughout this book, outside of the physical sciences, many indicators are arbitrarily concocted and their worth is only proven through practical experience, such as IQ, infant mortality, or coffee-rating schemes. Such proofs can take years.

THE INFLATION MEASUREMENT CONTROVERSY

Dan Palmer is a Canadian engineer who for more than a decade carefully recorded the grocery bill for his family of four. It rose from an average of $287 a month in August 1998 to $668 in August 2009. This is an average annual increase of 7.9 percent (using the geometric mean). According to the Bank of Canada's inflation calculator, his grocery bill should have risen to $341, an average annual increase of 1.6 percent. Mr. Palmer is understandably suspicious of official inflation measurements.

He is not alone. John Williams is an economist who runs a website known as Shadow Government Statistics.[2] On it he releases his "alternate Consumer Price Index." The Alternate CPI uses the method of measuring inflation that the US Bureau of Labor Statistics was using in the late 1970s, before making many changes to it. Williams's number is closer to Mr. Palmer's homegrown number: a 9.3 percent average annual change, compared to the BLS number of 2.6 percent for the same period.

The BLS says there is no need to worry if the experience of inflation of individual consumers differs from the CPI. Its website says that as "the CPI is a statistical average, it may not reflect your experience or that of specific families or individuals, particularly those whose expenditure patterns differ substantially from the 'average' urban consumer," which as we saw in chapter nine is a plausible explanation. The CPI is a weighted average of the prices of things that consumers buy, not just groceries. The relative weights of the items in the basket of an individual consumer will be different than the weights in the CPI. Another reason the BLS gives for differences in perceived inflation is that the prices of some frequently purchased goods such as food and gasoline may rise more rapidly than goods that are purchased less often, such as TVs. Economists at the BLS, in a paper apparently directed at Williams, say other explanations for the "apparent inconsistencies between the index and people's perceptions" are based on "misconceptions and myths."[3]

Williams does not buy it, and says that base political motives are at work. He says: "The reasons for the CPI changes have been stated clearly by political Washington: to reduce the deficit by cutting cost of living adjustments to Social Security."[4] His distrust is fueled by comments by politicians. The cochairs of President Obama's National Commission on Fiscal Responsibility and Reform said in a "Cochair's Proposal" in November 2010 that "current measures of inflation overestimate increases in cost of living" and that "adopting a more accurate measure of inflation would achieve savings government-wide." Katherine Abraham, the Commissioner of the BLS under the Clinton administration, was quoted as saying that Newt Gingrich, who along with other Republicans wanted to make changes to the way the CPI was calculated, told her, "If you could see your way clear to doing these things, we might have more money for BLS programs."[5] Gingrich is also quoted as saying that fixing the CPI index "would provide maneuvering room for budget negotiators."[6]

Williams's criticism echoes comments made almost two hundred years earlier by Joseph Lowe, who said that governments had an interest in the public not knowing that their money was depreciating. He said, "The interest of government, the greatest of all debtors, [is] to prevent the public from fixing its attention on the gradual depreciation of money,"[7] and "Our successive chancellors of the exchequer anticipated a continuance of this decline, and silently calculated on its producing a diminution in the pressure of the debt."[8]

There are many other critics of the BLS's inflation numbers: "The strongest criticism has not been concentrated in a single profession, academic discipline, or political group, but comes instead from an array of investment advisers, bloggers, magazine writers, and others in the popular press," according to two BLS economists.[9] Bill Gross,[10] managing director and founder of Pacific Investment Management Company, oversees the management of more than $1 trillion in securities. He argues that CPI numbers are "not reflecting reality at the checkout counter" and calls it a "con job" and the "total fiction that is government reporting of inflation."[11] Gross's argument is based on a comparison of US inflation figures with a foreign CPI composite. The US CPI is 3 to 4 percent lower, which he calls "a mite suspicious."

WHAT IS INFLATION? THE PROBLEM OF DEFINITION

Measuring inflation is an attempt to express in quantitative terms an idea that is not directly observable, but which many of us experience: a general increase in the supply of money at a faster rate than the supply of goods and services to purchase. This is called monetary inflation. The excess money may cause increases in the prices of the goods and services that people require for their daily lives. The excess money can also go into equities or real estate, inflating their values. Or it can cause speculative bubbles in the stock market or housing. Most attempts to measure inflation take the narrow view of price inflation, focusing only on the prices of goods and services.

Possibly the first attempt to measure inflation was by Bishop W. Fleetwood in his 1707 study *Chronicon Preciosum*.[12] His study was prompted by a statute enacted by All Souls College in Oxford when it was founded in 1440. The statute stated that a Fellow of the college, when admitted to Fellowship, had to swear to vacate it if his personal income increased beyond £5 per year. Fleetwood wondered whether a man could, in good conscience, take the oath even if he had a larger income, given that the value of money had fallen in the intervening 267 years.

To answer his question, Fleetwood created a basket of four commodities—corn, meat, cloth, and drink—and studied them over the previous six hundred years. He did not calculate an index or mean. He reckoned these commodities were the necessary staples of academic life. He concluded that £5 in 1440 was worth £30 in 1707, and that therefore a Fellow with such an income of £30 should have no moral compunction about accepting the Fellowship.

In 1764 an Italian professor of astronomy, Gian Carli, calculated the arithmetic mean of the ratios of prices of the items in his basket. His basket had three items: grain, wine, and oil. The next innovation was by Sir George Shuckburgh Evelyn (1751–1804) in 1798. Evelyn was a mathematician, astronomer, and Member of Parliament (the Shuckburgh crater on the moon carries his name). His basket contained "wheat, cattle in husbandry (horse, ox, cow, sheep hog), poultry (goose, hen, cock), butter, cheese, ale, small beer, beef and mutton, and labor in husbandry."[13] He did not weight the items in the basket, so a pound of butter had the same weight in his index as an ox. He included no manufactured goods, but he did include labor. He looked at the prices of items in his basket from 1050 to 1795 and projected forward to 1800. He set the year 1550 as his base year and gave it a value of 100. For each item in the basket, he expressed the prices in every other year relative to the base price in 1550. He then calculated, for each year, an index value. The index value was the arithmetic mean of the relative numbers for all the items in the basket.

Using the principles of geometric means we reviewed in chapter nine, I calculated the annual inflation rate with Evelyn's index data. It is shown in Figure 10.1. It is interesting to note that for five hundred years, inflation, according to Evelyn's basket and method, was less than half a percent per year. When it increased dramatically around the year 1550, it reached only about 1.5 percent per year by 1800. Yet the effects of such an increase in prices were sufficiently marked to force national attention to the hardships caused by fixed-price contracts.[14]

Arthur Young (1741–1820) introduced the idea of quality into measures of inflation. In a precursor to the modern controversy, Young said that the changes in price in Evelyn's index were not attributable solely to the loss of value of money but to increases in quality of the items in the basket. "Have there been no improvements in the breed of horses in the last fifty years? . . . If the animal, upon the whole, is improved, it would be a strange mode of showing a depreciation of money, by discovering that a better horse sells at a higher price."[15] He also objected to Evelyn's index on the grounds that the items in his basket were not well defined;

Figure 10.1   Annual inflation (%) based on Evelyn's index.

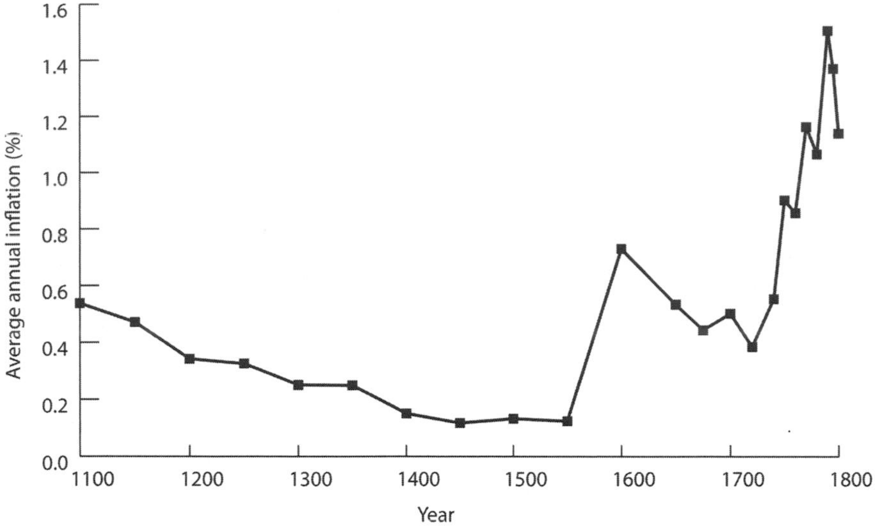

Source: Kendall.

important items such as manufactured items were omitted; and there was no weighting.

Young developed a different basket that included agricultural products, labor, wool, land, rent, houses, commodities such as timber, coal, and metal, and manufactured goods such as shoes, hats, and mops. He created what is perhaps the first weighted index by weighting the items in the basket by what he considered their importance, multiplying the price of wheat and labor by five, provisions four times, barley and oats twice, and so on. By his calculation, the rise in prices from one century to the next was 22.5 percent, "or only the tenth the part of the rise stated by Sir George [Evelyn]."[16]

Joseph Lowe published a book in 1823 in which he produced tables for determining the weights in the index.[17] Rather than use Young's subjective view of the importance of items to weight them in the index, he used weights that reflected the relative proportions purchased by the general public. He reckoned that these proportions would not change significantly over time—that consumers would not substitute products. This was not an outlandish assumption at the time. Today the problem of substitution underlies much of the modern suspicion about inflation. His basket contained items purchased by the British public on wheat, barley, oats, meat, woolens, cottons, linen, silk, leather, hardware, sugar, tea, and "all other heads of national consumption."[18]

Lowe believed that government indebtedness, particularly resulting from war, would increase the money supply, causing the depreciation of money. He attributed the sharp rise in prices seen in Evelyn's statistics to "the reign of Elizabeth, at the time when the American [precious metals] mines became productive on a large scale" and to our "defensive attitude toward Philip II"[19] (of Spain).

In the 19th century there was some subsequent debate about whether the weights should change with time, and whether the arithmetic or geometric means should be used.

Etienne Laspeyres (1834–1913), a German professor of economics and statistics, reinvented Lowe's method of weighting. His measure of price change was based on the weights of the items in the basket in the initial year. In other words, it measured change with a fixed basket. Another German academic, Hermann Paasche (1851–1925), a professor of political science, modified Laspeyres's weighting method, but used weights based on the relative amount of goods purchased in the period used to calculate the change in prices, irrespective of their weights in the initial year.

The United States Bureau of Labor Statistics (BLS) began developing the Consumer Price Index in World War I, for the reason given by Lowe almost one hundred years before regarding the "anomalies in regards to rents, salaries, wages &c." As in other wars, prices were increasing rapidly, and there arose a need for a means to calculate cost-of-living adjustments in wages. The BLS studied household expenditures in ninety-two industrial centers from 1917 to 1919[20] to determine an appropriate basket of goods, and the weights to assign the items in the basket. In 1919 the BLS began periodically collecting price information and began publishing separate indices for thirty-two American cities. Two years later the bureau began publishing a national index. It also estimated indices going back to 1913 using data on food prices, which it had started collecting as early as 1903.

Between 1919 and 2003, the Bureau of Labor Statistics comprehensively updated the way it calculated the Consumer Price Index six times. It made smaller changes to its methods more regularly. Many of the changes were fine tuning of themes that Lowe, Young, Laspeyres, and others had identified. For example, it used the same weights until 1940—assuming consumers purchased their items in constant proportion during that time. After 1940 it modified the weights based on a survey of consumer expenditures it conducted in 1934–1936. Thereafter the bureau started regularly surveying consumer expenditures to update the weights. It gradually expanded the areas across the country from which it sampled, broadened from cities and industrial centers to suburbs. It broadened the definition of "household," and broadened the eligibility of items for inclusion in the basket.

The three major changes that have generated the most criticism, and suspicion, were the switch to rental-equivalence as a way to measure the cost of shelter rather than housing prices (1983), hedonic regression (1998), and geometric means (1999). Of these, hedonic regression and geometric means generated the most criticism. The idea behind owner's equivalent rent is to calculate what the owner would pay to rent a similar house. The goal (a reasonable one) was to remove the investment portion of the cost of owning a house in the calculation of the index.

In 1995 the US Senate Financial Committee appointed a commission to study quality change and consumer substitution of items in the basket, and how they affected the CPI, in particular, whether they biased the CPI. Young's criticism that inflation measures did not adequately take into account price changes that were caused by changes in quality—in his example, changes in the quality of horses—thus became one of the prime motivations for a US Senate commission 183 years later. By 1995 the problem of quality changes was much more severe because products change so quickly compared to Young's time. Lowe's assumption that there was no substitution was also examined.

The commission's report, known as the Boskin Report,[21] which came out about one year later, estimated that the then-current method of measuring inflation had an upward bias of 1 percent. This bias is in the opposite direction of the CPI's critics, who claim it underestimates inflation. The report made several sweeping recommendations to address quality change and the measurement problems that arise when consumers substitute one product for another when prices change. One result of the commission's report was that the bureau greatly increased its use of hedonic regression to account for quality changes (the word "hedonic" comes from the Greek word *hedon,* which means pleasure).

The idea behind hedonic regression is to remove that part of an increase (or decrease) in price that results from an increase (or decrease) in quality rather than inflation. It is one of many methods used to account for changes in quality. The adjustments can push price up or down; for example, if a candy bar gets bigger but costs the same, the price (per ounce) is adjusted down, and if gets smaller and costs the same, it is adjusted up. The bureau uses hedonic regression when such simple methods do not work. It is based on a statistical technique known as multiple regression and is used to estimate the "market valuation of a feature . . . by comparing the prices of items with and without that feature."[22]

If a manufacturer stops making a particular model of television in the basket of goods that make up the CPI, the data collectors at the bureau put another one in its place that is similar. The new one will, however, have different characteristics. Suppose the new model has a better screen, and a higher price. The bureau might decide that the higher price results from the screen, not inflation. It will then calculate, using hedonic regression, the amount by which the screen increases the price. In one such case, both new and old models of 27-inch televisions were priced at $329, but the bureau decided the new screen was a quality increase worth $135. The bureau lowered the price of the television to $194, to account for the increase in quality, and put the lower-priced hedonically regressed television into the basket of goods it uses to calculate the CPI. If a characteristic is dropped from one model to the next, resulting in a price decrease, the bureau may compensate with an offsetting price increase to account for reduction in quality resulting from the loss of that characteristic. The bureau itself admits that hedonic regression relies on "some strong assumptions."[23] Critics point out that the consumer cannot ask for the adjusted price at the cash register, and must still pay $329 for their quality-enhanced TV.

According to the Organization for Economic Cooperation and Development, "the use of hedonic methods has been growing at an accelerating rate,"[24] "covering rent, apparel, computers, televisions, audio equipment, video cameras, VCR's and DVD players, refrigerators, freezers, and microwave ovens, college textbooks, washers and dryers.[25] It is now used for items in the CPI accounting for 32% of the weighting,[26] the largest of which is 'owners' equivalent rent," at 23 percent. Hedonic regression is used in the calculation of owners' equivalent rent to account for deterioration in the quality of dwellings.

A second major outcome of the Boskin Report was a recommendation to reflect consumers' substitution in the basket of goods by using geometric averages. Since Bishop Fleetwood, people measuring inflation had always used a fixed basket of goods, because they wanted to measure the value of money with respect to a fixed standard of living.

The authors of the Boskin Report thought that using geometric means would reduce the bias they reported in the measurement of inflation caused by substitution. As you will recall from chapter nine, geometric means are always less than arithmetic means (unless all the numbers making up the average are all equal, in which case the two means are the same). Critics charged that the whole purpose of the Boskin commission was to bring down reported inflation to protect the government from increasing social security payments to pensioners, veterans, and so on, because those are tied to inflation.[27]

The BLS provides a simple example.[28] Suppose a consumer buys four candy bars every week, two chocolate bars and two peanut bars, each for $1, for a total of $4. One year later the chocolate bars cost $4 each; the peanut bars remain $1 each. This consumer would have to spend $10 to buy the same candy bars. The Laspeyres index would calculate the increase as the ratio of $10 to $4, because it keeps the same proportions of each item in the basket. The Laspeyres calculation assumes that the consumer does not substitute chocolate bars for peanut bars when the price goes up. If they did, they could keep their weekly candy bar budget to $4 by buying only peanut bars. Thus $10 is an upper bound and $4 is a lower bound to the inflation the consumer experiences. With a geometric mean the weekly candy bar bill goes to $8. (The arithmetic and geometric weekly mean candy bar prices both start at $1 and increase to $2.50 and $2, respectively).

The BLS says that the objective of using geometric means is to calculate the "amount of money necessary to maintain a *constant* level of satisfaction" or constant standard of living. It says[29] that critics "erroneously assert" that it tracks a *declining* standard of living. The geometric means are only applied *within* narrow categories of products (such as candy bars), not *between* categories, such as candy bars and bread. Williams counters that after 2002 the weightings of the categories were changed every two years. Combined with geometric means, this turns the CPI into a "fully substitution-based index."[30] He contends that it is these methodological changes that cause people such as Dan Palmer to view inflation as being much higher than the officially reported numbers.

Figure 10.2 shows the annual change in the US CPI and core inflation rates from 1970 to 2006. Alongside these is the annual change in the "alternate CPI" produced by John Williams and published on his website Shadow Government Statistics.[31] Williams's Alternate CPI uses the methodology employed by the Bureau of Labor Statistics in the early 1980s, without any of the methodological changes that the Bureau introduced since then. The Alternate CPI is seen to be changing at an increasing rate as methodological changes are introduced, and as of 2006, at 10 percent annual increase, was almost 7 percent higher than the CPI.

The debate over the best way to measure inflation has been going on for three hundred years with no end in sight. Several important lessons can be drawn from that debate. First, when there is no clear definition of the measurement object, and particularly when the definition is constantly being revised to suit circumstances, suspicion is to be expected. Second, when there appears to be a motive for manipulating definitions and measurements, suspicion is almost guaranteed. Critics of official inflation statistics argue that this motive means there is a high probability the government

Figure 10.2   BLS Consumer Price Index versus John Williams's Alternate CPI.

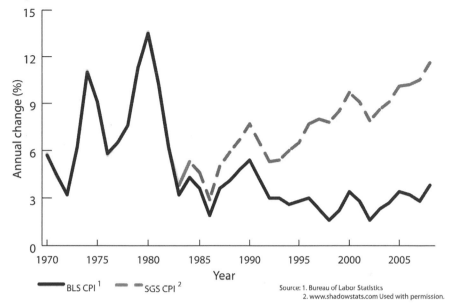

is misleading its citizens with its inflation measurements, because it will benefit financially from doing so. In such circumstances new measurements are unlikely to bring opposing views together; they are more likely to harden them into opposing camps.

The debate over measurements of inflation has remained civil. Even Williams says that he has been afforded a fair hearing. The debate over the measurement of global climatic temperature was far less civil.

THE CONTROVERSIES OVER MEASUREMENTS OF GLOBAL CLIMATIC TEMPERATURE

It is perhaps natural that the controversy over inflation measurements has remained civil. Many concepts in economics are nebulous compared to the hard sciences, leading inevitably to disagreements over definitions and numbers. The disagreements over the way to measure global climatic temperature have been characterized by deliberate attempts to destroy and/or protect the reputations of the scientists who take the measurements, so as to influence the probabilities that the public assigns to being misled.

The Climatic Research Unit at the University of East Anglia in England supplies global temperature measurements to the International Panel on

Climate Change (IPCC). When hacked emails from the CRU were re-leased, CRU scientists were accused of using "tricks" to hide a decline in temperature. Scientists whose findings ran contrary to the IPCC's were accused of being under the influence of the oil industry.

We saw in chapter three that it took centuries to find and standardize a way to measure temperature. This was done without having a precise defi-nition of what temperature was. We have a much more precise definition of temperature today. It is more difficult to define what we mean by global climatic temperature, as opposed to just temperature, yet I doubt that the definition is at the root of the controversy, as it is with measures of infla-tion. In chapter three we saw that temperature can only be precisely de-termined when a system, such as a pot of water, is in thermal equilibrium. When you crank up the heat on a cold pot of water, it very quickly goes out of equilibrium. The Earth's climate is not in equilibrium either; there are hot and cold parts and winds and ocean currents within and between them. But we can still use rougher definitions of temperature to measure whether pots of water or the climate are getting warmer or colder. After all, astronomers routinely measure the average temperatures of stars, and they are not in thermal equilibrium.

The source of the controversy has more to do with the difficulty of taking many, perhaps millions, of measurements and combining or averaging them somehow into a single stream of numbers, making inferences from these numbers about the global climatic temperature, and then proving through experience that the inferences from this stream of numbers are reasonable.

To see the difficulty, let's imagine an ideal situation on the imaginary planet Erg. Erg is nearly identical to Earth in geography and climate. Sev-eral thousand years ago Ergian scientists established a grid of temperature sensors across the surface of the planet. These sensors measured tempera-ture continuously every second since then. Every sensor is 100 feet away from its neighboring sensors, and 6 feet above the ground or water. They last thousands of years without needing to be changed, and are very ac-curate and precise.

Now, how do you average these temperatures?

In chapter nine we saw different ways of calculating an average of the stock market, and they all show different trends. We saw that there are many ways to calculate a class average, and each method produces differ-ent outcomes. So what is the right way to calculate the average tempera-ture of Erg's climate?

One Ergian scientist could point out that there are not an equal number of sensors in every square mile, when a square mile is seen from a bird's-eye view. There are fewer in flat square miles than hilly square miles, just like the contour lines on a map. This scientist might propose that averages should be calculated for square miles, and each square mile should be given equal weight. This means not every sensor gets equal weight in the overall average of square miles. Another Ergian scientist might point out that the air is less dense and has less heat capacity on the tops of mountains than at sea level. He might argue that a given temperature at high altitude represents less energy than the same temperature at sea level, and therefore sensors at high altitude should be given a smaller weight than sensors at sea level. The same argument could be used to give greater weights to measurements over water, because water has greater heat capacity than the ground.

Some Erg scientists might argue that the geometric mean is a better way to average the measurements than the arithmetic mean, because of its ability to dampen the effect of extreme values. I am sure the Ergian scientists, just like the physics teacher Rachel, would find many other ways to calculate an average Ergian temperature, all with plausible explanations. And it is quite possible that they would not always lead to the same inferences about the Ergian climatic temperature. How would the Ergian scientists know which is the best one to use? In extreme cases it would not matter. If Erg's sun were quickly warming up and baking the planet, all the different averages would go up. If its sun were dimming and losing energy, they would all go down. The problem is in the middle, when the solar energy fluctuates and the climate varies like the complex system it is.

We have seen many examples in this book of measurements or indicators that withstand the test of time. For example, the Apgar score has proven over several decades and millions of babies that it is an excellent indicator of neonatal health. This is the reality check in our four principles for reliable indicators.

The problem with the various averaging techniques for Ergian climate is that it is very hard to do a reality check when you only have one planet. There is no way to calibrate it either. We must rely on the intelligence, knowledge, reputation, and diligence of the Ergian scientists.

Earth scientists have the same problem. This was explained well by John P. Holdren. Holdren is a physicist and was a professor of environmental policy at Harvard before he became White House science advisor in the Obama administration. In an email exchange[32] with a journalist (released with the hacked CRU emails) about different contradictory scientific studies of global climatic temperature, he said that there were three ways to figure out who was right. First, if you had enough patience and scientific background, you could "penetrate the scientific arguments." Second, if

Figure 10.3   The four principles of measurement.

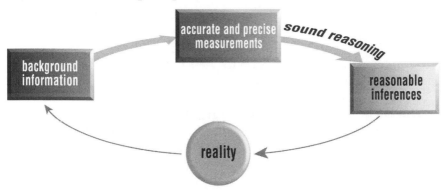

you did not have the patience and expertise, you could ask someone who does, "preferably somebody outside the handful of ideologically committed and/or oil-industry-linked professional climate-change skeptics." And third, if you could not use the other approaches, you could learn about the qualifications and reputations of the scientists making the claim, "at least to recognize that the odds strongly favor the proposition that the more experienced and reputable people are right."[33]

In other words, if you cannot judge the data and methods that back up a claim about climatic temperature, then assign a probability that you are being misled based on the reputation of the scientists who are making it. Unfortunately, the reverse of that principle has also been applied: attack a scientist's reputation to induce others to assign a high probability of being misled by him. Holdren did this indirectly when he referred to "ideologically committed and/or oil-industry-linked professional climate-change skeptics."

Of course none of these approaches amount to the sort of proof physicists usually require. A scientific argument is not proof, and as Holdren said in the same email, "It can be dangerous to assume that the more distinguished people are always right. Occasionally, it turns out that the opposite is true."

Earth scientists do not have the luxury of the intense temperature sensor grid available to our imaginary Ergian scientists. Instead they have scattered and unevenly distributed measurements of temperature that started at the beginning of the instrumental record, which was in the mid-19th century. Before that, there are no measurements of temperature. Of course 150 years or so of data is not enough to establish whether the globe is the warmest it has ever been in the last thousand or so years. So scientists are forced to measure other things that are thought to be strongly correlated with temperature, and then use them to make a reasonable inference about the ancient global climatic temperature. There are thus two types of global climatic temperature measurements: the instrumental record and the paleoclimate record.

THE CONTROVERSY OVER THE INSTRUMENTAL TEMPERATURE RECORD

By around 1850, after Kelvin had proposed the Kelvin temperature scale that is still in use today, people were systematically taking and recording temperature measurements in more and more places around the globe. We have records from about 110 locations, on land, around the world, that reported monthly average temperatures for the full year in 1850.[34] By the turn of the century, there were about ten times as many, and the number of stations continued to grow throughout the 20th century, reaching a peak of about 4,000 in 1970, and declining thereafter to about 1,000 today. We also have about 26,000 records of individual water temperature measurements from the sea surface taken by ships at sea in 1850. By the turn of the century that number had risen to 166,000 individual sea surface temperature recordings every year, and about 1.2 million today. This is the instrumental temperature record.

The main repository of the record is at the Climatic Research Unit (CRU) at the University of East Anglia in England. There, a group scientists, led by Professor Phil Jones, assemble and crunch the numbers to determine the global temperature "anomaly," which is used by the IPCC to report the global climatic temperature.

The CRU scientists divide the globe into grid boxes 5° of latitude high and 5° of longitude wide. Moving from the Greenwich Meridian at 0°, around the world and back, there are seventy-two bands 5° wide. From the North Pole to the South Pole, there are thirty-six bands 5° tall. In total, there are thus 2,592 grid boxes. At the equator, one of these grids is about 345 miles (550 km) on each side. As you near the poles, the grids are much smaller as the lines of longitude become closer and closer.

Jones and his group calculated the average monthly temperature in each of these grid boxes, for January to December, over the period from 1961 to 1990. This period they call the "normal period." They then calculated the anomalies by subtracting the normal values from the monthly temperature means. This they repeat for the entire instrumental record, for every grid box and every month of every year. Then they average the numbers. The results[35] are shown in Figure 10.4.

Figure 10.4   Monthly global temperature anomaly.

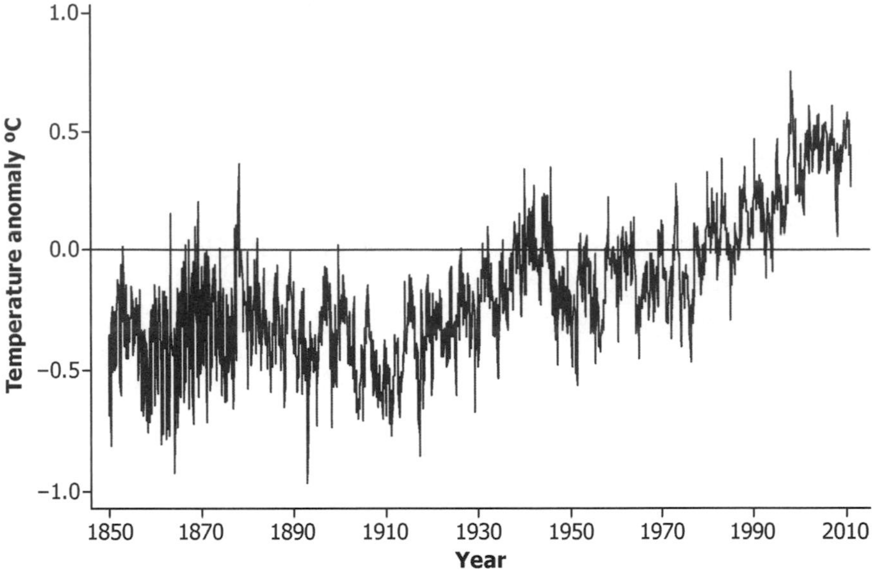

Source: Brohan et al., "Uncertainty Estimates."

The IPCC uses the chart from the Climatic Research Unit in its assessment reports. The 2007 report, of which Jones is one of the authors, says that "warming of the climate system is unequivocal, as is now evident from observations of increases in global average air and ocean temperatures," and that there was "very high confidence that the global average net effect of human activities since 1750 has been one of warming."[36]

THE CHALLENGE OF CALCULATING GLOBAL AVERAGE TEMPERATURE

Earthling scientists have a far more challenging task than their imaginary Ergian counterparts. They have to devise ways to correct for changing instruments, changing global coverage, changing mixes of sea and land temperatures, changing techniques, and heat island effects. Nonetheless, with millions of measurements, global coverage, consistently rising temperatures, and many reputable scientists, the IPCC says that the case is pretty well closed—the earth is warming.

The grid boxes get smaller as you move from the equator to the poles. To counteract this effect, Jones's group weights the anomalies according to their approximate surface area as a fraction of the surface of the globe.

The Climatic Research Unit scientists have attempted to quantify the uncertainties in the temperature anomalies—as in accuracy and precision, which we reviewed in chapter three. The problem is that a "definitive assessment of uncertainties is impossible,"[37] according to Phil Jones and Philip Brohan, in a joint study with their colleagues from the UK Met Office.

An important source of uncertainty comes from the thousands of thermometers that measured, and continue to measure, air and sea surface temperatures around the world. The thermometers used to make up the instrumental record were not all equal, as they were on Erg. They included instruments ranging from ship-borne thermometers in square-riggers in the 1850s, to the sophisticated devices in a modern meteorological station. They all make some errors of measurement, big or small. These measurement errors were not studied and recorded for use by today's climate scientists.

Many of the people who recorded temperatures over the years made adjustments to their records, either decreasing or increasing the recorded temperatures by a small amount. Suppose, for example, that a meteorological office decided to move one of its temperature reporting stations from the city, where it had been reporting temperatures for forty years, to an airport on the outskirts of the city, where it was cooler. The resulting temperature record would show a cooling. To correct this, they would subtract a small adjustment from the first forty years of the record so it more closely matched the new airport measurements. Adjustments could also be made for changing the time of day at which the temperature was measured, say from morning, when it is cool, to noon, when it is warm. And they could be made when the thermometer was replaced, if the old and new thermometers did not match. For most land-based thermometers, the amount of these adjustments, or even whether they were made, is unknown. For some, however, records were kept, and after analyzing these records, Jones and Brohan hypothesized that two-thirds of the adjustments were within 0.75°C.

There is much missing data in the instrumental record. This does not mean that temperature was recorded and the records lost, but that there are vast swaths of the planet where, at certain times, nobody measured the temperature. As the instrumental record grew, the percentage of grid boxes that had temperature measurements grew from around 20 percent in 1850 to more than 80 percent by 2010. You cannot calculate an average monthly temperature for a 5° by 5° grid if nobody took the temperature in that grid during that month. As Brohan and Jones put it (presumably without intending sarcasm), "In general, global and regional area-averages will have an additional source of uncertainty caused by missing data."

There are also a number of sources of bias in the measurements. One of the most important is the so-called urbanization effect: cities are warmer than the countryside. As cities have grown and sprawled since the beginning of the instrumental record, part of the measured increase in temperature is caused by cities replacing countryside. To correct for the urbanization bias you must try and get some idea of how big it is first. To do that you must measure it.

Brohan and Jones did not have the data necessary to make adjustments for urbanization for all their land stations, so they made a correction of 0.0055°C per decade for their entire data set.

Over the years meteorologists changed the enclosures that hold thermometers. This has added to the uncertainty. Thermometers that are used to report meteorological data are enclosed so that they are sheltered from the sun's rays. Since 1850, the design of these thermometer enclosures has changed. Whenever the enclosure is changed at a station, the temperature readings are biased up or down, by as much as 0.2°C. The problem is that there are few records that indicate when the enclosures were changed. Brohan and Jones thus adjusted all data "allowing for the simultaneous replacement across entire countries" from one type of enclosure to another.

The sea-surface temperatures present another set of problems and biases. Climate scientists blend water temperature measurements from sea with air temperature measurements from land, making "an implicit assumption that sea-surface temperature anomalies provide a good surrogate for marine air temperature anomalies."[38]

Over the years, the mariners switched from throwing wooden buckets over the edge to canvas buckets, and then rubber buckets, metal buckets, and other devices such as a leather and metal sampler the Germans used. Wooden and rubber buckets insulate the water more than canvas buckets, so the air temperature will have a greater effect, either heating or cooling, on the water in a canvas bucket. The speed of a ship with a bucket sitting on its deck affects the rate of heating or cooling of the water in the bucket because of the wind speed on deck. The difference is not insignificant, and can be seen by comparing a fast ship, going, say, 25 kilometers per hour or more and a slower ship going 14 kilometers per hour.[39] Experiments on ships in the tropical North Atlantic showed that a bucket can cool by as much as 1°C in ten minutes.[40]

To make a bias "correction" for the type of buckets sailors used, and the resulting bias in the measurement of the temperature of the sea, you have to know what types of bucket they were, how fast the ships were sailing, and how much heat is lost depending on the wind, the type of bucket, and the weather.

The problem is that usually sea surface temperature measurements are not accompanied by information on the speed of the ship or the type of the bucket. The British logbooks did not record the type of bucket, and Dutch records were destroyed in World War II.[41] To make up for the missing information, climate researchers use a variety of sources to estimate the proportion of each type of bucket and the proportion of fast and slow ships. They put it rather tersely when they said, "The choice of final corrections presents some difficulty." They decided to add a bucket correction that increased progressively from 0.11°C in 1856 to 0.42°C in 1941, and then fell abruptly to zero. After December 1941, they made no corrections at all, making an explicit assumption that bucket use rapidly dropped off. (Other research[42] showed that even by 1990, the end of the normal period, approximately a quarter of sea surface temperature measurements were still from buckets. Mariners had continued to use them for several more decades.)

In December 1941 there was a sudden increase in average sea surface temperature anomalies, of about 0.5°C, when the United States entered World War II. The US Navy switched to measuring sea surface temperatures from the engine intake water to avoid enemy detection.[43]

Eventually, more shipbuilders started putting thermometers in the engine intake water, which of course comes from deeper down than a bucket can go. In a bulk carrier, the intake water is 10 meters down, and in a passenger ship it is 4 meters down.[44] More recently, shipbuilders have installed sensors into the hulls of ships. Nonetheless, because of the warmth of the engines, some researchers found that the engine intake water is "systematically warmer" by "several tenths of a degree centigrade" than sea surface temperatures "measured using uninsulated buckets."[45]

In the late 1990s scientists from around the world began to discuss the need for better coverage of temperature and other data from the oceans. They conceived a program: a global array of buoys drifting through the oceans, transmitting their data to a satellite. They called the program "Argo," after the ancient Greek ship in which Jason sailed to capture the Golden Fleece, and the satellite "Jason." The first buoys were launched in 2001, and by 2007 the twenty-three nations cooperating in the program had achieved their goal of a global array of three thousand Argo buoys. The Argo program had three main impacts. It caused a huge increase in the number of sea temperature measurements. Measurements made by buoys are about 0.1° to 0.2°C cooler than measurements made by ships.[46] The buoys also changed the global coverage of sea surface temperature measurements. The routes ships have followed since the beginning of the instrumental record changed over time: most of the earliest records are dominated by sea routes from Europe, south through the Atlantic, and around the Cape of Good Hope to Asia. When the Suez and Panama Canals opened, entirely new sea routes opened. The buoys now measure the temperature continuously on a global grid.

As the number of sea temperature measurements increased, the opposite happened on land. This was caused by the collapse of the former USSR and a reduction in the number of US stations that report.[47] Even with the drop in US stations, there are still more stations reporting from the United States than from anywhere else.

AN ALTERNATE WAY TO AVERAGE THE INSTRUMENTAL TEMPERATURE RECORD

The IPCC's average temperature data doesn't jive with that of Vincent Courtillot, a French geomagneticist, director of the Institut de Physique du Globe in Paris and a former scientific advisor to the French Cabinet.

Figure 10.5   Number of land and sea temperature measurements.

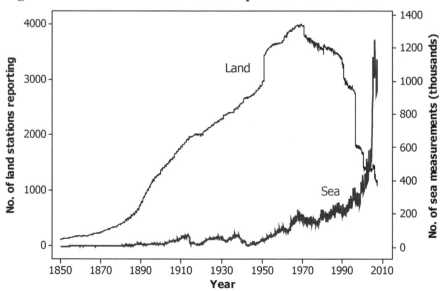

Source: Brohan et al., "Uncertainty Estimates."

Courtillot is the recipient of many French and International awards and honors, the author of dozens of scientific publications, and formerly a scientific advisor to the French cabinet. Courtillot has a very good reputation as a scientist.

Courtillot and Jean-Louis Le Mouël, another French geomagneticist, and three Russian colleagues first came into climate research as outsiders in 2005. The Earth's magnetic field responds to changes in solar output, so geomagnetic measurements are good indicators of solar activity. They thought it would be interesting to compare solar activity with climatic temperature measurements.

Their first step was to assemble a database of temperature measurements and plot temperature charts. To do that, they needed the raw temperature measurements that had not been averaged or adjusted in any way. The Climatic Research Unit provides its monthly mean data for each 5° grid, from 1850 to the most recent month, on its website. The data can be freely downloaded.

Courtillot asked Phil Jones, the scientist who runs the CRU database, for his raw data, telling him (according to one of the hacked emails), "There may be some quite important information in the daily values which is likely lost on monthly averaging." Jones refused Courtillot's request for data.[48] Generally in scientific research, scientists share their data so that others can verify their work.

Courtillot and his colleagues were forced to turn to other sources of temperature measurements. They found forty-four European weather stations that had long series of daily minimum temperatures that covered most of the 20th century, with few or no gaps. They removed annual seasonal trends for each series with a three-year running average of daily minimum temperatures. Finally they averaged all the European series for each day of the 20th century.

In 2008 he and three colleagues plotted an average temperature chart for Europe that shows a surprisingly different trend from that claimed by the CRU.[49] Aside from a very cold spell in 1940, the temperature was more or less flat for most of the 20th century, showing no warming while fossil fuel use grew. Then in 1987 it shot up by about 1°C and did not show any warming afterward (Figure 10.6).

Courtillot and his colleagues calculated temperature averages for the United States, which showed similar results. The warmest period was in 1930, slightly above the temperatures at the end of the 20th century. This was followed by thirty years of cooling, then another thirty years of warming (Figure 10.7).

Figure 10.6   European temperature average calculated by Courtillot and his colleagues.

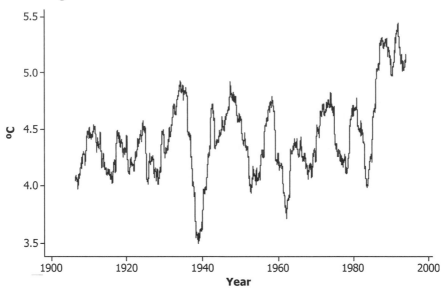

Source: Le Mouël et al., "Evidence for Solar Signature."

In their resulting article[50] they said the "USA and the European mean curves are rather different from the corresponding curves illustrated in the 2007 IPCC report." Their article also reported on a comparison of the disturbances in temperature, and compared them to a number of indicators of the sun, such as sun spots and magnetic fields. Their comparison showed reasonable correlations between the temperature disturbances with the solar indicators. They concluded that this was evidence that the sun was a significant factor in the temperature patterns that they observed and "should be a global feature."

We thus have two claims, as I referred to them at the beginning of this chapter, about global climatic temperature in the 20th century. The IPCC says that warming is unequivocal and most likely caused by humans. Courtillot and his colleagues said that when temperature averages were calculated differently the results were rather different than the IPCC, and that the sun may be playing a role in driving climate change.

The response to the article by Courtillot and his colleagues was a swift attack on his reputation. Raymond Pierrehumbert, a geoscientist at the University of Chicago and IPCC author, posted an article on the blog *Realclimate.org* attacking Courtillot, saying that Courtillot's articles "cross the line from the merely erroneous into the actively deceptive."[51] Based on this

Figure 10.7   North American temperature average calculated by Courtillot and his colleagues.

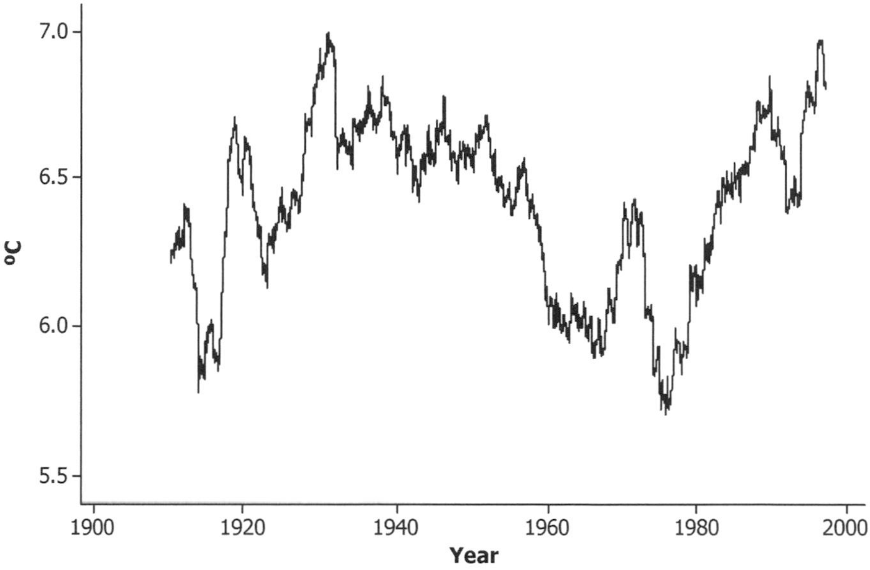

Source: Le Mouël et al., "Evidence for Solar Signature."

post there were simultaneous articles in three French daily newspapers[52] that called him a "climate skeptic" and suggested he may have been deliberately fraudulent. Courtillot was forced to defend himself in front of colleagues, his institute, the president of the *Centre National de la Recherche Scientifique*, and at the first meeting in 2008 of the *Académie des Sciences*[53] after the accusations were made. Courtillot called it a series of "lies and slandering"[54] and a campaign of defamation. (He and his colleagues subsequently published more papers with stronger conclusions.[55]) The accusation of deception and fraud was a direct attack on Courtillot's reputation.

Courtillot and his colleagues reported that they had measured the global climatic temperature a new way, and found that the planet's temperature was *not* changing in a way consistent with human influence. The new information received by the public and the broad scientific community was not as follows:

> Professor Courtillot has conducted a careful scientific analysis, using great caution to prevent errors. The global temperature is not changing the way the IPCC says it is, and the change is consistent with solar influence.

The new information was instead:

> Professor Courtillot *claims* that he has conducted a careful scientific analysis, using great caution to prevent errors, and says this shows that the global temperature is not changing the way the IPCC says it is, and the change is consistent with solar influence.

Different people have different background information about Courtillot. Upon this background information they base the probability they assign to being misled by Professor Courtillot. And for this reason, the initial attacks on Courtillot appear to have been intended to impugn his reputation so that people would assign a high probability that they were being misled.

Likewise, the information from Professor Jones and other IPCC scientists was:

> The IPCC scientists *claim* they have carefully analyzed millions of temperature measurements, and found that the climate is unequivocally warming because of human influence.

THE CONTROVERSY OVER THE PALEOTEMPERATURE RECORD

In April 1998, Michael Mann, Raymond Bradley, and Malcolm Hughes published an article in the prestigious journal *Nature*[56] that showed global temperatures for the previous six centuries—going back farther than the instrumental record, before either thermometers or a calibration scale for temperature had been invented, and before Santorio Santorio first quantified temperature in 1612. The graph became known as the "hockey stick," because it looked like a hockey stick laid down on its side with the blade pointing up to the right, the blade representing the recent increase in temperatures.

Mann and his colleagues claimed that "Northern Hemisphere mean annual temperatures for three of the past eight years are warmer than any other year since (at least) AD 1400," a statement that galvanized concern over the very future of the planet from around the globe. A year later, they published another paper[57] in the journal *Geophysical Research Letters* that extended the hockey stick back another four hundred years, to AD 1000.

In 2001, the International Panel on Climate Change published its third assessment report on climate change.[58] The report prominently featured the second graph that Mann and his colleagues had produced. Within a few years the hockey stick had become an iconic symbol[59] of the apparently dangerously warming planet.

For a long time, scientists had used information contained in the growth rings of trees, corals, the layers in sediments, and other things with annual patterns that are laid down and preserved with time, to study climate variability.

Scientists call the data from the trees, corals, ice, and similar annually changing things "proxies" for climate. Mann and his coworkers made a bold new claim: that they could use these proxies to actually reconstruct past temperatures from years before thermometers were even invented or were in common use. To do this they developed a way to combine the proxies into a new, smaller, set of numbers. They then compared these new numbers with measurements of temperature during the period of about 150 years when the proxies and the thermometer measurements overlapped. This period they called the training period. They used the results of the comparison to estimate the temperature before the training period. They likened their method to a calibration of the proxies. With their calibrated proxies they could read the temperature in the past, they claimed.

A tree grows more when it gets lots of water and sunlight. Its leaves suck up the carbon dioxide from the air, and when they are struck by sunlight, turn it into sugars and other molecules that form the building blocks of the wood. When conditions are good, the tree lays down more wood and the rings are larger. When they are poor, the rings are smaller. The child looking at the rings on a tree stump can thus tell the good years and the bad. The rings measure the quality of the growing conditions of one year relative to other years.

Ice cores contain clues to past climate in the ratios of isotopes of oxygen and other common atmospheric atoms. Isotopes are versions of atoms with slightly different weights.

Atmospheric processes, such as changes in temperature, tend to separate the two isotopes slightly, so that the ratio between them changes depending on the conditions. By taking ice cores from glaciers in Antarctica, Greenland, and mountains around the world, scientists can determine when the climate warmed and cooled, based on the layers of annual snowfall and the ratios of the isotopes.

Mann and his colleagues also used measurements from coral. Corals produce annual bands of calcium carbonate mineral. The ratio of oxygen isotopes changes when the water temperature changes. The oxygen isotope ratio of coral from the open ocean can thus be used to create a measure of changes in ocean temperature and salinity.[60]

Mann and his coworkers developed what they called a "new statistical approach reconstructing global patterns of annual temperature."[61] The difficulty they were trying to overcome was to calibrate the global information in the proxies to global temperature measurements from thermometers. By doing so, they hoped, they could read the global mean temperature in the past.

Calibration procedures for measurement instruments make minimal—if any—use of statistics because the calibration is direct and physical, such as placing a thermometer in ice water to find zero degrees centigrade, and in boiling water to find 100 degrees; or placing a known one-kilogram weight on a scale to find the one-kilo mark. Mann and his coworkers were trying to calibrate a century and a half of measurements from more than one hundred proxies from the training period. They used a statistical technique known as "principal component analysis" to combine these into the smaller set of numbers.

They used statistical techniques to fit a linear relationship between the principal components for the instrumental temperature record, and the new principal components for the proxies over the training period from 1902 to 1980. In essence, they were calibrating the principal components of their basket of proxies to the principal components of millions of temperature measurements. Figures 3.7 to 3.10 in chapter three demonstrate the basic concept for finding this relationship, where the measured temperatures are the standard and the proxies are the measured values.

Once they had established a linear relationship between the instrumental record and the proxies, they used the equations to back-calculate the mean temperature in the Northern Hemisphere from 1400 to the start of the training period. They then tacked the mean temperature that they calculated from the instrumental record on to the end. The graph (Figure 10.8) showed variable but relatively flat temperatures for most of that (blended) period, and a rapid increase in temperature during the second half of the 20th century.

Two years after the hockey stick graph appeared in the International Panel on Climate Change 2001 report, five American scientists, led by Willie Soon and Sallie Baliunas,[62] published a paper that reappraised the methods used to reconstruct past climate. They started their paper with a review of historical evidence of two prominent past climatic events, the Medieval Warm Period, which occurred roughly between AD 800 and 1300, and the Little Ice Age, which occurred roughly between AD 1300 and 1900. These events were known from the documentary record, from such things as books and paintings, and from other scientific studies.[63] In 1990, in its First Assessment Report, the International Panel on Climate Change had published a graph that showed these periods. It dropped it

Figure 10.8   Hockey stick temperature proxy reconstruction and instrumental record.

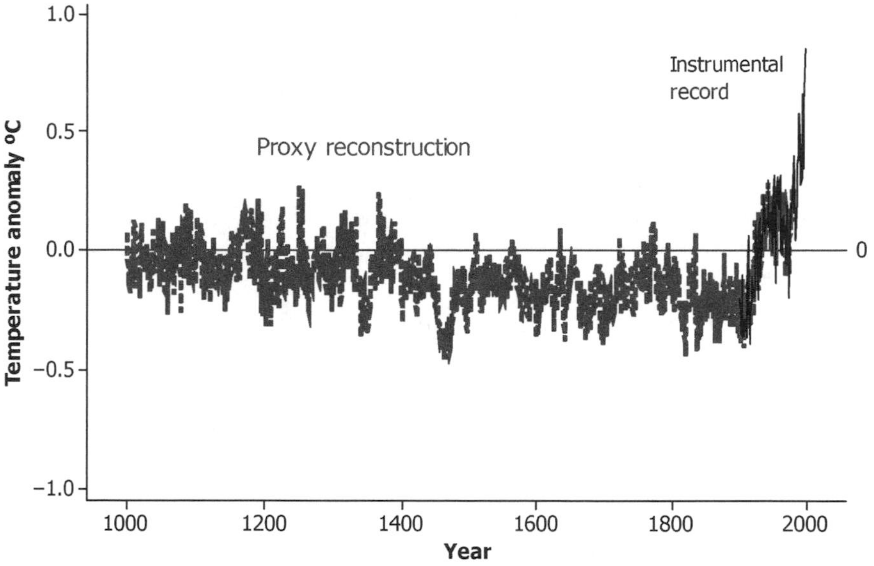

Source: Mann, Bradley, and Hughes, "Northern Hemisphere."

after that, and in its 2001 report, featured Mann's hockey stick graph instead. The Medieval Warm period would have been roughly at its warmest around the year 1000—the year that Mann's reconstruction started. Neither the Medieval Warm period nor the pronounced cold temperatures of the Little Ice Age were discernible on the hockey stick, which was fairly straight except for the blade.

Soon and Baliunas and their colleagues took an entirely different approach to examining past climate. They called Mann's work "mainly a mathematical construct." Rather than trying to calibrate a basket of global proxies against global temperatures measurements by using a novel but obscure statistical procedure, they selected more than one hundred proxies with at least five hundred years of data that various other researchers had created and analyzed. Each researcher had calibrated their proxy to temperature using local information for that proxy. They thus had a separate calibration for each proxy. They reviewed the analyses conducted by the original researchers, but did not blend them into a single data stream. They dubbed their work a "non-quantitative and very 'low-tech' study." The graphical displays Soon and his team developed preserved much of the structure of the original data, rather than trying to create an indicator that blended it. The graphs displayed boxes superimposed on a map of the globe. The size of the boxes indicated the strength of the answer to the questions as to whether there were discernible climate anomalies during the Little Ice Age, the Medieval Warm Period, and the 20th century that was the warmest.

They concluded that the "Medieval Warm Period and Little Ice Age are widespread climatic anomalies" and that the "20th Century does not contain the warmest or most extreme anomaly of the past millennium in most of the proxy records."

Their approach was similar in many respects to Winston Churchill's graphs showing the state of readiness of the home defenses against German invasion. Rather than trying to calculate an overall readiness number, which hid important structural information in the measurements, they maintained the basic structure of the data in the chart.

The premise of Soon and his team was that local temperature trends differ significantly: it can be getting warmer in one part of the planet while

Figure 10.9   One of the Soon and Baliunas's graphs, this one regarding the Little Ice Age. The chart answers the question, "Is there an objectively discernible climatic anomaly during the Little Ice Age (1300–1800 AD) in this proxy record?"

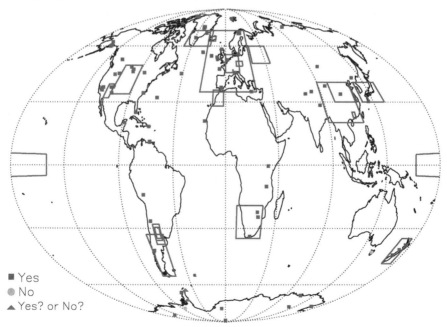

■ Yes
● No
▲ Yes? or No?

Source: Soon et al., 2003, "Reconstructing Climatic and Environmental Changes."

it is cooling in another. When you blend two temperature streams, you cancel out many of these opposing trends. Therefore proxies should be calibrated locally, and not against a mathematical composite of global temperatures, and analyzed individually. Furthermore, tree rings and glaciers are not thermometers, and respond to many climate signals, including wetness or dryness.

It did not take long for their paper to become known to mainstream journalists. A few weeks after it appeared, in an article in the *Seattle Post Intelligencer,*[64] Jeff Nesmith described the authors as tools of the oil and coal industry who were deploying a strategy to attack the credibility of climate science and create an impression that scientists were deeply divided on the issue. Nesmith quoted one critic: "The contradictory statements of a tiny handful of discredited scientists, funded by big oil and big coal, represent a deliberate—and extremely reckless—campaign of deception and disinformation."

The five smeared scientists were from the Harvard-Smithsonian Center for Astrophysics, Mount Wilson Observatory, the Center for Climatic Research at the University of Delaware, and the Center for the Study of Carbon Dioxide and Global Change. Their funding had come from three US government sources, including the National Oceanic and Atmospheric Administration, and from the American Petroleum Institute. Nowhere in Nesmith's article was there any criticism of their scientific method or conclusions, nor acknowledgement of the government funding they received.

In July, Mann and twelve other scientists, including Bradley, Hughes, and Jones, shot back[65] at the paper by Soon and Baliunas in a commentary in the journal *EOS.* They stated that the claim of Soon and Baliunas was "inconsistent with the preponderance of scientific evidence." They claimed there were three fundamental problems with their methodology. First, they claimed that the way Soon and Baliunas defined warm anomalies might have been wet or dry anomalies instead. Second they claimed that by looking at large time intervals, such as those wide enough to capture the Medieval Warm period and the Little Ice Age, Soon and Baliunas might only be showing the natural flow back and forth or warmth from one part of the planet to another. And finally, they attacked the low-tech approach, saying that it is essential that temperatures be "quantitatively compared." They finished by stating that while healthy debate about the "details of past climate change exists," the conclusion that the late 20th century was the warmest of the millennium was the "robust consensus view." They also allowed that "it remains a challenge to reduce uncertainties and properly synthesize global means."

Later that summer, Senator James Inhofe, R-Oklahoma, chair of the Senate Environment and Public Works Committee, asked Soon, Baliunas, and Mann to testify at a hearing of the committee. Dr. Soon testified that proxy records used in hundreds of climate studies have a high degree of uncertainty and that local and regional climatic shifts such as the Medieval Warm Period or the Little Ice Age are more important than average global temperatures. In an answer to Senator James Jefford at the hearing, Soon said that "the quality of knowledge about climate science or any other subject of interest must be judged on its own merits, and does not and must not be determined by invoking the amount of formal schooling or consensus viewpoints."

At the hearing, Dr. Mann dismissed Dr. Soon's findings, criticizing him for failing to assess global temperatures. Mann also criticized the editor of the journal for publishing Soon's paper, claiming he "frequently publishes [opinion] pieces in newspapers attacking the International Panel on Climate Change."[66]

Shortly after the hearing, one of Soon's coauthors, David Legates, came to the defense of Soon and Baliunas in an article in the *Washington Times*.[67] He claimed they were victims of a "vicious campaign behind the scenes to smear two leading scientists" and others associated with their paper. He said that if this had remained "merely a disagreement about science and research methods" there would not be much of an issue. Instead, he said, it turned into a "scientific lynching."

Clare Goodess and Hans von Storch were two of ten editors of the journal *Climate Research*, which published one of the versions of Soon and Baliunas's paper. When it came out, they received "numerous unsolicited complaints and critiques of the paper from many leading members of the international paleo- and historical climatology community."[68] They raised their concerns with the editor who had approved the Soon and Baliunas paper, Chris de Freitas, who in turn accused them of "a mix of a witch-hunt and the Spanish Inquisition." Von Storch wanted to publish an editorial on the review process leading to publication of the paper. The publisher replied that all ten editors would have to agree on the content of the editorial. Some of the editors did not see a problem with the paper by Soon and Baliunas, nor with the review process, and would not agree to an editorial that put its credibility in doubt. On the day that Senator Inhofe began his hearings, half the journal's editors, including von Storch and Goodess, resigned in protest.

Soon, Baliunas and Legates[69] published an article to defend their research. Mann and twelve others responded alongside it, accusing them of "promoting myths" and using language such as "straw man arguments" and the "ill-conceived, largely subjective approach" of Soon and Baliunas. In response, Soon said of these remarks, "Mann et al.'s last words were another sad attempt to smear and confuse the public."[70]

"CLIMATEGATE" AND THE ATTACKS ON IPCC SCIENTISTS

On November 17, 2009 a computer hacker broke into the computers at the CRU and retrieved thousands of emails, which were subsequently posted on the Internet and shortly after in the media. Many of them gave the impression that researchers were trying to show that the temperature was increasing. One email advised against selecting a different period for the normals (1961–1990), saying "anomalies will seem less positive than before if we change to newer normals, so the impression of global warming will be muted."[71] Another from Phil Jones said that "I've just completed Mike's Nature trick of adding in the real temps to each series for the last 20 years (i.e., from 1981 onwards) amd [sic] from 1961 for Keith's to hide the decline."[72]

Within days leading scientists who had contributed to the IPCC reports were attacked. For example, Eduardo Zorita, a climate scientist at a German research institute, said that Phil Jones and Michael Mann should be "barred from the IPCC process" because any assessments in which they took part would no longer be credible. The emails, he said, showed climate science was "full of machination, conspiracies, and collusion" and showed "very troubling professional behavior."[73] Patrick Michaels, a climatologist at the Cato Institute, was accused in the emails of engaging "in vicious public attacks on the reputations of individual scientists." In response he wrote[74] that the release of emails comes "to resemble Watergate" and that "this is not a smoking gun; this is a mushroom cloud." British politician Lord Lawson said the "reputation of British science has been seriously tarnished." One of the scientists who were attacked said[75] Michaels was engaging in "vicious public attacks on the reputation of individual scientists" because he wanted to "influence opinion."

Shortly afterward, there were a number of inquiries and reviews on the work of the CRU, which quotes some of their conclusions on its website. They defend the reputations of the CRU scientists: "The scientific reputation of Professor Jones and CRU remains intact," from the House of Commons Science and Technology Committee. The US Environmental Protection is also quoted: "Careful examination of the emails and their full context shows that the petitioners' claims are exaggerated and are not a material or reliable basis to question the validity and credibility of the body of [climate] science."

REPUTATIONS CAN MATTER AS MUCH AS MEASUREMENTS

I started this chapter by asking whether measurements can resolve opposing views or controversial claims. They can do so only in two circumstances. The first is when the reputation of the person making the claim is irrelevant because other evidence can be sought and weighed. This is the way research in the hard sciences such as physics and chemistry is done. The second is when the reputation of the person making the claim is beyond reproach. In any other circumstances, reputation matters, because it is used to assess the credibility of the claim. It is a natural, if unfortunate, aspect of any controversy that some people attack their opponent's reputation to improve the credibility of their own claims.

Gallup, a polling firm, does an annual survey to measure the public's opinion about global warming. One of the questions they ask is whether people think the seriousness of global warming is exaggerated. Between 2005 and 2009 (before the hacked emails), about one-third of Americans said it was. In 2010, that shot up to almost half of Americans. One of the possible reasons Gallup gave for the increase was "controversies over the integrity of the data."

The credibility of measurements depends on reputation in business life as much as it does in society at large. It is necessary but not enough to have careful analytical procedures. It is equally important to air and resolve any concerns about the persons using them.

TOOL BOX

- The more a measurement is free from personal influences such as reputation, the better it is.
- Do you trust measurements because you trust the process by which or the persons by whom they were obtained? In the latter case, don't be surprised if some people mistrust the measurements because they do not trust those persons, and if the measurements polarize people into opposing camps.

- You must first resolve concerns about reputation before resolving controversies or doubts that arise over claims that are based on measurements
- Whenever an average or index number is used, remember that there may be many possible and often contradictory ways to construct it. The reputation of the person who constructs it does not make it right or wrong. It must be proven through experience.

ELEVEN

Misleading Ourselves with Measurements of Risk

I, at any rate, am convinced that He does not throw dice.

—Albert Einstein (1879–1955)

On the east bank of the East River, opposite the economically depressed town of Stellarton, Pictou County, Nova Scotia, lies the abandoned site of the Westray coal mine. All that is left today is a large field, surrounded by rolling farms and scrubby forest, a few miles south of the Northumberland Strait in the Gulf of St. Lawrence.

On April 9, 1992, the Canadian Institute of Mining, Metallurgy, and Petroleum awarded the Westray Mine the coveted John T. Ryan Award. The institute grants the award every year to the mine that had the lowest accident frequency during the previous calendar year in all of Canada. Westray had won for being the safest coal mine in Canada in 1991. This award assumes, falsely as it will be shown, that the mine with the lowest accident frequency is the safest.

On May 9, 1992, the mine exploded, killing twenty-six miners. Why did it explode despite having a statistical record as the safest mine? The tragic explosion graphically illustrates the misleading nature of measurements that are claimed to measure risk.

Throughout this book I have emphasized the critical importance of background information when using measurements. When it comes to risk, there is a twist: the measurements are part of the background information. To illustrate this I have reconstructed the events leading to the

Westray mine explosion based on the testimony at the judicial enquiry run by Justice Peter Richards that followed.

The mine was one of eight that, over two hundred years, had mined coal from the rich Foord seam. The Foord is low in sulfur but high in explosive methane gas. Local historian James Cameron reckons that 576 miners were killed between 1866 and 1972 in Pictou County,[1] many of them on the Foord seam. In 1873, Henry S. Poole, Inspector of Mines, in the Annual Report of the Nova Scotia Department of Mines, wrote that the Foord seam was especially dangerous "on account of the liability of cutting heavy feeders of gas."[2]

"Continuous miners" are gigantic earth-eating machines, with a drum of spinning teeth—which the miners call heads—15 feet wide, each head about a foot long, that chew into the coal face and spew coal backward to be brought to the surface by shuttle cars.

On Wednesday, May 6, Wayne Cheverie, an industrial mechanic at Westray, was working underground.[3] He noticed that the coal face was "gassing out." The day after, on Thursday, May 7, Cheverie took the day off for some personal business in Halifax, the capital of Nova Scotia, about a two-hour drive away.

While he was away, toward the end of the day, a rock fell on the continuous miner and sheared off a vital cable on the methanometer. The built-in safety device immediately shut down the continuous miner, stopping production. Arnie Smith, the fire boss, asked Mick Franks, an industrial electrician and one of Wayne's coworkers, to fix it. Mick fixed the obviously damaged cable but could still not get the methanometer to work. The safety device would not let the continuous miner start.

"Well, can you jump it out?" Arnie asked. "I'll give Buddy the handheld."

Jumping it out would defeat the safety shut-off so that the continuous miner could continue to cut coal, even in the presence of high methane levels. Arnie was proposing that Buddy, the operator that day, would use the handheld methanometer to measure methane levels, and would shut down the miner himself if they went too high. Mick reluctantly jumped out the methanometer. When his shift was finished, he went to the surface. Before he left, he wrote in big bold letters on his tradesman's report, "No methanometer on the miner," and told the electrician taking over the shift that it needed to be fixed immediately.

The methanometer was fixed to the continuous miner to measure methane concentrations in the air around it. When methane reaches a concentration in air of 1.25 percent or more it can explode. The methanometer was designed to shut off the spinning heads before the gas seeping from the coal face got to a high enough concentration in the air around the heads to ignite.

On the morning of Friday, May 8, Wayne Cheverie returned to the mine. He soon met Mick walking up Southwest 2-A Road, deep underground.

Minutes before, Mick had found out from one of the underground workers that the methanometer had not been fixed during the night shift. Mick had promptly challenged his supervisor, who told him, "Don't worry about the methanometer on the miner, just get underground and assist Andrew with tramming the machines into the North Mains."

Wayne could tell from Mick's demeanor that he was quite upset. "What's the matter?" Wayne asked him.

"The continuous miner working in our section is cutting coal with no methanometer working on it," Mick replied, in a manner that confirmed Wayne's impression.

Wayne became, in his own words, "quite irate and scared at the same time." He knew that they had been gassing out the day before, and if those conditions were the same, then the miner would not kick itself out and they were putting themselves in grave danger.

Wayne promptly sought out and found Arnie Smith.

"I'm sick and tired of having safety Number Two at Westray," he said, implying that production was Number One. Arnie responded that they had four more shuttle cars to fill with coal before they could pull the miner.

"That's bullshit," Wayne retorted. "If you send it back into another cut without repairing the methanometer, I'm going to leave the mine. And I'm going to the Department of Mines, to the mine's inspector, and then to The Evening News."

"If you leave the mine, Wayne, you're fired," Arnie said.

"Fired or dead, that's not much of a choice, is it?" Wayne replied.

"You won't have a leg to stand on, Wayne. According to the Coal Mines Regulation Act, there's no methanometer required on the miner—you'll get yourself fired for nothing," Arnie answered, and strutted off. Wayne stood there for a long moment, pondering what to do. While he was standing there, Arnie's boss, Glyn Jones, walked by.

"Glyn, I'm not trying to cause any trouble here, but I'm afraid," Wayne said. "We were gassing out steady. I wasn't here yesterday, but we were gassing out steady the day before and now we're in the heading cutting coal with no methanometer. I'm afraid. All we want to do is fix this and we were told that we can't take the machine out of production. And I threatened to walk out, and Arnie told me if I walked out I would get fired."

Glyn told him that he could have the miner for fifteen or twenty minutes to try and fix it. Wayne got hold of Mick. They grabbed their tools and went down to the miner. They hurriedly took the covers off the right-hand side of the machine—they knew this would make it take longer to put the machine back together, giving Mick more time to work on the methanometer. Wayne would explain that he was fixing one of the hydraulic hoses that had been leaking on the right side. When they had the covers off, Arnie came by to see what they were doing.

"Hey, Mick—I want you to recalibrate the methanometer to 1.5 percent," Arnie said.

Mick refused. If he recalibrated, the methanometer would cut out the miner when the gas concentration reached 1.5 percent, which could be high enough for the heads to ignite the methane if they caused a spark.

Arnie grabbed a screwdriver, and went into the cab of the miner to recalibrate it himself. Normally, calibrating a methanometer involves using a small vial that contains methane gas at a mixture of 1.25 percent methane gas in air, to make sure the instrument cuts out at the right concentration. Arnie did not have a vial; he was doing the recalibration visually. After a few minutes of fiddling around, Arnie hopped out of the cab and told Mick he had changed it. He stayed there and waited until Wayne and Mick had the continuous miner running again, and ordered the operator to put it back into production.

Such was the condition of the methanometer early on the morning of May 9.

Shortly after five that morning, the operator of one of these machines was at the working face of SW2-1 Road of the Westray Mine, a mile underground. He was working the same face where Wayne Cheverie had noticed the gassing out three days earlier.

The operator saw a flame. While they were cutting into the coal, the spinning heads had hit some hard rock, probably pyrites. With the same effect as a cigarette lighter, a few dull orange sparks shot out, and ignited the methane gas that was seeping from the coal.

When the sparks flew from the heads of the continuous miner, a rolling flame erupted, rapidly traveling along the underground roadways, consuming all the oxygen it found and leaving a deadly trail of carbon monoxide in its wake. When the operator saw the flame, he jumped off to grab his survival equipment, but to no avail—he did not have enough time before the flame, the oxygen-deprived air, and the carbon monoxide combined to kill him.

As the flame rushed through the mine's tunnels, turning corners, encountering mining equipment and fans from the mine's ventilation system, its pressure built up until it exploded. The explosion, and the shock wave that rushed ahead of it, stirred up coal dust, which became airborne. The extreme heat from the methane explosion that closely followed the shock wave caused an even more violent coal dust explosion, which "moved rapidly through the entire mine, causing death and devastation in a matter of a few seconds,"[4] in the words of Justice Richards in his report on the public inquiry. When the shock wave reached the surface, it blew off the top of the mine entrance, and caused windows to shatter and houses to shake in nearby towns.

Twenty-six miners were now dead.

Only six days after the explosion, the Premier of Nova Scotia announced a public inquiry and appointed Justice Richards of the Nova Scotia Supreme Court to head it. After several years of delays caused by court challenges to the commission by the mining company, Curragh, that owned Westray, Justice Richards began hearings in October 1995. Justice Richards delivered his report in December 1997. He called it "The Westray Story, A Predictable Path to Disaster."

It was predicted by Wayne Cheverie because he had relevant background information. It was not predictable with measurements used by the Canadian Institute of Mining, Metallurgy, and Petroleum, which suggested the opposite—that the mine was the safest coal mine in Canada. These measurements made no use of background information. The declaration, or inference, that it was the safest coal mine in Canada was based entirely on the frequency of past accidents.

CAN RISK BE MEASURED?

Peter Bernstein, in his popular book[5] *Against the Gods: The Remarkable Story of Risk,* claims that "without numbers, there are no odds and no probabilities; without odds and probabilities, the only way to deal with risk is to appeal to the gods and the fates." Bernstein describes the history of attempts to measure risk. He says that "real-life situations often require us to measure probability ... from sample to universe. In most instances, we have to estimate probabilities from what happened after the fact."[6]

There are a limited number of circumstances where probability can be determined from past events. There are many people, however, who think that probability *must* be measured entirely from past records. This view is based on two intuitively appealing but false premises. The first false premise is that probability is a physical property like other physical properties of nature. Thus, according to this view, the probability that a coin will turn up heads when flipped is a physical property of the coin, such as its weight or mass, the circumstances of the experiment, and the nebulous concept of randomness. Bernstein, for example, refers to events that are "truly random" and "an event that is the result of cause and effect."[7] The second false premise is that we can, indeed we must, measure the probability of an event from its frequency, just as we can measure other physical properties of nature. We can, supposedly, measure the probability that somehow—although it is never explained how—belongs to the coin, by flipping it many times and counting the frequency of heads.

British economist and mathematician John Maynard Keynes[8] (1883–1946) dubbed this view of probability the "frequency theory of probability." Those that espouse it are called "frequentists."

The physicist E. T. Jaynes (1922–1998), argued that the frequency theory of probability conflicts with physics, because it requires one to ignore professional knowledge that scientists have about real phenomena, and because it requires "utter contempt" for the known laws of physics.[9] Research in physics and other sciences is a search for the causes of observed effects. The frequency theory is based on the premise that there are random events that are presumably, and rather bafflingly, without cause.

Running a business and managing risk based on a theory that is contemptuous of the laws of physics is not smart. To understand how to use probability to manage risk, you have to understand what probability is. There is a warning, though: if you have been trained in frequentist thinking, such as what is taught in most university statistics courses or Six-Sigma courses, you will find that this explanation conflicts with your understanding of statistics and probability. Some readers may be happy to learn why statistics never made sense to them. For the rest: get used to it. The laws of physics are a solid foundation for managing risk. You will have to unlearn some of your statistical training.

Bruno de Finetti (1906–1985) was an iconoclast amongst statisticians. He said[10] that probability does not exist as a property of nature, but only subjectively in the minds of people: "The abandonment of superstitious beliefs about the existence of Phlogiston, the Cosmic Ether, Absolute Space and Time, . . . of Fairies and Witches, was an essential step along the road to scientific thinking. Probability, too, if regarded as something endowed with some kind of objective existence, is no less a misleading misconception, an illusory attempt to exteriorize or materialize our true probabilistic beliefs."

WHAT IS PROBABILITY?

The need for probabilistic reasoning stems not from randomness but from incomplete knowledge, resulting in our uncertainty. For example, suppose I hold up a coin in my right hand in front of a friend and then hide it behind my back. I bring my left hand behind my back, and shuffle the coin back and forth between my hands. Then I bring both hands forward toward him, fists clenched, holding it in my right hand. I ask my friend to assign to a probability to the coin being in my right hand.

Most people will answer that it is one-half because they are uncertain about its whereabouts, and have no reason for thinking the coin is in one hand over another. For *them* the probability is one-half. But for me it is not. I *know* it is in my right hand. I am certain it is there. I do not need to rely on probability to characterize my knowledge that it is in my right hand. The probability that it is in my left hand is zero. I am certain it is *not* there. My assignment of the probability is different from that of my friend's because my state of knowledge is different: I know more than my friend knows about the coin's whereabouts.

Suppose that I now open my hands and show my friend the coin lying in my right palm. His assignment of the probability promptly changes. It is now the same as mine. The coin, though, has not changed. Our initial views of the probability were different because our states of knowledge were different. Our subsequent views of the probability were the same because we had the same state of knowledge.

Once I tried this trick with a small rock rather than a coin. To my surprise, my interlocutor answered that it was highly probable it was in my right hand. When I asked him why, he replied that he could see it was not as tightly closed as the left. It was in my right hand. The extra piece of information successfully broke the symmetry in his state of knowledge in favor of my right hand.

These two examples illustrate a fundamental principle about probability: probabilities may change when our state of knowledge changes, and we become more, or less, certain; frequencies, on the other hand, do not. I am not claiming that probability and frequency cannot, under certain well-defined circumstances, be related. My claim is that the two are not the same and must be carefully distinguished.

In this sense, probability is a descriptive device that fills the gap left by missing information. The Portuguese philosopher Baruch Spinoza (1632–1677) believed that probability arises solely out of the limitations of our knowledge. Keynes argued that probability is a branch of logic that enables you to relate a body of evidence with a proposition. (The proposition, in the above case, was that the coin was in my right hand.) Keynes argued that if you have evidence, which, through some rational argument, leads you to believe in a proposition, you can say that the proposition is probable. This line of thinking has a long pedigree from Bayes through Laplace, Jeffreys, and, most recently, to E. T. Jaynes.

The view that probability is a way to relate a body of evidence to a proposition with an argument is dubbed, rather misleadingly, the "subjective" view of probability. It is not called subjective because it is subject to personal belief or whim. It is subjective because it is an expression of rational belief, or state of knowledge, formed by a rational argument using evidence or data which one knows (or believes) to be true. Everyone holding the same evidence and using rational arguments will assign the same probability.

Propositions, with a few exceptions with which we are not concerned here, are either true or false. "The Westray mine will not blow up" is a proposition. "This man will not default on his mortgage" or "This company's stock will go up" are also propositions. When we are uncertain about whether a proposition is true or false, our only recourse is to state the degree of our belief in the proposition based on the information at hand. As that information changes, the degree of our belief changes.

Take the proposition, "This man will not default on his mortgage." If the man has a steady, high income, a high credit rating, and a good employment record, it is rational to argue based on those facts, and to believe based on that argument, that it is plausible that he will repay his mortgage, and thus that it is plausible the proposition is true.

Take the proposition that "this mine will not blow up." Now suppose it is known by some miners that the mine is in a coal seam that emits methane, which, over the last two centuries, has often exploded, killing hundreds of miners. They also know the managers violate elementary safety precautions designed to prevent explosions. It is rational for them to argue based on those facts, and to believe based on that argument, that it is plausible that the mine will explode, and thus that the proposition is false.

Probabilities are used in quantum mechanics to describe such phenomena as the photoelectric effect, in which electrons are emitted at unpredictable times when a steady laser is shone on a sheet of metal. These probabilities do not justify a belief in a randomness property of nature, but, as Jaynes argues, "express the incompleteness of human knowledge." We do know that the laser light causes the electrons to appear, though we do not know what causes them to appear when they do. Perhaps someday we will. A presumed "randomness property," which presumes some events occur without cause, contradicts the underlying premise of scientific research. That is not a strong foundation upon which to measure risk.

Jaynes developed probability theory into a branch of extended logic about propositions with unique rules for conducting inference and plausible reasoning of any kind, based on all the information at hand, including observed frequencies. His work was based on the work of Richard Threlkeld Cox (1898–1991), a professor of physics at Johns Hopkins University. Cox's theorem, which now bears his name, showed that degrees of belief in propositions can be, indeed must be, represented by probability.

Arguments about propositions are either deductive or plausible. Jaynes kicks off his description of extended logic with a description of the difference between deductive and plausible reasoning. Plausible reasoning is the foundation of probability theory, and thus of any discussion of risk.

Jaynes used the conventions of George Boole (1815–1864), a British mathematician and logician, in formalizing his extended logic. Boole invented what we now call Boolean algebra, which is the theoretical basis for modern computers. He was in the same camp as Jaynes with respect to the nature of probability, saying that "probability is always relative to our actual state of information and varies with that state of information."[11]

Jaynes highlighted two types of deductive arguments and three types of plausible arguments. To illustrate, consider a man sitting in the basement of his house, where he is unable to observe the weather. From time to time an observer sitting on the porch outside hollers information about the weather to the man in the basement.

First Deductive Argument

If A is true then B is true. Thus if I know that A is true, I can deduce that B is true.

For example, suppose proposition A is that it is raining. Proposition B is that it is cloudy. The observer yells that it is raining. The man in the basement deduces that it is cloudy—the argument is certain and conclusive. Note that this is logical deduction, not physical causation: the rain does not cause the clouds, but he can deduce from the rain that it is cloudy.

Second Deductive Argument

If A is true then B is true. Thus if I know that B is false, I can deduce that A is false.

The observer says there are no clouds around (B is false). The man in the basement deduces (A) that it is not raining—again with certainty.

First Plausible Argument

If A is true then B is true. Thus if I know that A is false, B becomes less plausible.

The observer says that it is not raining outside. The man in the basement believes that it is less plausible that there are clouds around.

Second Plausible Argument

If A is true then B is true. Thus if I know that B is true, A becomes more plausible.

The observer says that the sky is overcast (B). The man in the basement believes that it is more plausible that it is raining (A).

An even weaker plausible argument is as follows:

Third Plausible Argument

If A is true then B becomes more plausible. Thus if I know that B is true, A becomes more plausible.

Suppose proposition A is that it is raining, as before. Proposition B is that there is lightning. The man in the basement hears a clap of thunder. He knows lightning occasionally occurs without rain (meteorologists call rainless lightning "dry lightning"). The man can thus not deduce from the thunder clap that it *is* raining. He believes, however, that it is more *plausible* that it is raining. Jaynes gives a clever example[12] to illustrate the third plausible argument and to show that we often use this form of plausible reasoning.

> Suppose some dark night a policeman walks down a street, apparently deserted. Suddenly he hears a burglar alarm, looks across the street, and sees a jewellery store with a broken window. Then a gentleman wearing a mask comes crawling out through the broken window, carrying a bag which turns out to be full of expensive jewellery. The policeman does not hesitate at all in deciding that this gentleman is dishonest.

In the policeman's case, proposition A was that the man was a thief. Proposition B was that the man wore a mask, broke the window, crawled through it and removed jewelry in a bag. The policeman did not *know* that the man was a thief. According to the third plausible argument, if proposition B is true, proposition A is more plausible. He believed it to be very plausible that the man was a thief because he had data that he thought showed proposition B to be true. But it may not be. As Jaynes says:

> There may have been a perfectly innocent explanation for everything. It might be, for example, that this gentleman was the owner of the jewellery store and he was coming home from a masquerade party, and didn't have the key with him. However, just as he walked by his store, a passing truck threw a stone through the window, and he was only protecting his own property [by placing the jewellery in a bag and removing it].

The policeman believed Proposition B to be true because of his own experience with and background information about thieves. His reasoning that the gentleman was dishonest makes sense to us because of it. What, Jaynes asks, if that experience (and background information) had been different, and that policemen encountered such situations regularly while on the beat? The policemen would soon ignore most masked men crawling out of stores with bags of goods.

We use such background information subconsciously and continually in our daily lives when we assess plausibility. Any system of assessing plausibility that does not make use of background information can easily lead to assessments that contradict common sense—as with our policeman. Jaynes said that one of the three basic desiderata of plausible reasoning is that the assignment of plausibility should correspond qualitatively with common sense.

People have a knack for arranging similar propositions in order of plausibility. We may be able to readily argue that there is a greater plausibility of being hit by a car when crossing Elm Street than Oak Street; or of losing money investing in oil stocks than computer stocks. We can do this without assigning a numerical value to the plausibility of every argument. But we cannot readily compare plausibilities of dissimilar propositions. For example, we cannot readily say whether the plausibility of being hit by a car crossing Elm Street is greater than losing money investing in oil stocks.

People find it difficult, however, to assign numerical values to probabilities. To compare the plausibility of any two propositions, we need some method of assigning numerical values to them. Another of Jaynes's desiderata of plausible reasoning was that degrees of plausibility should be represented by real numbers. Of his three desiderata, this is the only one that may be relaxed somewhat. Contrary to what Bernstein said (that without numbers one must appeal "to the gods and the fates"), it is very difficult in some cases to assign numerical values to plausibilities, and it is not always possible. Keynes argued that it would be futile to even attempt it in all situations: "Whether or not such a thing is theoretically conceivable, no exercise of the practical judgment is possible, by which a numerical value can actually be given to the probability of every argument," he wrote.[13] Jaynes said it was "an open-ended problem, since there is no end to the complicated information that might be contained in [proposition] B."

Jaynes's third and final desideratum was consistency. By this he meant principally that equal states of knowledge should produce the same assignment of plausibility, no matter what path was taken to arrive at them.

The two strong deductive arguments set lower and upper bounds on the numerical values: we can assign zero to represent impossibility, or "not true," and one to represent certainty, or "true." The assignment of any value in between impossibility and certainty to the plausibility of a proposition, while respecting Jaynes's desiderata, results in what Jaynes calls probabilities. The colloquial meaning of probability is closer to what Jaynes means by plausibility. I will henceforth maintain Jaynes's distinction for clarity.

A key concept of probability is the concept of exchangeability, introduced by Bruno de Finetti. It explains how the frequency theory works in certain conditions, even though it is fundamentally wrong as a theory of probability.

De Finetti's thinking was as follows. Suppose you have a potentially infinite series of future events, such as coin flippings. Take any finite sequence from that series, such as getting heads on the first, third, fourth, fifth, and eighth flip, and tails on the rest of the first ten flips. You assign a probability to that specific sequence based on what you know about the coin-flipping experiment. At the same time, you write down on a piece of paper the exact result of the experiment, such as HTHHHTTHTT. Now suppose you lose the piece of paper and you remember the *number* but not the *order* of heads and tails in the sequence. If this does not change your probability assignment, and would not change it for any other finite sequence, the series is exchangeable. Exchangeability in effect deprives each toss from its individuality regarding its position in the sequence; all that matters is that it is H or T. So you can see how a coin-flipping sequence could easily be exchangeable. In fact, it is well-nigh impossible to make it not exchangeable, unless, for example, someone, during the sequence of flips, could increase his ability to produce heads at will.

Now take your favorite baseball team, which you hope is also potentially an infinite series. You pick a sequence of ten games next summer when you are away on holiday. You write down on a piece of paper the locations and teams, and the exact result of the sequence, such as WLW-WWLLWLL (W means win and L means lose). You assign a probability to this particular sequence of five wins in ten games. Just before you start your holiday, you learn that your team's first game will not be against the Red Sox in Boston, but the Cubs in Chicago. The other games' location and teams have also been changed. Would the new knowledge change your probability assignment for the new sequence of games? I bet it would. If so, the series is not exchangeable; the individuality of the event, expressed by the name of the opponent, matters.

As a demonstration of this concept, suppose that even with the new series of games, your team wins and loses exactly in the sequence you had originally predicted. You would be shocked! This, too, shows that the series is not exchangeable.

If the exchangeability conditions are met, and you have no useful background information about your series, you can assign the probabilities from the frequencies you observe by doing an experiment with a long sequence. However, if you have cogent background information, like Wayne Cheverie did, that can be quantified or scaled, such as in a bond rating, then you cannot calculate probability this way. This is an extremely important point in understanding how to assign probability.

In the above coin-flipping example, the ability to produce an excess number of heads is equivalent to a high degree of control. Let me illustrate briefly what I mean by degree of control. You can do this yourself with little effort. Use a large coin, such as a silver dollar or a medallion. Place your clenched fist firmly on your desk or table, your thumb on top, ready to flip the coin. Put the coin over your thumb and try to flip it so that it does a slow 180-degree flip in the air as it slides off your thumb. If it starts heads up, it should land tails up. With a bit of practice you should be able to get quite good at it and get the result you want almost every time. Even if the coin is biased you can learn to control your flipping so that you can call your shots accurately.

You might complain that this result is too simple. In other words, if you believe that the probability of getting heads is a physical property of the coin, you would be inclined to object that there is not enough randomness in such an experiment to measure it. But how high must the coin be tossed and how fast should it spin before that mysterious randomness appears in the experiment for such a presumed physical probability to be measurable? No one has an answer to that question.

An American magician turned probabilist, Persi Diaconis, figured out how he could carefully control the flipping of a coin and built a small machine to do it.[14] He and his colleagues vigorously flipped coins with their machine and found that they tended to land facing the same way they started—in accordance with their predictions based on the physics of coin movement. (Diaconis confessed that magicians do this intuitively in their tricks.) They even found that when humans flip coins they came up 51 percent of the time the way the coins started—a slight tendency. It was an elegant demonstration of what is obvious to the physicist—flipping coins follow the laws of physics, and with sufficient understanding of the laws and accurate control over the experiment one can make a coin flip any way one wants. Granted, most people when flipping a coin are unable to control the outcome. This does not justify a belief in randomness—it merely illustrates that the typical person does not have much control over a coin when flipping it.

This belief in randomness has a quasi-religious overtone to it, with its supposed ability to explain away physical phenomena with comforting and authoritative words. An accomplished statistician with whom I once had the pleasure of working, and who authored several respected books before his well-deserved retirement, even called the deity of randomness "Grits," which he always took great pleasure in explaining, after a pregnant pause in which he teased his audience's anticipation with his mischievous smile, stood for the "Great Randomizer in the Sky."

Jaynes did a coin-flipping experiment that was similar to the one Diaconis did. His results for four different methods are shown in Table 11.1.

These experiments show that it is meaningless to talk about the probability of getting heads when flipping coins as if the probability belonged to the coin. This is the sort of fuzzy thinking that Jaynes says is contemptuous of the laws of physics. The probability of getting heads expresses what you know about your ability to get heads—in other words, your degree of control. If that matches the frequency, you are in the happy situation where your state of knowledge describes your degree of control. If you continue to have no control toss after toss, then the tosses are exchangeable and a probability assignment of one-half makes sense. And if you have perfect control, and know you do, a probability assignment of one, or 100 percent, also makes sense. In both cases, as you flip the coin more and more, the average frequency will tend to get closer to the probability. In fact, under perfect control, the frequencies will mirror exactly the probability.

You are in a stickier situation if someone hands you a bent coin. Suppose he tells you that he has flipped it vigorously (i.e. with little control)

Table 11.1   Jaynes's Coin Flipping Experiment

Method	No. heads	No. flips
One	99	100
Two	0	50
Three	0	100
Four	54	100

Source: E. T. Jaynes, *Probability Theory: The Logic of Science* (Cambridge: Cambridge University Press, 2003), 321.

hundreds of times. It came up roughly two-thirds of the time on one side (i.e., heads or tails) and one-third on the other side (i.e., tails or heads). He does not tell you on *which* side it came up most frequently. That is all you know about this coin.

He now tells you he is going to flip it another hundred times. What probability will you assign to getting heads? The symmetry in your knowledge once again should lead you to assign a probability of one-half to getting heads, even though you know that the frequency of heads you will get if you flip it hundreds of times is very unlikely to be one-half of the total flips and will be closer to either two-thirds or one-third. In this case the probability and the frequency diverge.

BOND RATINGS

The US bond rating agencies Moody's, Standard & Poors, and Fitch's are in the business of selling ratings that describe the plausibility of default of the securities they rate. Good ratings are highly coveted by governments and corporations that sell bonds and similar securities to raise funds for their operations, as it means they will pay less interest to the bondholders. Ratings play a central role in modern, global finance.

The rating systems Moody's and the other agencies use are proprietary, so we do not know specifically how they determine the rating for a security. But we do know some basic things about them. They assess the legal contract between the issuer of the bond and the purchaser, the assets that are pledged, the working capital and liquidity of the issuer, redemption rights on the bond, the nature of protection covenants, and so on. The rating agencies also assess the strategies of the companies and governments issuing bonds. They look at their competitiveness and economic situations, and their financial and accounting policies. Finally, they look at industry fundamentals, demographic factors, and any topics of concern that might affect their ability to repay.

This is their body of knowledge. It comprises both background information and measurements: indeed, the measurements are *part* of the background information. A bond rating is an assignment of plausibility to the proposition that a bond issuer will repay principle and interest. The ratings agencies evaluate the body of knowledge to assign a rating that characterizes their informed opinion on the bond issuers' ability to repay principal and interest.

Their rating system applies Jaynes's third plausible argument. Consider proposition A for any issuer of a bond: "The issuer will not default and will repay principal and interest." Proposition B could be summarized as, "The issuer has sound finances." If an issuer does not default, it is more plausible that the issuer has sound finances. Thus if they know that an issuer has sound finances, it becomes more plausible it will not default.

A similar rating scheme for the safety of mines—or any other industrial operations—would be far more useful than a safety measurement based on frequency. Consider proposition A: the operation will not kill or injure its workers. Proposition B is that the operation has an effective safety system. If there were a way to evaluate a safety system and determine that it was effective, it would become more plausible that the operation will not kill or injure its workers. Yet lost-time injury frequency is used almost universally in industry to measure safety and to grant safest plant awards[15] based on the lowest frequency in the last year. While the frequency and the probability of injury are not unrelated, we saw in the case of Westray that they are not the same. It is as if individual bond issuers' ratings were based only on the frequency of their past defaults.

The bond ratings system describes the rating agencies' state of knowledge. This state of knowledge is based on evidence, and background information. The rating is the result of a rational argument that uses this knowledge, regarding the plausibility of default. This is a subjective view, in the sense I have defined subjective, of the plausibility of default: their system describes their state of knowledge and not some unseen property of the bond issuer that the rating agencies reveals with their ratings. Although measurements may be included in the body of knowledge, the ratings are thus not a measurement of risk but a rating scale that enables one to rank bonds, from the lowest plausibility of default to the highest.

The bond rating agencies state that their ratings are opinions: for example, "A Standard & Poor's credit rating represents Standard & Poor's opinion as of a specific date on the creditworthiness of an obligor in general or with respect to a particular financial obligation."

The ratings are actually more than opinions: they are descriptions of states of knowledge. They are somewhere in between opinions and facts, as they are rational beliefs formed by making an argument based on the material facts. The "arguments" are the proprietary rating methods used by the rating agencies. With the same facts and with logical—that is Bayesian—arguments, two rating agencies should make the same rating.

What is the relationship between the rating and the frequency of default? If Moody's rates a bond AAA and it defaults, does this mean their rating was wrong, or even fraudulent? Should the ratings tell us what frequency of defaults to expect?

The rating agencies track the bonds they rate and publish the frequency of defaults. (See Figure 11.1, which uses data taken from Standard and Poor's.[16])

Does this mean that a bond with a triple-A rating has a near-zero probability of default, and a bond with a triple-C rating has a 22 percent chance? Well, they might come close, but only if the condition of exchangeability is met.

Through a careful analysis of each of the bonds they rate, bond-rating agencies group them into rating groups such as AAA, AA, or C according to their similarity on a variety of characteristics. They assign the same

Figure 11.1   Bond ratings and default frequencies.

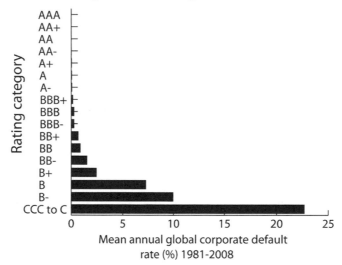

Source: Standard and Poor's LLC

plausibility of default for each bond within each group. Within a group their knowledge is exchangeable. In other words, all the companies within a rating group are indistinguishable with respect to their essential characteristics, and, therefore, have the same assignment of plausibility of default. It would not matter if they changed the names of the companies within a group: their assignment of plausibility would remain unchanged because of their common characteristics. This is how Richard Cantor, head of ratings research at Moody's at the time, together with Eric Falkenstein, expressed the concept of exchangeability in layman's terms in a research paper[17] on rating consistency for bonds rated by Moody's:

> Securities that are currently rated single-A are generally expected to perform similarly to one another and similarly to how A-rated securities have performed in the past.

In other words, it doesn't matter whether you look at old or new securities, or what the security is called, any security with the same rating has the same plausibility of default.

There will always be some differences in the securities, but the differences have (or should have) a nonquantifiable effect on the plausibility of default. Some bonds within a rating category may eventually default sooner than others[18] (exchangeability implies that we don't know which) but overall, if their rating method is any good at all, for rating purposes we can consider them exchangeable.

If the frequencies of default stay consistent over a long period of time within a rating group, this suggests that the agencies have a degree of knowledge that matches their degree of control. In this case, the "control" is the influence of the economy on the liquidity of the bond issuers. Their knowledge is the information they have about the economy, the issuers, the rating scheme itself, and their ability to classify bond issuers into exchangeable groups.

What happens when there is a systemic change in the economy that causes more defaults? They have a bent coin. Suppose they suspect, for example, that the frequency of default for bonds will soon go up, but they do not know by how much or by how much it will differ for AAA rated bonds or CCC rated bonds. Suppose they don't know what information they need to figure that out. Their knowledge no longer matches the degree of control (i.e., the control of the economy on the bond issuers). They cannot change their rating scheme to account for the expected change in the frequency of default even if they think that the probabilities assigned to ratings and the corresponding frequencies of default will diverge. It may be that the ratings that were made before the systemic change are exchangeable, and those made after the change are exchangeable. But ratings made before will not be exchangeable with those made after the change.

Such systematic changes occur all the time. Between 1970 and 1999, the default rates for speculative grade securities rated by Moody's dropped from 9 percent in 1970, down to around 1 percent between 1971 and 1981. They climbed up to over 10 percent by 1991, dropped to 2 percent, and slowly started climbing again.[19] With every major swing, there were systemic changes in the economy. In 1991, for example, junk bond financing was very tight and overall macroeconomic conditions were weak, causing higher defaults of junk bonds.

Cantor and Falkenstein comment on these variations by saying:

> Annual default rates for specific rating categories fluctuate much more widely than would be expected if their *true underlying default probabilities* were constant over time [emphasis mine].

Not quite. The way they said it, they appear to be falling into the trap of thinking that securities have a true underlying probability. But as we have seen, probability is a description of a state of knowledge, not a true property of a security or a coin that can somehow be measured. The probability (plausibility) is represented by a rating. The agencies assign the rating based on their state of knowledge. Probability and frequency are not the same; ratings and default rates are not the same.

One can no more measure the probability than assign the frequency, as Jaynes put it. And one can no more measure the rating than assign the default rate.

Their rating scheme takes the knowledge they have about companies and the economy and uses it to assign a rating, which is basically an assignment of probability. What they should have said is something like this:

> If we could adjust our rating scheme quickly enough to account for systemic changes in the economy, annual default rates for specific rating categories would fluctuate much less widely than they do now.

To speak of "true underlying default probabilities" is to suggest that securities have a probability "property" and that they default for "random" reasons; that instead of economic and physical causes, the Great Randomizer in the Sky—Grits—is the cause. It leads to a futile search for Grits's probability by attempting to measure it from the frequency of defaults of the securities. It is the same mistake people make when they think they can *measure* the probability that a coin-flip will turn up heads. It's de Finetti's Phlogiston.

We saw that we change our assignment of probability if we change our state of knowledge. A change in our state of knowledge does not, however, cause the frequencies to change. The frequencies, nevertheless, can give us a useful clue that our state of knowledge is more (or less) incomplete than we thought. This is how we learn how the world works: by studying those situations where our plausible arguments fail. When the default rate for a certain class of bonds suddenly climbs (or drops), this tells us that the rating scheme no longer reflects economic reality. Frequencies thus play a useful, even a critical, role in plausible reasoning, enabling us to constantly update our knowledge and thus our assignments of probability.

Many of the people who rely on the ratings are confused about the nature of probability. When a highly rated or well-known firm defaults, a common reaction is to claim the rating agencies made a mistake, or worse, that they cooked the rating because they were in a conflict of interest with the company they rated. If a rating of AAA meant certainty that there would be no default, then the claim would make sense. But that is not what the rating means.

Putting aside for a moment the possibility of deception or fraud, such claims are based on the mistaken belief that there is some kind of objective probability and one can measure it. These claims confuse measurement with plausible (or probabilistic) reasoning. If probability were a physical property of some sort that could be measured, like temperature, one could claim that the measurement was mistaken if the bond issuer defaulted. But it is not—it is a description of a state of knowledge about a proposition. If a thermometer says the water is 50°F just before the pond freezes, it is mistaken. If a rating agency rates a bond AAA just before it defaults, it is not, or not necessarily, mistaken.

Does this mean that ratings can be cooked with impunity, making the numbers meaningless? Anyone who uses probability faces this problem. Ultimately it comes down to openness and experience with reality. Those who propose a probability assignment or rating must be prepared to open the books on the basis of their assignment and submit it to scrutiny, and their assignments (or ratings) should withstand the test of time (our reality check in our four principles for reliable measurement).

We use plausible reasoning when we are uncertain about something. It could be something in the past, present, or future. The reason the bond rating agencies rate bond issuers is because we are uncertain about their ability to repay principal and interest on the bond. Their rating indicates their degree of rational belief that the issuer will not default, given the information they have about the companies.

It is reasonable to believe in the plausibility of rain if there are dark clouds outside, even if it is not raining. Or, if all I know about an urn is that it contains black and white beads in a ratio of two to one, it is rational for me to assign a probability of two-thirds that I will draw a black bead when I put my hand in the urn. My probability assignment was not mistaken if the bead subsequently turns out to be white. It is thus perfectly reasonable for a person to believe a proposition A to be plausible when A is in fact, though without his knowledge, false, if the information they have about the proposition B upon which A depends is true, and if the argument for believing that A is plausible is rational.

Likewise if a rating agency rates a bond as AAA, it is—or should be—indicating its rational belief that it is highly plausible that the issuer will not default. If the issuer subsequently defaults, the agency did not make a mistake by giving them an AAA rating, if the information upon which it based its rating was true, and if it properly applied its own methodology.

It is, however, not rational for me to assign a probability of one-half to drawing a black bead when I know that black and white beads are in a proportion of two to one. Neither would it be rational for a bond rating agency to rate a bond AAA if the raters knew the bond issuer were on the brink of default, even though they have a good record.

In 2007 a giant real estate bubble burst in the United States, and many bond issuers defaulted. The bubble had been pumped up by interest rates that fell from 6 percent in 2001 to just over 1 percent a year later, in the wake of the terrorist attacks in New York and Washington. With the cost of borrowing so low, demand for housing jumped. To finance the boom, financiers created new and complex instruments known as "structured finance" products, including collateralized debt obligations, or CDOs, which were rated by the rating agencies.

Banks created CDOs through separate companies they set up called special-purpose entities (also called special purpose vehicles or structured investment vehicles), which were conveniently outside the reach of banking regulators and off their balance sheets—reducing the stress on regulatory capital. The entities would then invest in mortgages or other types of loans.

The banks would invest a small amount of their own money into the entities to put up equity, and raise the rest by selling notes to investors. The notes were divided into "tranches," or slices. The senior tranches paid the lowest return, but their investors were paid back first. If there were losses from defaults that were greater than the equity, the lowest tranches took the first hit. For this higher risk they received the highest return. If losses were greater still, the middle or mezzanine tranches took it. The mezzanine tranches paid a slightly lower return than the lowest tranche, because the mezzanine tranche offered investors some protection. The senior noteholders were supposed to take a loss only if the losses from all defaults were greater than the value of all the lower tranches. Once the defaults beat up the lower tranches, the upper tranches started getting smacked.

Satyajit Das,[20] an author of reference books on financial derivatives, called CDO tranching "the black art of dissimulation." Suppose there are one hundred loans of $10 million each, creating a $1,000 million CDO. Each loan may itself be repackaged into other loans and mortgages. Das gives an example in which the equity tranche is $20 million, the mezzanine tranche is $30 million, and the senior tranche is $950 million. The equity tranche takes the risk of the first two of *any* of the one hundred loans defaulting. The mezzanine tranche takes the risk of any of the next three defaults. Instead of diversifying risk, this method concentrates it. (In practice there could be many more tranches.)

Tranching allowed financial wizards to create different levels of credit risk. With a thick equity tranche, the lower notes had lower risk. The more and thicker the tranches, the higher the rating on the top tranches because of the protection offered by the lower tranches. This was the basic structure of the CDO. But it got increasingly complicated as financial engineers created a myriad list of financial derivatives on the basic structure.

The rating agencies worked closely with big banks on structuring the CDOs and other structured finance products, and then provided ratings for each of the tranches. They generated enormous fees doing this. Between 2002 and 2007 Moody's revenue went from $1 billion to $2.3 billion; its stock price climbed from $20 to a peak of $72. The top tranches usually got AAA ratings.

In the search for returns in an era of low interest rates, many of the underlying loans were mortgages to people who were high credit risks. These mortgages became known as "subprime." In 2005 and 2006, up to half of the securities in some CDOs were subprime mortgages.[21] Interest rates were low, the economy was strong, and default rates of mortgages were at that time very low.

In 2007 the whole structure started to unravel in what became known as the credit crunch. It started when two highly leveraged Wall Street hedge funds that had invested heavily in subprime mortgages announced that they were having trouble meeting margin calls. The ratings of some of the CDOs in which they had invested had been downgraded.

Depending on the distribution of loan quality in the bottom tranches, defaults in those tranches could affect ratings in the upper tranches differently. In some CDOs a 2 percent default rate in the lower tranche could require that only 2 percent of AAA rated bonds in the top tranche be downgraded. In a CDO with a different distribution, the ratings of up to 40 percent of the top tranche could be downgraded.[22]

The banks had raised money for the special-purpose entities with short-term asset-backed commercial paper. The mortgages held by the CDOs, however, were long-term. After the first few downgrades, investors stopped buying the commercial paper. Charles Morris, an author on the credit crunch, said it was a shout from buyers that, "We don't trust you and don't know what you're doing with our money." The *Financial Times* called it a buyers' strike. Over the course of the next year, the banks had to take hundreds of billions of dollars in write-downs on securities that had been highly rated. Millions of homeowners across the United Stated defaulted on their mortgages when interest rates went up. The venerable US investment bank Bear Stearns and the British bank North Rock both had to be rescued from collapse. Lehman Brothers, a 150-year-old institution, collapsed. Merrill Lynch, another respected investment firm, had to be bought up by Bank of America to stave off disaster. The US government funneled hundreds of billions to the banks to rescue them and stop the contagion of toxic assets from spreading. Governments around the world did the same; some governments nationalized banks.

The rating agencies were blamed immediately. The Securities and Exchange Commission launched a review of the rating agencies. United States Senator Richard Shelby, a member of the Senate Banking Committee, said that the credit rating agencies must "shoulder some responsibility." The *Economist*[23] magazine said they were "vulnerable to punishment for their role in the credit crisis, largely thanks to the generous ratings they doled out on dubious mortgage-linked securities." They were accused of being in a conflict of interest because they were paid by the companies they rated, and provided advice on the structure of the products they were rating.

The agencies defended themselves. Vickie Tillman, executive vice president of Credit Market Services for Standard & Poor's, in an article titled "Don't Blame the Rating Agencies," which she published in the *Wall Street Journal,*[24] wrote that "the fundamental service provided by a rating agency such as S&P is to issue an independent opinion on the creditworthiness of securities, which speaks to the likelihood that investors will receive payments of interest and principal on time. Our ratings are based on the facts available to us at the time these opinions are made."

Were the rating agencies to blame? It is the same sort of plausible reasoning Jaynes's policeman used when he saw a masked gentleman crawling out of the jewelry store with a bag of jewelry. Proposition A is, in this case, that the rating agencies gave bogus ratings. Proposition B was that the agencies were in a conflict of interest and were influenced by the big fees they earned by the banks. We do not *know* that the ratings were bogus. According to the third plausible argument, if proposition B is true, proposition A is more plausible. The agencies' critics believed it to be very plausible that the ratings were bogus because they had data that they thought showed proposition B to be true.

But like Jaynes's policeman, perhaps there is another explanation.

In the years before the credit crunch several powerful corporate executives had been sent to jail after the major corporations they ran collapsed into financial scandal. Certainly this background information about fraud and other nefarious financial practices would lend credence to proposition B. Yet there is other background information that reduces the plausibility of proposition B, as in Jaynes's men with masks and bags of jewelry.

This background information has to do with the way people reason about probability. When they do, they do so using a small number of rules or strategies that simplify the thought processes involved. These strategies are useful, but can lead to severe and systematic errors.[25]

Two Israeli researchers, Amos Tversky and Daniel Kahneman, dubbed their theory that explains these strategies "prospect theory." Apparently they chose the name because it was catchy, not because it had anything to do with managing risk. Their research started with an investigation into the rules or strategies people use when making decisions involving risk and uncertainty. They noticed that their decisions contradicted economic models about how rational people should behave. They eventually won the Nobel Prize in economics for their work, although Tversky died before the award was granted.

In one of their seminal papers, published in 1974,[26] Tversky and Kahneman described another example of how a simple rule can lead to systematic errors:

> The apparent distance of an object is determined in part by clarity. The more sharply the object is seen, the closer it appears to be. This rule has some validity, because in any given scene the more distant objects are seen

less sharply than nearer objects. However, the reliance on this rule leads to systematic errors in the estimation of distance. Specifically, distances are often overestimated when visibility is poor because the contours of objects are blurred. On the other hand, distances are often underestimated when visibility is good because the objects are seen sharply. Thus, the reliance on clarity as an indication of distance leads to common biases.

Tversky and Kahneman called one of the rules "anchoring." "In many situations," they wrote, "people make estimates by starting from an initial value that is adjusted to yield the final answer." The initial value is the anchor. In a simple example, a group of high school students were given five seconds to evaluate the product

$$8 \times 7 \times 6 \times 5 \times 4 \times 3 \times 2 \times 1$$

A second group was given five seconds to evaluate the product

$$1 \times 2 \times 3 \times 4 \times 5 \times 6 \times 7 \times 8$$

The median estimate for the first group was 2,250. For the second group it was 512. The correct answer is 40,320. In both groups, the results of the first few multiplications created an anchoring effect. In the first group, the first few multiplications were higher than in the second, leading to the impression that the entire product would be higher.

The effect of anchoring is particularly important when assigning probabilities in situations where there are many possible outcomes. To illustrate, consider three events involving drawing beads from urns. Suppose there are three urns, each filled with a very large number[27] of red and white beads.

In the first urn, the beads are in equal proportion. The event of interest is the drawing of a single red bead with one draw, which is called an elementary event. The probability assigned to this event is 50 percent.

In the second urn, 90 percent of the beads are red and 10 percent are white. The event is the drawing of seven red beads in succession. This is a joint event, because *all* the beads must be red for the event to occur.

In the third urn, 10 percent of the beads are red and 90 percent are white. The event is the drawing of at least one red bead in seven draws. This is a disjoint event, because *any* of the beads could be red for the event to occur.

Tversky and Kahneman described a study in which the events were described to subjects in pairs. The subjects were asked to bet on the event in each pair that they thought had the highest probability. The subjects preferred to bet on the joint event over the elementary event, and on the elementary event over the disjoint event. They bet wrong for each pair—the probability of the disjoint event (52 percent) is higher than the elementary event (50 percent), which is higher than the probability of the joint event (48 percent).[28]

They concluded that people tend to assign too high a probability to joint events and too low a probability to disjoint events. The reason is that the "stated probability of the elementary event provides a natural starting point" for the assignment of the probabilities of both the joint and disjoint events. Typically, people do not adjust far enough from the starting point when they assign probabilities, hence the term "anchoring." (The probability of a single red bead, the elementary event, is the lowest in the third urn—10 percent—but the probability of the disjoint event—at least one red bead—is the highest at 52 percent.)

Even mathematically competent people underestimate disjoint probabilities because of anchoring. For many years I have taught courses on statistics in industry to engineers, scientists, and managers. I have enjoyed asking the participants to guess the probability of getting pregnant over a ten- or twenty-year period with a method of contraception that was supposedly 98 percent effective. Most of them would promptly answer that it was 2 percent.

I explained to them what that 98 percent meant. In studies of 1,000 women who used the method for a year, usually about 980—or 98 percent—did not get pregnant and 20 did. That is the frequency. If the women were exchangeable (no pun intended) it might even be reasonable to treat it like the probability, too, for an individual woman using the method and about whose personal life you knew nothing else.

Now suppose you had a huge urn that was filled with 98 percent white beads and 2 percent red beads. If you draw one bead every year, what's the

Table 11.2   Tversky and Kahneman's Experiment

No. draws	No. red beads drawn	Probability	Type of event	Urn contents
One	One	50%	Elementary	Beads in equal proportion
Seven	Seven	48%	Joint	90% red, 10% white beads
Seven	One	52%	Disjoint	10% red, 90% white

Source: Amos Tversky and Daniel Kahneman, "Judgment under Uncertainty: Heuristics and Biases," *Science* 185 (1974): 1124–1131.

probability that in ten or twenty years you'll get at least one red bead—or get pregnant? It is 18 percent for ten years, and 33 percent for twenty years. That amounts to "effectiveness" of 82 percent and 67 percent, a far cry from 98 percent.

Most of the young women would take careful notes of my explanation, only to return the next day, having explained the calculation to their husbands and boyfriends, to ask me to explain it once again, and more slowly.

Disjoint events occur regularly in complex situations in which only one failure is needed for an entire failure to occur. (That's certainly the case with contraception!) A nuclear reactor can fail if only one component of the thousands of components that make up a reactor fail. The multimillion-dollar Reactor Safety Study conducted by the US Nuclear Regulatory Commission in 1975 made just this mistake when assessing the probability of a core meltdown. A subsequent review of the study by the commission, just before the Three Mile Island nuclear disaster, concluded that it was "overconfident."[29]

The CDO structure was similar to a nuclear reactor or a method of contraception: The probability of any single security defaulting, when there are many securities, is higher than the probability of a given single, "elementary" default. If *any* of the securities in the equity tranche, for example, defaulted, the equity investors had to take the hit. It is a disjoint event. Say there are ten BB-rated securities within a tranche: if you rated the plausibility of *any* default within the tranche you would have to give it something lower, perhaps a C rating.

When defaults occurred, they moved up the tranches. As the protection offered by the lower tranches collapsed, buyers went on strike, and the agencies eventually had to downgrade the ratings of the top tranches, setting off a chain of events leading to the credit crunch.

Unlike the Westray disaster, where a fault in a methanometer led to an explosion, defaults in loans led to an implosion. As one part of the incredibly complex financial structure imploded, other parts were weakened and fell with it, or threatened to. Unlike Westray, which exploded in seconds, the collateralized debt obligations imploded slowly, taking more than a year, and taking big banks with them. By the autumn of 2008, venerable banks such as Bear Stearns and Lehman Brothers were gone, and the US and British treasuries had taken equity positions in the major banks to prop up their capital. The world's largest insurance company, American Insurance Group, was bailed out by the US government, and Congress authorized an extraordinary $700 billion bailout package to keep the country's banks afloat.

Tversky and Kahneman found that both lay people and experts are too confident in their own judgments about risk. Although the psychological reasons are not well understood, it appears to be because people are not aware that they have made some shaky assumptions. The overconfidence results from several misunderstandings, including failing to understand how complex systems function as a whole, and failure to understand how people respond to safety measures. The structured finance products and the subprime loans were rated individually, but they worked together as a whole system—when one part was weakened, all the others were weakened.

There are possibly more decisions made at the subconscious level than we would like to believe.

People often react to safety measures by taking more risks—for example, dams and levees encourage people to build homes in the flood plain. The tranche system, by creating AAA rated top tranches on top of baskets of securities that had a high proportion of low-quality loans and subprime mortgages, encouraged the financial wizards to take more risks. The levees were made of sand.

Time may tell which explanation is right—that the rating agencies were influenced by the fees or they made the same sort of mistakes as other experts and laypeople when rating risk. It would be ironic to make those same mistakes when assigning a high probability to the proposition that the agencies were so influenced.

VALUE AT RISK

The mistaken idea that risk can be measured made another significant contribution to spectacular losses in the banking industry around the same time. It was an easy trap to fall into, one that millions of people before and surely millions after will also fall into, from all walks of life. It is the same sort of thinking that led the Canadian Institute of Mining to call Westray Mine the safest coal mine in Canada, except that it had the imprimatur of advanced mathematical backing and sophistication. The measure is known as "value at risk."

Value at risk is based on an understanding about a statistical distribution typically known as the "normal" distribution, or bell curve, or Gaussian, that is gravely mistaken. The mistake is the "universal tendency to think of probability distributions in terms of frequencies," as Jaynes put it. Most people are familiar with the general shape, although the numerical values of the axes may be unfamiliar.

Figure 11.2   Standard Gaussian distribution.

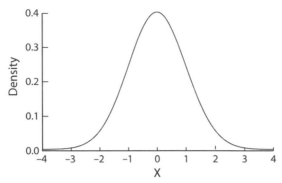

The distribution had first been described by a French mathematician named Abraham de Moivre in 1733. He made little use of it, and did not understand its significance.[30] It was Gauss who derived the distribution in a new way in 1809. Gauss was concerned about the slight differences he found when he analyzed repeated measurements of the position of celestial objects such as stars. Even though he took the measurements very carefully and with the same method each time, he got a slightly different result with each attempt. He reasoned that each of these measurements had a small error in it relative to the celestial object's true position. He pondered how he could use these different values to estimate the position of the celestial object. Ideally he wanted a method that would cause the errors to cancel each other out. If they did, he would maximize the likelihood of estimating a celestial object's position. Gauss searched for a mathematical proof that whatever method he picked did indeed cancel out the errors and maximize the likelihood of estimating the object's position.

His proof was based on two things Gauss knew about the errors. First, he knew that the errors varied around a fixed point. This point was defined by the measurement method. If his method was good, and he believed it was, this fixed point would be the same as the object's position. If there was, in addition to the individual errors, a constant error in his method that affected all measurements equally, the fixed point would differ from the object's position by that constant amount, but it would still be fixed, and the measurements would still vary around it. A viewfinder on a sharp-shooter's pistol that aimed slightly to the right is an example of this kind of additional constant error (or bias).

The second thing he knew was that the probabilities of these errors being greater than any particular number were equal. As the number gets bigger, the probability of any error being bigger than that number gets smaller. Another way to say this is that the *rate* at which the probability decreases was the same for all the errors. This rate is closely related to what is called the standard deviation.[31]

With this knowledge, and a rather clever bit of mathematical maneuvering, Gauss showed that the best estimate[32] of position was the arithmetic mean. He also showed that the only distribution that described the two things he knew and for which the arithmetic mean of the measurements gave this best estimate was the one that now bears his name.

Gauss's result is of fundamental importance and is widely misunderstood by workers in all fields. As we have seen, there is a general—and incorrect—tendency to think of probabilities as frequencies, instead of descriptions of states of knowledge. This tendency extends to probability distributions such as the Gaussian, which are also generally viewed in terms of frequencies, or as ways of characterizing frequency distributions of measurements.

This faulty line of thinking goes something like this: take a set of data—and check it to see if it is "normally distributed" with one of the ubiquitous statistical tests available on desktop computers. If the test shows the general shape of the frequency distribution is not too far from a bell shape, which the computer draws using the mean and standard deviation of the data, then assume the data are normal, irrespective of your background knowledge of the process that produces the data. Then you can use the distribution to "estimate probabilities" about what will happen in the long run if you keep getting the same sort of data. With the Gaussian distribution, the probability of a measurement being less than one standard deviation from the mean is about two-thirds. The probability of it being less than 2.6 standard deviations away is 99 percent.

But the Gaussian distribution does not describe data, or measurements that you have taken and the frequencies with which they vary from their mean. It is not an assumption about the physical world and the measurements you can get from it. Nor is it an assumption about the distribution of data or of error frequencies that you would obtain in the long run.

It is, rather, a description of a state of knowledge: a fixed mean and a fixed standard deviation. The continuous distribution that describes this state of knowledge without assuming anything more is the Gaussian. It is a useful distribution not because we have measurements and can examine their frequencies, but because we do not. The frequency distribution of the data we have before us does *not* have to have a Gaussian distribution for the Gaussian distribution to be useful. The Gaussian describes a state of knowledge, not frequencies of data. Nor does the frequency distribution of a future, imagined, set of data have to be Gaussian.

What matters is our state of knowledge about the process that generates the data, and the actual data we have in hand. The errors present in actual data we have in our hands will determine how close the arithmetic mean of this data is to the mean of the thing we are measuring. If our knowledge about the process that generates data is that we have a fixed mean and standard deviation, then these errors will gradually cancel each other out the more measurements we take.

If we learn something that leads us to believe the mean, or the standard deviation, are not constant, then the probabilities we calculated from the assumed assigned normal distribution of the data will no longer be consistent with our state of knowledge, and are thus not a valid description of our state of knowledge. We have a bent coin.

Anyone who mixes up frequency and probability will go on blindly believing the fanciful probabilities they calculate from the Gaussian distribution they assume for their data, probabilities that are inconsistent with their own knowledge of what is going on.

That is basically what the banks do with value at risk.

Its purpose is to find the amount of money they call the value at risk on its trading floor on any trading day, and that they will lose with a probability of 1 percent.

The raw data for the calculation of value at risk are daily trading losses and gains. The banks calculate the mean and standard deviation from this data over various time frames. They make this calculation by employing, knowingly or not, the catechism of frequentist statisticians, first enunciated by Ronald A. Fisher, "let the data speak for themselves," as if there were no other relevant background information about the patterns of trading losses than their recent frequencies. Then, by assuming the future losses and gains will follow the Gaussian distribution, they calculate the loss that would be exceeded with a 1 percent probability.

The banks confuse the frequency distribution of trading losses with the probability distribution. They make the usual mistake of thinking they can measure probability from frequencies rather than assign it based on their state of knowledge, which includes past trading losses. Put more simply, they do not make sufficient use of their collective knowledge and experience about what is happening in the market and on their trading floor to manage their risks. Their assignment of probabilities should be done in a way similar to how the rating agencies assign probabilities. Instead, banks rely too heavily on calculations of meaningless probabilities.

Value at risk assumes they have a series in which the future will behave as the past in two coarse features: the mean and standard deviation of the trading losses. In fact they know darn well these two values are not constant. If they were there would be no need for risk management departments in any banks. It was perfectly reasonable for Gauss and the legions of scientists who followed him to believe their measurement errors were constant in those coarse features. It is wishful thinking to believe this for the wild and bumpy gyrations of financial markets whose variations are driven by people, not small errors in refined measurement instruments. There is no justification for a Gaussian probability distribution for a fixed mean and standard deviation over time. Generally banks calculate a value-at-risk for one-day or rolling ten-day (or similar) holding periods, and track it as a measure of risk, as if it were a speedometer on a dashboard. Like we saw in chapter six, such calculations and dashboard displays may be meaningful representation of risk for small linear bits of complex systems. A Gaussian probability assignment might make sense for such short time periods, in other words, to calculate a probability of a loss in the next twenty-four hours if the future behaves as the past. But they do not make sense to represent the risk in the whole system. Keynes said about such misuse of probability theory: "It is hard to think of an example in which the frequency conditions are even approximately satisfied."[33]

The markets, Keynes also said, are irrational, and will remain so longer than you can remain solvent. A particularly good illustration of this was Long Term Capital Management (LTCM), a $7 billion hedge fund founded in 1994 by several accomplished financiers, including two Nobel Prize winners. In early 1998, the fund managers ran their portfolios so that their daily value at risk was around $45 million. Over the course of the year there were fundamental changes in the markets related to the Asian financial crisis and the Russian moratorium on their debt—a phase change, as we discussed it in chapter six. Their portfolios were not structured to adapt to these changes. A positive feedback cycle developed. Their value at risk kept climbing up. They could not restructure their portfolios for the new regime. By September, the fund had lost 92 percent of its value.

The markets that the banks model with value at risk are like the streams we looked at in chapter eight. Modeling them with a constant average and standard deviation is like pretending that a raging torrent of a river, with wild rapids and plunging cataracts, is a placid lake. A constant standard deviation and mean might make sense for only a small stretch of river over a short time.

The value-at-risk measures were entrenched in the Basel II international banking accords on capital adequacy in 2004. By then, value-at-risk frequency histograms and charts were a standard feature of most banks' annual reports. The Canadian Imperial Bank of Commerce, for example, reported in its 2007 annual report that its average value at risk was about $15 million. It said: "We hold positions in traded financial instruments to meet client investment and risk management needs. . . . Traded instruments are recorded at fair value and include debt and equity securities, as well as interest rate, foreign exchange, equity, commodity and credit derivative products." By June 2008, its write-downs on these products had reached nearly $7 billion and the bank was facing another $2 billion in charges. A Swiss bank, UBS, had write-downs of about $40 billion.

The banks are thus courting disaster with their clients' and investors' money, and the risk managers with their spreadsheets are leading the way. The *Economist*[34] magazine said that "value at risk is programmed to instill complacency."

Das tells a story that illustrates how value at risk is misused in the banks and how bank risk managers believe in measuring probability from frequency.

A risk manager was hauled up before the board of directors and called upon to explain why the bank had lost more than $250 million in a single day when its value at risk was only $75 million. "The model must be wrong," complained one of the directors. "No, definitely not!" the risk manager countered. "Our risk models run at the 99 percent confidence level. The fact that we lost more on this one day actually proves that our risk models are working perfectly as intended. We should lose more than our measured risk one day in every 100."

The risk manager was masking the same logical errors as those who apply statistical process control charts to processes that they know are changing (see chapter eight). The risk manager's reasoning was something like: If the mean trading loss does not change, than 99 percent of all future losses can be expected to be less than the value at risk. He is concerning himself with:

The probability of a loss greater than the value at risk, if the mean trading loss does not change.

But he is forgetting, or ignorant of, the part of the sentence after the comma. What he should be worried about this time is:

The probability that there has been some systemic change in trading risk, given that we just lost $250 million.

I suspect that if he incorporated other background information, as we did in the tube-cutting example, he would have found that the probability of a systemic change, given the $250 million loss, was quite high. The risk manager's argument was based on the same flawed frequentist reasoning we have seen elsewhere. Suppose there is no systemic change in trading, and further suppose the Gaussian distribution was the correct way to assign probabilities to losses (which it is not): the probability of a loss of $75 million or more is 1 percent. But if he is going to use that flawed reasoning, then by the same flawed reasoning, the probability of a loss of $250 million would be one in 2.5 million (or 0.4 parts per million). An event with such a low probability is virtually certain not to happen.

The director should have replied to this risk manager, "There are two explanations for this $250 million loss. One, it had a 1 in 2.5 million chance of happening, and through bad luck, it happened. Or two, there has been a systemic change in trading risk. Which one do you think is more likely?"

SIMPLE, NEAT, AND RECKLESS: ONE SIZE DOES NOT FIT ALL

The Greek mythological figure Icarus escaped from the island of Crete with his father Daedalus, who was an inventor and craftsman. Daedalus made wings of feathers and wax that he affixed to their backs. He warned his son not to fly too close the sun, as the wax would melt, and not too close to the sea, as the wings would dampen and would be hard to fly. But when Icarus became airborne the exhilaration of flying seduced him, and he flew so high that his wings melted and he crashed to his death in the sea. And like Icarus, the exhilaration nurtured by the imaginary mathematical precision of modern risk measurement techniques seduced bankers and financiers.

When Justice Richards said that the Westray mine story was a predictable path to disaster, he was saying that, given the evidence, and given the rational arguments of the experts and employees at the testimony, the explosion was probable. He was not relying on the frequency theory to measure fictitious probabilities. Neither was that lonely miner, Wayne Cheverie.

Bayesian methods provide a way to overcome the limitation of the frequency theory. They enable you to formally incorporate background information into an assignment of probability. The statistical process control chart, the way it is widely taught and applied, is based on the frequency theory of probability. In the statistical process control example I illustrated in chapter eight, we saw that by incorporating background information we calculated a very different, and more realistic, probability than the one-size-fits-all SPC chart. The same principle applies to any determination of risk based on an assignment of probability. Bayesian methods are a way of formally updating opinions based on new evidence. They recognize that when it comes to risk, or any other matter involving probability, we have varying degrees of beliefs in propositions. We cannot measure whether or not they are true, or the degree to which they are true.

The apparent advantage of the frequentists' methods is that they sell many one-size-fits-all "tools," such as many enterprise-wide software packages that make such claims as the ability to "calculate your company's aggregate risk." Just feed in the numbers. Simple, neat, and reckless.

E. T. Jaynes says that the "superiority of Bayesian methods is now a thoroughly demonstrated fact in a hundred different areas,"[35] while the frequentist methods are useful for "simple, idealized problems" in "special cases" with no relevant background information. The *Economist* magazine reports that there has been a "blossoming of 'Bayesian' methods" in many fields.[36]

Physicists know that to determine the probability of truth of any scientific claim they *must* incorporate background information into their calculations. They are natural Bayesians.

The challenge of Bayesian methods is that they are more difficult to apply to calculate probabilities, precisely because there is no single tool that fits all situations. In important cases, such as the survival of a bank, this should not be an impediment.

Our brains are wired as Bayesians. We learn by updating our background information with new information. When we assess the risk of jaywalking across a busy street, we incorporate background information about that street, about jaywalking, and about our own abilities, with new information about the state of the traffic on the street at the moment we stand there. Such decision making in the face of risk can be formalized, as it is in bond ratings, by laying out the relevant background information that must be considered, and the way of considering it, when assigning plausibility. As in daily life, it is not always necessary to assign numerical values, and it is sometimes be very difficult to do.

This is a far better approach than the false succor of "measured" probabilities based on the idealized frequency theory, which you should have no hesitation in thoroughly rejecting.

CLOSING THE LOOP

The aim of this book was to reveal the hidden traps and potentially misleading nature of measurements that can make or break a business. The four criteria for reliable measurement are meant to help you achieve it. They will help you spot misleading indicators and develop reliable ones.

Who should use the criteria? Who takes measurements that can make or break a business? Who relies on them?

Many of the examples we used in the book came from science, engineering, medicine, education, quality control, economics, government, and other fields. To a business professor, chief financial officer, or investment adviser, some of these might not seem closely related to business performance measurement, which is more often conceived of in terms of financial performance.

The challenges faced by a vice president, accountant, chief executive officer, economist, or bond rating agency when they devise a method or measurement, and then draw inferences from those measurements, are very similar to the challenges faced by a process engineer, quality assurance technician, laboratory chemist, or safety officer. They are all part of business, and the four criteria for reliable measurement apply equally them all. Likewise, the measurement challenges faced by climate scientists, particle physicists, and high school teachers are similar.

We have conceived of "business" broadly and used such a wide range of examples to show the universality of the principles and the broad range of people who can apply them. There is nothing special about measurement in business compared to measurement in any other field, except, perhaps, the consequences of relying on misleading indicators.

TOOL BOX

- You cannot measure the risk that something will happen anymore than you can assign the frequency with which it will happen.
- There is a limited number of circumstances where probability can be determined from past events. Don't fall into the trap of thinking that probability must be or should be determined this way.
- Do not believe in random causes, an incoherent concept. The idea of randomness is just a way to express the incompleteness of human knowledge.

- Probabilities express a state of knowledge. For risks that you assess, develop methods that describe what information should be included in the body of knowledge to assign a probability, and how to consider that information.

- If you have frequency information such as bond defaults, trading losses, and lost time accidents, include it in the body of knowledge. Do not think of this information as a way to measure risk—it is not. It is only a small part of your body of knowledge, and not nearly as important as it is made out to be.

- Be wary of one-size-fits-all tools and software that claim they can measure your business risk. They cannot.

- In daily life we do not use numerical assignments of probability, but qualitative assignments of plausibility based on our background information, experience, and judgment. That works in business too.

- Learn how the world works by studying those situations where your plausible arguments fail.

Notes

CHAPTER ONE

1. Maurice G. Kendall, "The Early History of Index Numbers," *Review of the International Statistical Institute* 37, no. 1 (1969): 1–12. (Lowe is referred to on page 5.)

2. Peter Drucker, *Management: Tasks, Responsibilities, Practices* (New York: Harper & Row, 1985), 498.

3. Graeme J. N. Gooday, *The Morals of Measurement* (Cambridge: Cambridge University Press, 2004), 4.

4. "Happiness Inc.," *Wall Street Journal,* March 18–19, 2006.

5. Gooday, *The Morals of Measurement,* 142.

6. Alert readers will ask how this loss could be measured and against what standard. The details can be found at the BIPM website, www.bipm.fr.

7. News Focus, "A Most Unbearable Weight," *Science,* May 7, 2004, 812.

8. David Kestenbaum, "Recipe for a Kilogram," *Science,* May 7, 1998, 823–824.

9. Sally Croft, "Keeping the Kilo from Gaining Weight," *Science,* May 12, 1995, 804.

10. National Center for Children in Poverty, http://www.nccp.org/cat_8.html.

11. Phil Rosenzweig, *The Halo Effect . . . and the Eight Other Business Delusions that Deceive Managers* (New York: Free Press, 2007), 173.

CHAPTER TWO

1. "Shortchanged? Census, State Differ on Pinal County's Headcount," *Arizona Republic,* Phoenix, March 17, 2006, B1.

2. http://www.census.gov/popest/topics/methodology/2005_st_co_meth.pdf.

3. Graeme Smith, "From Russia with Hate," *Globe and Mail,* Toronto, April 26, 2006.

4. Doug Anderson, personal communication, May 13, 2011.

CHAPTER THREE

1. P.H. Sydenham, *Measuring Instruments, Tools of Knowledge and Control* (New York: Peter Peregrinus, 1979), 219.

2. The usual habit in naming measurement units is to use a capital letter when it is based on the name of a person, as in the capital "K" used for degrees Kelvin. Originally, Linnaeus's unit was a small "c" for centigrade, but through usage and bad habit, it became capitalized. To maintain the convention, it was decided to name the unit after Celsius and keep the capital C, even though Celsius's contribution to the development of the temperature scale was trivial.

3. Theodore M. Porter, *Trust in Numbers* (Princeton: Princeton University Press, 1995), 18.

4. Miguel Rubi, "The Long Arm of the Second Law," *Scientific American* 299, no. 5 (2008): 62–67.

5. Joseph Kestin, *A Course in Thermodynamics* (New York: Taylor & Francis, 1979).

6. Rubi, "Long Arm," 64.

7. The temperature at which liquid, solid, and gas are in equilibrium at sea level—for water this is 0.01°C.

8. Werner von Siemens, *Recollections* (Munich: Piper Verlag GmbH, 2008). Originally 1892.

9. Graeme J.N. Gooday, *The Morals of Measurement* (Cambridge: Cambridge University Press, 2004).

10. Ibid., 251.

11. Ibid.

12. Adam Silverman, "Former UVM Professor Sentenced to Jail for Fraud," *Burlington Free Press*, June 29, 2006.

13. Porter, *Trust in Numbers,* 33.

14. http://www.ec.gc.ca/pdb/npri/documents/2004ToolBox/docs/sect_2_3_1_e.cfm.

15. Paul J. Nietert, Andrea M. Wessel, Chris Feifer, and Steven Ornstein, "Effect of Terminal Digit Preference on Blood Pressure Measurement and Treatment in Primary Care," *American Journal of Hypertension* 19 (2006): 147–152.

16. D. Wingfield, J. Cooke, L. Thijs, J.A. Staessen, A.E. Fletcher, R. Fagard, C.J. Bulpitt, Syst-Eur Investigators, "Terminal Digit Preference and Single Number Preference in the Syst-Eur Trial: Influence of Quality Control," *Blood Pressure Monitoring* 7, no. 3 (2002): 169–177.

CHAPTER FOUR

1. www.investowords.com.

2. Martin D. Weiss, "Crisis of Confidence," manuscript presented at the National Press Club, Washington, DC, June 11, 2002.

3. James T. McClave and Terry Sincich, *Statistics,* 10th ed. (Upper Saddle River, NJ: Pearson Prentice Hall, 2006), 7.

4. Surely the authors meant that we should ask more than one registered voter to rate the president's performance.

5. "Less than Meets the Eye," *Economist,* August 12, 2006, 47.

6. Daniel Koretz and Sheila Barron, "Test-Based Accountability Systems: Lessons of Kentucky's Experiment," RB-8017 (Santa Monica, CA: RAND Corporation, 1999).

7. Atul Gawande, "The Score," *New Yorker,* October 9, 2006.

8. M. Finster and M. Wood, "The Apgar Score Has Survived the Test of Time," *Anaesthesiology* 102, no. 4 (2005): 855–857.

CHAPTER FIVE

1. Peter Drucker, *Management: Tasks, Responsibilities, Practices* (New York: Harper & Row, 1974), 496.

2. H.M. Parsons, "What Happened at Hawthorne?" *Science* 183 (1974): 922–932.

3. Malcolm Wright and J. Scott Armstrong, "The Ombudsman: Verification of Citations: Fawlty Towers of Knowledge?" *Interfaces* 38, no. 2 (March–April 2008): 125–139.

4. Atul Gawande, "The Score," *New Yorker,* October 9, 2006.

5. Friedrich Pukelsheim, "Robustness of Statistical Gossip and the Antarctic Ozone Hole," *Institute of Mathematical Statistics Bulletin* 19, no. 4 (1990): 540–543.

6. J.C. Farman, B.G. Gardiner, and B.G. Shanklin, "Large Losses of Total Ozone Reveal Seasonal ClO/Nox Interaction," *Nature* 315 (1985): 207–210.

7. Maureen Christie, "Data Collection and the Ozone Hole: Too Much of a Good Thing," *Proceedings of the International Commission on the History of Meteorology* 1, no. 1 (2004): 99–105.

8. Benjamin Graham, *The Intelligent Investor* (New York: Harper & Row, 1973).

9. P.M. Deechow and Weili Ge, "The Persistence of Earnings and Cash Flows and the Role of Special Items: Implications for the Accrual Anomaly," *Review of Accounting Studies* 11 (2006): 253–296. The 19 percent figure is based on the average frequency of special items in Deechow and Ge's Table 3.

10. By Ronald Fisher, the godfather of frequentist statistics.

CHAPTER SIX

1. Robert S. Kaplan and David P. Norton, *The Balanced Scorecard* (Boston: Harvard Business School Press, 1996), 24.

2. Ibid., 10.

3. Masaaki Imai, *Kaizen: The Key to Japan's Competitive Success* (New York: Random House, 1986).

4. Phil Rosenzweig, *The Halo Effect and the Eight Other Business Delusions that Deceive Managers* (New York: Simon and Schuster, 2007), 97.

5. Richard Gallagher and Tim Appenzeller, "Beyond Reductionism," Science 284, no. 5411 (April 1999): 79.

6. Thomas Sowell, *Knowledge and Decisions* (New York: Basic Books, 1980).

7. Henry Regier, personal communication, October 20, 2006.

8. Gareth Morgan, *Images of Organization* (Newbury Park, CA: SAGE, 1986).

9. John C. Avise, "Evolving Genomic Metaphors: A New Look at the Language of DNA," *Science* 294 (2001) : 86–87.

10. Sowell, *Knowledge and Decisions,* 11.

11. Chris Meyer and Rick Ross, *Performance Dashboards*, in *The Dance of Change,* ed. Peter Senge et al. (New York: Doubleday, 1999), 314.

12. Bill Gates, "A Robot in Every Home," *Scientific American* 296, no. 1 (January 2007): 58–65.

13. Satya Chakravorty, "Six-Sigma Programs: An Implementation Model," *International Journal of Production Economics* 119 (2009): 1–16.

14. John Bangs and Carlos Hart, *Factory Management* (New York: Alexander Hamilton Institute, 1942), 19.

15. Peter Pande, Robert Neuman, and Roland Cavanagh, *The Six-Sigma Way* (New York: McGraw-Hill, 2000), 223.

16. Sowell, *Knowledge and Decisions,* 220.

17. John Goodier, "Fishermen and Their Trade on Canadian Lake Superior: One Hundred Years," *Inland Seas, Quarterly Journal of the Great Lakes Historical Society* 45 (1989): 284–306.

18. John Goodier, "Native Lake Trout Stocks in the Canadian Waters of Lake Superior Prior to 1955," *Canadian Journal of Fisheries and Aquatic Science* 38, no. 12 (1981): 1724–1737. © 2008 NRC Canada or its licensors. Reproduced with permission.

19. For example, the Canadian New Democratic Party's policy for addressing economic security is for the government to develop "job-supporting sector strategies for industries from auto to aerospace to agriculture."

20. Henry A. Regier and Jennifer L. Nielsen, "Sustaining Salmonid Populations: A Caring Understanding of the Naturalness of Taxa," *American Fisheries Society Symposium* 43 (2004): 203–211.

21. I put "health" in quotes because it is a value judgment. Within any of the bounds in which life is possible and a self-organizing system exists, even rotting masses of algae, the same self-organizing behavior of complex systems takes place.

22. "Weights and Measures," *Economist,* December 16, 2006.

23. Anthony Atkinson, John Waterhouse, and Robert Wells, "A Stakeholder Approach to Strategic Performance Measurement," *Sloan Management Review* 38, no. 3 (1997): 25–37.

CHAPTER SEVEN

1. Winston S. Churchill, *The Gathering Storm,* Book 2, *The Twilight War* (London: The Reprint Society, 1948; 12th impression, 1956), 377.

2. M.M. Postan, *British War Production* (Her Majesty's Stationery Office, 1952). Published online at http://www.ibiblio.org/hyperwar/UN/UK/UK-Civil-WarProduction/.

3. Winston Churchill, speech to the House of Commons, June 18, 1940.

4. Jacques Bertin, *Sémiologie graphique: Les diagrammes, les réseaux, les cartes,* 2nd ed. (Paris: Mouton, 1973).

5. Robert S. Kaplan and David P. Norton, *The Balanced Scorecard* (Boston: Harvard Business School Press, 1996), 136.

6. Chris Meyer and Rick Ross, "Performance Dashboards," in *The Dance of Change,* ed. Peter Senge et al. (New York: Doubleday, 1999), 317.

7. Edward Tufte, *The Visual Display of Quantitative Information* (Cheshire, CT: Graphic Press, 1983).

8. Ibid., 191.

9. Peter Drucker, *Management: Tasks, Responsibilities, Practices* (New York: Harper and Row, 1974), 500.

10. Bertin, *Sémiologie graphique,* part 2, chapter 1, "Les diagrammes."

11. Kurt Eichemwald, *Conspiracy of Fools* (New York: Broadway Books, 2005), 429.

12. Roger Slater, *Integrated Process Management* (Boston: McGraw Hill, 1991).

13. Chris Argyris and Donald Schon, *Organizational Learning: A Theory of Action Perspective* (Reading MA: Addison-Wesley, 1978).

14. Kaplan and Norton, *The Balanced Scorecard.*

15. Phil Rosenzweig, *The Halo Effect and the Eight Other Business Delusions that Deceive Managers* (New York: Simon and Schuster, 2007), 13.

CHAPTER EIGHT

1. Ovid (43 BC–AD 17), *Metamorphoses,* trans. David Raeburn (London: Penguin, 2004).

2. Satya Chakravorty, "Six Sigma Failures: An Escalation Model," *Operations Management Research* 2 (2009): 44–45.

3. For details on how to do this, refer to any of the many texts on the topic, such as Douglas C. Montgomery, *Introduction to Statistical Quality Control* (New York: John Wiley & Sons, 1991).

4. Three-sigma control limits.

5. Steven Pinker, *The Blank Slate: The Modern Denial of Human Nature* (New York: Penguin, 2002), chapter 12.

6. Ibid., 203.

7. Donald J. Wheeler, *Understanding Variation* (Knoxville, TN: SPC Press, 1993), 27.

8. For technical details on how this is done, see, for example, George E. P. Box, Gwilym M. Jenkins, and Gregory Reinsel, *Times Series Analysis: Forecasting and Control* (Upper Saddle River, NJ: Prentice Hall, 1994), chapter 13.

9. http://waterdata.usgs.gov.

10. Paul Samuelson, "Science and Stocks," *Newsweek*, September 19, 1966, 92.

CHAPTER NINE

1. John Maynard Keynes, *A Treatise on Probability* (New York: Dover Phoenix Books, 2004; originally published 1921).

2. Peter Bernstein, *Against the Gods: The Remarkable Story of Risk* (New York: Wiley, 1998).

3. Sam Roberts, "For Young Earners in the Big City: A Gap in Women's Favor," *New York Times,* August 3, 2007.

4. This effect was noticed and published by Carl Bialik, "The Mystery of the Median," *Wall Street Journal,* August 6, 2007.

5. For example, $1/2 + 1/3$ is not equal to $(1+1)/(2+3)$

6. "A Hero Last Year, Justice Takes a Seat," *New York Times,* October 12, 1996.

7. Charles Dow, "Watching the Tide," *Wall Street Journal,* January 31, 1901.

8. Dow Jones Indexes, *Dow Jones Industrial Average Methodology,* brochure on www.djindexes.com, 2011.

9. *Value Line's Ranking System Performance,* http://www.valueline.com.

10. www.standardandpoors.com.

11. The funds in this category were defined by globefund.com as "a minimum 90% weight in equities. In addition, the fund must have a minimum weight of 85% in U.S. equities. The fund's average capitalization must exceed the mid-cap threshold." The funds were: AGF American Growth Class, AIC Value, AIM American Growth, Altamira U.S. Larger Company, Beutel Goodman American Equity(R), Beutel Goodman Private US Equity(R), BMO U.S. Growth, CDA U.S. Small Cap (Trimark)(R), CI American Equity, CI American Value, CI Synergy American, CI Synergy American Corporate Class, CIBC U.S. Equity Index, CIBC U.S. Index RRSP, Clarica MVP

U.S. Equity(C), Co-operators U.S. Equity VA(C), Elliott & Page American Growth, Ethical American Multi-Strategy, Ferique American(R), Fidelity Growth America-A, Fidelity Growth America-B, Frk Tmp US Rising Dividend-F, GGOF American Equity Fund Ltd Class, GGOF American Equity Fund Ltd Mut, GWL US Equity (G) DSC, GWL US Equity (G) NL, HSBC U.S. Equity-I(R), Investors U.S. Large Cap Growth-C(R), Investors U.S. Large Cap Value-C(R), Investors U.S. Opportunities-C(R), Leith Wheeler U.S. Equity(R), London Life U.S. Equity (LC), Mackenzie Univ US Growth Leaders, Mawer U.S. Equity, MB American Equity(R), McLean Budden American Equity(R), MD U.S. Large Cap Growth(R), Millennia III American Equity 1, ML Ser R Class A U.S. Equity(C), MLCAP Class A Amer Growth & Income(R), MLCAP Class A S&P 500 IdxUS$ cl(R), MLIA Class A Amer Growth & Income(C), MLIA Class A S&P 500 IdxUS$ cl(C), MLIP Class A Amer Growth & Income(C), MLIP Class A S&P 500 IdxUS$ cl(C), North Growth U.S. Equity(R), PH&N U.S. Equity-A(R), PH&N U.S. Growth-A(R), Quadrus Mac Unv U.S. Gro Leaders, RBC U.S. Equity, Renaissance U.S. Equity Growth, Renaissance U.S. Index, Scotia American Growth, Scotia American Stock Index, Scotia CanAm Stock Index, Standard Life US Equity-A(R), Talvest U.S. Equity, TD North American Dividend-I, TD U.S. Blue Chip Equity, TD U.S. Index (US$), TD U.S. Quantitative Equity-I, Trans IMS Can-Am(C), United-US Equity Value Pool Class W(R).

12. TD US$ Index fund, from www.tdwaterhouse.ca.

13. Bernstein, *Against the Gods,* 286.

14. Keynes, *Treatise on Probability,* 206.

15. Calculated as follows: $(1-(1.15\text{x}1.12\text{x}1.08\text{x}1.11\text{x}0.8)^{1/5})100\%$.

16. Calculated as $(1-(2+0.5)/2) \times 100\%$.

17. Calculated as $(1-(2\text{X}0.5)^{1/2})\text{X}100\%$.

18. The harmonic mean is calculated by dividing the number of rates you are averaging by the sum of the reciprocals of the rates. In this example it would be $3/(1/50+1/100+1/50)$.

19. This calculation is valid if the components are in parallel.

CHAPTER TEN

1. Daniel T. Willingham, "Trust Me, I'm a Scientist," *Scientific American* 304, no. 4 (May 2011): 12.

2. www.shadowstats.com.

3. John S. Greenlees and Robert B. McClelland, "Addressing Misconceptions about the Consumer Price Index," *Monthly Labor Review* 131, no. 8 (August 2008): 3–19.

4. John Williams, personal communication, March 29, 2011.

5. Sam Zuckerman, "Economist Challenges Government Data," *San Francisco Chronicle*, May 25, 2008.

6. Robert D. Hershey Jr., "Panel See a Corrected Price Index as Deficit Cutter," *New York Times*, September 15, 1995.

7. Joseph Lowe, *The Present State of England in Regard to Agriculture, Trade and Finance* (London: Longman, Rees, Orme, and Browne, 1823), 346.

8. Ibid., 342.

9. Greenlees and McClelland, "Addressing Misconceptions."

10. Timothy Aeppel, "An Inflation Debate Brews Over Intangibles at the Mall," *Wall Street Journal,* May 17, 2005.

11. Bill Gross, *Investment Outlook* (newsletter), June 2008.

12. Maurice G. Kendall, "The Early History of Index Numbers," *Review of the International Statistical Institute* 37, no. 1 (1969): 1–12; William Fleetwood, *Chronicon Preciosum* (London, 1745), cited in Kendall, "Early History," 1. Much of the material describing the history of measures of inflation is drawn from Kendall.

13. Kendall, "Early History," 4.

14. Ibid.

15. Arthur Young, "An Inquiry into the Progressive Value of Money in England, Etc." (London: MacMillan, 1812). Quoted in Kendall, "Early History," 5.

16. Quoted in Kendall, "Early History," 5.

17. Lowe, *Present State,* appendix to chapter X.

18. Ibid., 96.

19. Ibid., 317, 318.

20. BLS Handbook of Methods, chapter 17, "The Consumer Price Index," http://www.bls.gov/opub/hom/. Accessed October 21, 2011.

21. U.S. Advisory Commission to Study the Consumer Price Index, 1996.

22. Greenlees, "Addressing Misconceptions."

23. Dennis Fixler, Charles Fortuna, John Greenlees, and Walter Lane, *The Use of Hedonic Regressions to Handle Quality Change: The Experience in the U.S. CPI*, paper presented at the Fifth Meeting of the International Working Group on Price Indices, Reykjavik, Iceland, August 1999.

24. Brent Moulton, *The Expanding Role of Hedonic Methods in the Official Statistics of the United States,* Organization for Economic Cooperation and Development, STD/NA(2001)21, Paris, France.

25. David Johnson, Stephen Reed, and Kenneth Stewart, "Price Measurement in the United States: A Decade after the Boskin Report," *Monthly Labor Review,* May 2006, 10–19.

26. Ibid.

27. For example, Jim Puplava, "The Big Picture," *Financial Sense Newshour,* November 17, 2007, http://www.financialsense.com/fsn/BP/2007/1117.html#billmurphy.

28. Greenlees and McClelland, "Addressing Misconceptions," 6.

29. Ibid.

30. John Williams, *Response to BLS Article on CPI Misconceptions,* September 10, 2008. Published online at www.shadowstats.com.

31. www.shadowstats.com.

32. www.eastangliaemails.com, 1066337021.txt. Accessed April 16, 2011.

33. http://www.whitehouse.gov/files/documents/ostp/press_release_files/holdren_email.pdf. Accessed April 17, 2011.

34. P. Brohan, J. J. Kennedy, I. Harris, S. F. B. Tett, and P. D. Jones. "Uncertainty Estimates in Regional and Global Observed Temperature Changes: A New Dataset from 1850," *Journal of Geophysical Research* 111 (2006): D12106. doi:10.1029/2005JD006548.

35. Ibid. Graph represents Hadcrut3 monthly means.

36. *Summary for Policy Makers,* a report of working group 1 of the IPCC, 2007.

37. Brohan et al., "Uncertainty Estimates."

38. Ibid.

39. N. A. Rayner, P. Brohan, D. E. Parker, C. K. Folland, J. J. Kennedy, M. Vanieck, T. J. Ansell, and S. F. B. Tett, "Improved Analyses of Changes in Sea Surface Temperature Measured in Situ since the Mid-Nineteenth Century: The HadSST2 Dataset," *Journal of Climate* 19 (2006): 446–469.

40. Chris Folland and D. E. Parker, "Correction of Instrumental Biases in Historical Sea Surface Temperature Data," *Quarterly Journal of the Royal Meteorological Society* 121, no. 533 (1995): 319–367. DOI: 10.1002/qj.49712152206

41. Ibid.

42. E. C. Kent, S. Woodruff, and D. I. Berry, "Metadata from WMO Publication No. 47 and an Assessment of Voluntary Observing Ship Observation Heights in ICOADS," *Journal of Atmospheric and Oceanic Technology* 24 (2006): 214–234.

43. Folland and Parker, "Correction of Instrumental Biases."

44. Kent, Woodruff, and Berry, "Metadata from WMO," 232, Table 5.

45. D. E. Parker, C. K. Folland, and M. Jackson, "Marine Surface Temperature: Observed Variations and Data Requirements," *Climatic Change* 31 (1995): 559–600.

46. Rayner et al., "Improved Analyses," 466.

47. Phil Jones, personal communication, January 15, 2008.

48. Vincent Courtillot, personal communication, January 29, 2008.

49. Jean-Louis Le Mouël, Vincent Courtillot, Elena Blanter, and Mikhail Shnirman, "Evidence for a Solar Signature in 20th-Century Temperature Data from the USA and Europe," *Comptes Rondu Geoscience* 340 (2008): 421–430.

50. Vincent Courtillot, Yves Gallet, Jean-Louis Le Mouël, Frédéric Fluteau, and Agnès Genevey, "Are There Connections between the Earth's Magnetic Field and Climate?" *Earth and Planetary Science Letters* (2007): 253, 328–339.

51. Raymond Pierrehumbert, "Les Chevaliers de l'Ordre de la Terre Plate, Part II: Courtillot's Geomagnetic Excursion," December 18, 2007, www.realcimate.org.

52. See for example, "Une étude 'climato-sceptique' soulève des soupçons de fraude," *Le monde,* December 21, 2007.

53. Vincent Courtillot, personal communication, February 4, 2008.

54. Vincent Courtillot, personal communication, October 7, 2009.

55. Ibid.

56. Michael Mann, Raymond Bradley, and Malcolm Hughes, "Global-Scale Temperature Patterns and Climate Forcing over the Past Six Centuries," *Nature* 392 (April 1998): 779–787.

57. Michael Mann, Raymond Bradley, and Malcolm Hughes, "Northern Hemisphere Temperatures during the Last Millenium: Inferences, Uncertainties, and Limitations," *Geophysical Research Letters,* March 15, 1999.

58. Intergovernmental Panel on Climate Change, *Climate Change 2001: The Scientific Basis* (Cambridge: Cambridge University Press, 2001).

59. Richard Kerr, "Yes, It's Been Getting Warmer in Here Since the CO2 Began to Rise," *Science* 312 (2006): 1854.

60. Committee on Surface Temperature Reconstructions for the Last 2,000 Years, National Research Council, *Surface Temperature Reconstructions for the Last 2,000 Years* (Washington, DC: National Academies Press, 2006), http://www.nap.edu/catalog/11676.html.

61. Mann, Bradley, and Hughes, "Global Scale Temperatures."

62. Willie Soon, Sallie Baliunas, Craig Idso, Sherwood Idso, and David Legates, "Reconstructing Past Climate and Environmental Changes of the Past 1000 Years: A Reappraisal," *Environment and Energy* 14, no. 3 (2003): 233–296.

63. P. D. Jones, T. J. Osborn, and K. R. Briffa, "The Evolution of Climate over the Last Millennium," *Science* 292, no. 662 (2001): 662–667.

64. Jeff Nesmith, "Foes of Global Warming Theory Have Energy Ties," *Seattle Post Intelligencer,* June 2, 2003.

65. Michael Mann, C. M. Ammann, R. S. Bradley, K. R. Briffa, T. J. Crowley, M. K. Hughes, P. D. Jones, M. Oppenheimer, T. J. Overpeck, J. T. Overpeck, S. Rutherford, K. E. Trenberth, and T.M.L. Wigley, "On Past Temperatures and Anomalous Late 20th Century Warmth," *Eos, Transactions American Geophysical Union* 84, no. 27 (2003): 256.

66. David Legates, "Global Warming Smear Targets," *Washington Times,* August 26, 2003.

67. Ibid.

68. Clare Goodess, "Stormy Times for Climate Research," *Scientists for Global Responsibility Newsletter* 28, November 2003. Online newsletter published at www.sgr.org.uk.

69. Willie Soon, Sallie Baliunas, and David Legates, "Comment on 'Past Temperatures and Anomalous Late-20th Century Warmth,'" *Eos, Transactions American Geophysical Union* 84, no. 44 (2003): 473–476.

70. Willie Soon, personal communication, April 29, 2011.

71. East Anglia Confirmed Emails from the Climate Research Unit—Searchable, www.eastangliaemails.com, 105019698.txt, accessed April 28, 2011.

72. East Anglia Confirmed Emails from the Climate Research Unit—Searchable, www.eastangliaemails.com, 942777075.txt, accessed April 28, 2011.

73. Eduardo Zorita, "Climategate: Now Eduardo Zorita Speaks Out," *Climateresearchnews.com,* November 28, 2009.

74. Patrick Michaels, "Climate Scientists Subverted Peer Review," *Washington Examiner,* December 2, 2009.

75. East Anglia Confirmed Emails from the Climate Research Unit—Searchable, www.eastangliaemails.com, 1255095172.txt, accessed April 28, 2011.

CHAPTER ELEVEN

1. *Westray Coal Mine Disaster,* http://newscotland1398.ca/westray/wray-menu.html.

2. Ibid.

3. Justice K. Peter Richard, Commissioner, *The Westray Story: A Predictable Path to Disaster; Report of the Westray Mine Public Inquiry* (1997). Testimony of Wayne Cheverie. Published online on the authority of the Lieutenant Governor in Council of the Province of Nova Scotia by the Westray Mine Public Inquiry, Halifax, Nova Scotia, http://www.gov.ns.ca/lae/pubs/westray/.

4. Ibid., chapter 6.

5. Peter Bernstein, *Against the Gods: The Remarkable Theory of Risk* (New York: Wiley, 1996).

6. Ibid., 120.

7. Ibid., 197.

8. John Maynard Keynes, *A Treatise on Probability* (New York: Cosimo, 2006). Original edition 1920.

9. E. T. Jaynes, *Probability Theory: The Logic of Science* (Cambridge: Cambridge University Press, 2003), 317.

10. Bruno de Finetti, *Theory of Probability,* vol. 1 (New York: Wiley, 1975).

11. George Boole, "On a General Method in the Theory of Probabilities," in Keynes, *A Treatise on Probability,* 90.

12. Jaynes, *Probability Theory,* 3.

13. Keynes, *A Treatise on Probability,* 27.

14. Persi Diaconis, S. Holmes, and R. Montgomery, "Dynamical Bias in the Coin Toss," *Siam Review* 49, no. 2 (2007): 211–235. doi:10.1137/S0036144504446436.

15. See for example, Philip Green and A. Dobriyal, "Which Is the Safest Mill in Canada?" *Pulp & Paper Canada* 100, no. 11 (1999): 17–19.

16. *Understanding Standard & Poor's Rating Definitions*, June 3, 2009, Table 1. Online brochure published by Standard & Poors at http://www.standardandpoors.com/ratings/en/us/.

17. Richard Cantor and E. Falkenstein, "Testing for Rating Consistency in Annual Default Rates," *Journal of Fixed Income* 11, no. 2 (September 2001): 36–51. ISSN: 10598596; DOI: 10.3905/jfi.2001.319296.

18. Ibid.

19. Ibid., chart 1.

20. Satyajit Das, *Traders, Guns and Money: Knowns and Unknowns in the Dazzling World of Derivatives* (Harlow: Prentice Hall Financial Times, 2006).

21. Charles Morris, *The Trillion Dollar Meltdown* (New York: Public Affairs, 2008).

22. Ibid.

23. "Status Cuomo," *Economist,* June 5, 2008.

24. Vickie Tillman, "Don't Blame the Rating Agencies," *Wall Street Journal,* August 31, 2007.

25. Amos Tversky and Daniel Kahneman, "Judgment under Uncertainty: Heuristics and Biases," *Science* 185 (1974): 1124–1131.

26. Ibid.

27. Large enough that the probabilities associated with sampling without replacement and sampling with replacement are very close, for the purpose of simplifying the illustration.

28. Elementary event: the red and white beads are in equal proportion; therefore the probability of a single red bead is 50 percent. Joint event: the probability of a red bead in a single draw is 90 percent, or 0.9. The probability of seven red beads in a row is thus 0.9 X 0.9 X 0.9 X 0.9 X 0.9 X 0.9 X 0.9, which is equal to 0.48, or 48 percent. Disjoint event: The probability of a red bead in a single draw is 10 percent. The only other alternative to getting at least one red bead in seven draws is getting seven white beads. The probability of getting a single white bead is 90 percent. The probability of getting seven white beads is thus 48 percent and thus the probability of getting at least one red bead is 52 percent.

29. Paul Slovic, Baruch Fischhoff, and Sarah Lichtenstein, "Facts versus Fears: Understanding Perceived Risk," in *Judgment under Uncertainty: Heuristics and Biases*, ed. Daniel Kahneman, Paul Slovic, and Amos Tversky (Cambridge: Cambridge University Press, 1982).

30. Jaynes, *Probability Theory*, 203.

31. It is the reciprocal of the standard deviation. See Jaynes, *Probability Theory,* equation 7.16.

32. "Best" in the sense that it is what we now call the maximum likelihood estimate.

33. Keynes, *A Treatise on Probability,* 107.

34. "Professionally Gloomy," *Economist,* May 17, 2008.

35. E. T. Jaynes, *Probability Theory,* xxii.

36. "In Praise of Bayes," *Economist,* September 28, 2000.

Bibliography

Aeppel, Timothy. "An Inflation Debate Brews over Intangibles at the Mall." *Wall Street Journal,* May 17, 2005.

Argyris, Chris, and Donald Schon. *Organizational Learning: A Theory of Action Perspective.* Reading, MA: Addison-Wesley, 1978.

Atkinson, Anthony, John Waterhouse, and Robert Wells. "A Stakeholder Approach to Strategic Performance Measurement." *Sloan Management Review* 38, no. 3 (1997): 25–37.

Avise, John C. "Evolving Genomic Metaphors: A New Look at the Language of DNA." *Science* 294 (2001): 86–87.

Bangs, John, and Carlos Hart. *Factory Management.* New York: Alexander Hamilton Institute, 1942.

Bernstein, Peter. *Against the Gods: The Remarkable Theory of Risk.* New York: Wiley, 1996.

Bertin, Jacques. *Sémiologie graphique.* Paris: Mouton, 1967.

Bialik, Carl. "The Mystery of the Median." *Wall Street Journal,* August 6, 2007.

BLS Handbook of Methods. Bureau of Labor Statistics. http://www.bls.gov/opub/hom/.

Box, George, E. P. Gwilym, M. Jenkins, and Gregory Reinsel. *Times Series Analysis: Forecasting and Control.* Upper Saddle River, NJ: Prentice Hall, 1994.

Brohan, P. J., J. Kennedy, I. Harris, S. F. B. Tett, and P. D. Jones. "Uncertainty Estimates in Regional and Global Observed Temperature Changes: A New Dataset from 1850." *Journal of Geophysical Research* 111 (2006): D12106. doi:10.1029/2005JD006548.

Chakravorty, Satya. "Six Sigma Failures: An Escalation Model." *Operations Management Research* 2 (2009): 44–45.

Chakravorty, Satya. "Six-Sigma Programs: An Implementation Model." *International Journal of Production Economics* 119 (2009): 1–16.

Christie, Maureen. "Data Collection and the Ozone Hole: Too Much of a Good Thing." *Proceedings of the International Commission on the History of Meteorology* 1, no. 1 (2004): 99–105.

Churchill, Winston S. *The Gathering Storm.* Book 2: *The Twilight War.* London: The Reprint Society, 1948. 12th impression, 1956.

Churchill, Winston S. *Their Finest Hour.* Book 1: *The Fall of France.* London: The Reprint Society, 1949. Ninth impression 1956.

Committee on Surface Temperature Reconstructions for the Last 2,000 Years. *Surface Temperature Reconstructions for the Last 2,000 Years.* Washington, DC: National Academies Press, 2006. http://www.nap.edu/catalog/11676.html.

Courtillot, Vincent, Yves Gallet, Jean-Louis Le Mouël, Frédéric Fluteau, and Agnès Genevey. "Are There Connections between the Earth's Magnetic Field and Climate?" *Earth and Planetary Science Letters* 253 (2007): 328–339.

Croft, Sally. "Keeping the Kilo from Gaining Weight." *Science,* May 12, 1995.

Deechow, P. M., and Weili Ge. "The Persistence of Earnings and Cash Flows and the Role of Special Items: Implications for the Accrual Anomaly." *Review Accounting Studies* (2006): 11.

Dow, Charles. "Watching the Tide." *Wall Street Journal,* January 31, 1901.

Dow Jones Indexes. *Dow Jones Industrial Average Methodology.* Brochure. www.djindexes.com. 2011.

Drucker, Peter. *Management: Tasks, Responsibilities, Practices.* New York: Harper & Row, 1974.

Eichemwald, Kurt. 2005. *Conspiracy of Fools.* New York: Broadway Books, 2005.

Farman, J. C., B. G. Gardiner, and B. G. Shanklin. "Large Losses of Total Ozone Reveal Seasonal ClO/Nox Interaction." *Nature* 315 (1985): 207–210.

Finster, M., and M. Wood. "The Apgar Score Has Survived the Test of Time." *Anaesthesiology* 102, no. 4 (2005): 855–857.

Fixler, Dennis, Charles Fortuna, John Greenlees, and Walter Lane. *The Use of Hedonic Regressions to Handle Quality Change: The Experience in the U.S. CPI.* Paper presented at the Fifth Meeting of the International Working Group on Price Indices Reykjavik, Iceland, August 1999.

Fleetwood, William. *Chronicon Preciosum.* London, 1745.

Folland, Chris, and D. E. Parker. "Correction of Instrumental Biases in Historical Sea Surface Temperature Data." *Quarterly Journal of the Royal Meteorological Society* 121, no. 533 (1995): 319–367. DOI: 10.1002/qj.49712152206.

Gallagher, Richard, and Tim Appenzeller. "Beyond Reductionism." *Science* 284, no. 5411 (1999): 79.

Gates, Bill. "A Robot in Every Home." *Scientific American* 296, no. 1(2007): 58–65.

Gawande, Atul. "The Score." *New Yorker,* October 9, 2006.

Gooday, Graeme J. N. *The Morals of Measurement.* Cambridge: Cambridge University Press, 2004.

Goodess, Clare. "Stormy Times for Climate Research." *Scientists for Global Responsibility Newsletter* 28, November 2003.

Goodier, John. "Fishermen and Their Trade on Canadian Lake Superior: One Hundred Years." *Inland Seas, Quarterly Journal of the Great Lakes Historical Society* 45 (1989): 284–306.

Goodier, John. "Native Lake Trout Stocks in the Canadian Waters of Lake Superior Prior to 1955." *Canadian Journal of Fisheries and Aquatic Sciences* 38, no. 12 (1981): 1724–1737.

Graeme, J. N. Gooday. *The Morals of Measurement.* Cambridge:Cambridge University Press, 2004.

Graham, Benjamin. *The Intelligent Investor.* New York: Harper & Row, 1973.

Greenlees, John S., and Robert B. McClelland. "Addressing Misconceptions about the Consumer Price Index." *Monthly Labor Review*, August 2008.

Gross, Bill. *Investment Outlook* (newsletter). June 2008.

"Happiness Inc." *Wall Street Journal,* March 18–19, 2006.

"A Hero Last Year, Justice Takes a Seat." *New York Times,* October 12, 1996.

Hershey, Robert D., Jr. "Panel See a Corrected Price Index as Deficit Cutter." *New York Times*, September 15, 1995.

Imai, Masaaki. *Kaizen: The Key to Japan's Competitive Success.* New York: Random House, 1986.

Intergovernmental Panel on Climate Change. *Climate Change 2001: The Scientific Basis.* Cambridge: CUP, 2001.

Johnson, David, Stephen Reed, and Kenneth Stewart. "Price Measurement in the United States: A Decade after the Boskin Report." *Monthly Labor Review* (May 2006): 10–19.

Jones, P. D., T. J. Osborn, and K. R. Briffa. "The Evolution of Climate over the Last Millennium." *Science* 292 (2001): 662–667.

Kaplan, Robert S., and David P. Norton. *The Balanced Scorecard.* Boston: Harvard Business School Press, 1996.

Kendall, Maurice G. (1969), "The Early History of Index Numbers." *Review of the International Statistical Institute* 37, no. 1 (1969): 1–12.

Kent, E. C., S. Woodruff, and D. I. Berry. "Metadata from WMO Publication No. 47 and an Assessment of Voluntary Observing Ship Observation Heights in ICOADS." *Journal of Atmospheric and Oceanic Technology* 24 (2006): 214–234.

Kerr, Richard. "Yes, It's Been Getting Warmer in Here Since the CO2 Began to Rise." *Science* 312 (2006): 1854.

Kestenbaum, David. "Recipe for a Kilogram." *Science* 280, no. 5365 (1998): 823–824.

Kestin, Joseph. *A Course in Thermodynamics.* New York: Taylor & Francis, 1979.

Keynes, John Maynard. *A Treatise on Probability*. (New York: Dover Phoenix Books, 2004. Originally published 1921.)

Koretz, Daniel, and Sheila Barron. "Test-Based Accountability Systems: Lessons of Kentucky's Experiment." RB-8017. Santa Monica, CA: RAND Corporation, 1999.

Legates, David. "Global Warming Smear Targets." *Washington Times,* August 26, 2003.

Le Mouël, Jean-Louis, Vincent Courtillot, Elena Blanter, and Mikhail Shnirman. "Evidence for a Solar Signature in 20th-Century Temperature Data from the USA and Europe." *Comptes Rendu Geoscience* 340 (2008): 421–430.

"Less Than Meets the Eye." *Economist,* August 12, 2006.

Lowe, Joseph. *The Present State of England in Regard to Agriculture, Trade and Finance.* London: Longman, Rees, Orme, and Browne, 1823.

Mann, Michael, C.M. Ammann, R.S. Bradley, K.R. Briffa, T.J. Crowley, M.K. Hughes, P.D. Jones, M. Oppenheimer, T.J. Osborn, J.T. Overpeck, S. Rutherford, K.E. Trenberth, and T.M.L Wigley. "On Past Temperatures and Anomalous Late 20th Century Warmth." *Eos, Transactions American Geophysical Union* 84, no. 27 (2003): 256.

Mann, Michael, Raymond Bradley, and Malcolm Hughes. "Global-Scale Temperature Patterns and Climate Forcing over the Past Six Centuries." *Nature* 392 (April 1998).

Mann, Michael, Raymond Bradley, and Malcolm Hughes. "Northern Hemisphere Temperatures during the Last Millenium: Inferences, Uncertainties and Limitations." *Geophysical Research Letters* 20, no. 6 (1999).

McClave, James T., and Terry Sincich. *Statistics,* 10th ed. Upper Saddle River, NJ: Pearson Prentice Hall, 2006.

Meyer, Chris, and Rick Ross. "Performance Dashboards." In *The Dance of Change,* ed. Peter Senge et al. New York: Doubleday, 1999.

Michaels, Patrick. "Climate Scientists Subverted Peer Review." *Washington Examiner,* December 2, 2009.

Morgan, Gareth. *Images of Organization.* Newbury Park, CA: SAGE, 1986.

"A Most Unbearable Weight." *Science,* May 7, 2004, 812.

Moulton, Brent. *The Expanding Role of Hedonic Methods in the Official Statistics of the United States.* Paris, France: Organization for Economic Cooperation and Development, STD/NA, 2001.

Nesmith, Jeff. "Foes of Global Warming Theory Have Energy Ties." *Seattle Post Intelligencer,* June 2, 2003.

Nietert, Paul J., Andrea M. Wessel, Chris Feifer, and Steven Ornstein. "Effect of Terminal Digit Preference on Blood Pressure Measurement and Treatment in Primary Care." *American Journal of Hypertension* 19 (2006): 147–152.

Ovid. *Metamorphoses.* Trans. David Raeburn. London: Penguin Books, 2004.

Parker, D.E., C.K. Folland, and M. Jackson. "Marine Surface Temperature: Observed Variations and Data Requirements." *Climatic Change* 31 (1995): 559–600.

Parsons, H. M. "What Happened at Hawthorne?" *Science* 183 (1974): 932.

Pierrehumbert, Raymond. "Les Chevaliers de l'Ordre de la Terre Plate, Part II: Courtillot's Geomagnetic Excursion." *www.realcimate.org*. December 18, 2007.

Pinker, Steven. *The Blank Slate: The Modern Denial of Human Nature*. New York: Penguin, 2002.

Plackett, L. *Studies in the History of Probability and Statistics,* vol. 2. New York: Macmillan, 1977.

Porter, Theodore M. *Trust in Numbers*. Princeton: Princeton University Press, 1995.

Postan, M. M. *British War Production*. London: Her Majesty's Stationery Office, 1952.

Pukelsheim, Friedrich. "Robustness of Statistical Gossip and the Antarctic Ozone Hole." *Institute of Mathematical Statistics Bulletin,* 19, no. 4 (1990): 540–543.

Rayner, N. A., P. Brohan, D. E. Parker, C. K. Folland, J. J. Kennedy, M. Vanieck, T. J. Ansell, and S. F. B. Tett. "Improved Analyses of Changes in Sea Surface Temperature Measured In Situ since the Mid-Nineteenth Century: The HadSST2 Dataset." *Journal of Climate* 19 (February 1, 2006).

Regier, Henry A., and Jennifer L. Nielsen. "Sustaining Salmonid Populations: A Caring Understanding of the Naturalness of Taxa." *American Fisheries Society Symposium* 43 (2004): 203–211.

Richard, K. Peter. *The Westray Story: A Predictable Path to Disaster. Report of the Westray Mine Public Inquiry.* 1997. Published online on the authority of the Lieutenant Governor in Council of the Province of Nova Scotia by the Westray Mine Public Inquiry. Halifax, Nova Scotia. http://www.gov.ns.ca/lae/pubs/westray/.

Roberts, Sam. "For Young Earners in Big City, a Gap in Women's Favor." *New York Times,* August 3, 2007.

Rosenzweig, Phil. *The Halo Effect … and the Eight Other Business Delusions that Deceive Managers.* New York: Free Press, 2007.

Rubi, Miguel. "The Long Arm of the Second Law." *Scientific American* 299, no. 5 (2008): 62–67.

Samuelson, Paul. "Science and Stocks." *Newsweek,* September 19, 1966.

"Shortchanged? Census, State Differ on Pinal County's Headcount." *Arizona Republic,* March 17, 2006.

Siemens, Werner von. *Recollections*. Munich: Piper Verlag GmbH, 2008. Originally 1892.

Silverman, Adam. "Former UVM Professor Sentenced to Jail for Fraud." *Burlington Free Press*, June 29, 2006.

Slater, Roger. *Integrated Process Management.* Boston: McGraw Hill, 1991.

Smith, Graeme. "From Russia with Hate." *Globe and Mail* (Toronto), April 26, 2006.

Soon, Willie, Sallie Baliunas, Craig Idso, Sherwood Idso, and David Legates. "Reconstructing Past Climate and Environmental Changes of the Past 1000 Years: A Reappraisal." *Environment and Energy* 14, no. 3 (2003).

Soon, Willie, Sallie Baliunas, and David Legates. Comment on "Past Temperatures and Anomalous Late-20th Century Warmth." *Eos, Transactions American Geophysical Union* 84, no. 44 (2003): 473–476:

Sowell, Thomas. *Knowledge and Decisions*. New York: Basic Books, 1980.

Sydenham, P. H. "Measuring Instruments: Tools of Knowledge and Control." New York, NY: Peter Peregrinus, 1979.

Tufte, Edward. *The Visual Display of Quantitative Information*. Cheshire, CT: Graphic Press, 1983.

"Une étude 'climato-sceptique' soulève des soupçons de fraude." *Le monde,* December 21, 2007.

Value Line's Ranking System Performance. October 21, 2011. http://www.value line.com/About/Ranking_System.aspx.

"Weights and Measures." *Economist,* December 16, 2006.

Weiss, Martin D. "Crisis of Confidence." Manuscript presented at the National Press Club, Washington, DC, June 11, 2002.

Wheeler, Donald J. *Understanding Variation*. Knoxville, TN: SPC Press, 1993.

Williams, John. *Response to BLS Article on CPI Misconceptions*. September 10, 2008. Published online at www.shadowstats.com.

Willingham, Daniel T. "Trust Me, I'm a Scientist." *Scientific American* 304, no. 4 (2011): 12..

Wingfield, D., J. Cooke, L. Thijs, J. A. Staessen, A. E. Fletcher, R. Fagard, C. J. Bulpitt, Syst-Eur Investigators. "Terminal Digit Preference and Single Number Preference in the Syst-Eur Trial: Influence of Quality Control." *Blood Pressure Monitoring* 7, no. 3 (2002): 169–177.

Wright, Malcolm, and J. Scott Armstrong. "The Ombudsman: Verification of Citations: Fawlty Towers of Knowledge?" *Interfaces* 38, no. 2 (2008): 125–139.

Young, Arthur. "An Inquiry into the Progressive Value of Money in England, Etc." 1812.

Zorita, Eduardo. "Climategate: Now Eduardo Zorita Speaks Out." *Climateresearchnews.com.* November 28, 2009.

Zuckerman, Sam. "Economist Challenges Government Data." *San Francisco Chronicle*, May 25, 2008.

Index

About the Authors

Philip Green is currently chairman and CEO of First Resource Management Group, Inc. and is president of Greenbridge Management Inc. For over twenty-five years he has advised major corporations and government agencics on statistical and measurement issues across the United States, Canada, South America, Europe, and Asia. Green has published in the business, financial, and scientific press and has a master's degree in statistics from McMaster University in Ontario, Canada.

George Gabor, now retired, was professor of statistics at Dalhousie University in Halifax, Nova Scotia, since 1977. His published works include the book *Recursive Source Coding* as well as many scholarly articles. Gabor's latest research focused on uncovering serious logical flaws in the classical statistical methods that medical researchers, scientists, universities, and businesses teach and use.